They Left Their Hearts
in San Francisco

ALSO BY BILL CHRISTINE

Bill Hartack: The Bittersweet Life of a Hall of Fame Jockey (McFarland, 2016)

They Left Their Hearts in San Francisco
The Lives of Songwriters George Cory and Douglass Cross

BILL CHRISTINE

McFarland & Company, Inc., Publishers
Jefferson, North Carolina

Library of Congress Cataloguing-in-Publication Data

Names: Christine, Bill, author.
Title: They left their hearts in San Francisco : the lives of
　　songwriters George Cory and Douglass Cross / Bill Christine.
Description: Jefferson, North Carolina : McFarland & Company, 2017 |
　　Includes bibliographical references and index.
Identifiers: LCCN 2017046493 | ISBN 9781476669007
　　(softcover : acid free paper) ∞
Subjects: LCSH: Cory, George, 1920–1978. | Cross, Douglass. |
　　Composers—United States—Biography. | Lyricists—United States—
　　Biography.
Classification: LCC ML410.C8248 C5 2017 | DDC 782.42164092/2
　　[B]—dc23
LC record available at https://lccn.loc.gov/2017046493

British Library cataloguing data are available

ISBN (print) 978-1-4766-6900-7
ISBN (ebook) 978-1-4766-3081-6

© 2017 Bill Christine. All rights reserved

No part of this book may be reproduced or transmitted in any form or by any means, electronic or mechanical, including photocopying or recording, or by any information storage and retrieval system, without permission in writing from the publisher.

Front cover image: George Cory (left) and Douglass Cross met during World War II. This photo was taken in the 1960s, at Claramae and Frank Turner's Belli Acres in upstate New York. Ms. Turner sang "I Left My Heart in San Francisco" years before Tony Bennett (photograph courtesy of Albert and Bea Thomas); *background* Golden Gate Bridge in San Francisco © 2017 Jorge Villalba/iStock

Printed in the United States of America

McFarland & Company, Inc., Publishers
　Box 611, Jefferson, North Carolina 28640
　　www.mcfarlandpub.com

For my wife Pat
and all the tunesmiths everywhere

Table of Contents

Preface	1
1. The Puzzling Death of George Cory	5
2. Walter K. Hinton	17
3. Westward, Ho	30
4. Douglass Cross Writes a Will	36
5. A Song Grows in Brooklyn	43
6. Woulda, Coulda, Shoulda	52
7. The George Cory Ensemble: Here Today, Gone Tomorrow	61
8. "The Phantom": Tony Bennett's Secret Weapon	71
9. "The middle of nowhere"	82
10. December 28, 1961	90
11. String Along with Mitch	99
12. The Battle of San Francisco	112
13. City Ditties	122
14. Suppositions	131
15. Old Man River	140
Appendix I: Douglass Cross' and George Cory's Wills	153
Appendix II: Other One-Hit Wonders	159
Appendix III: The Richest Songs of All Time	167
Chapter Notes	173
Bibliography	187
Index	193

Preface

They wrote a song that has sold an estimated fourteen million records for Tony Bennett alone, yet George Cory and Douglass Cross lived lives that have rarely been explored. They lived in two of the largest cities, New York and San Francisco, yet no one recognized them. No one, that is, but Ralph Sharon, an accomplished jazz pianist who saw them walking down the street in Manhattan one day and tucked some of their sheet music in his pocket. That chance meeting made millionaires out of the songwriters and revived Tony Bennett's flagging career.

The more I looked into the lives of Cory and Cross, the more I realized how chancy, unappreciated and tragic they were. The more I inquired, the more I was intrigued. Almost every phone call, every interview, produced new and fascinating tidbits that cried out for further scrutiny. While Bennett continues to feature "I Left My Heart in San Francisco" anytime he performs, all the way into his 91st year, Cory and Cross were, before now, no more than part of a puzzler that Alex Trebek might have used on *Jeopardy!* While at least one biography has been written about Bennett—he's written a few memoirs of his own—Cory and Cross never attracted such interest. The most ever written about them came when they died, and those day-after stories came and went, victims of the Yesterday's Newspaper Syndrome. The stories saying George Cory was a suicide were incorrect; the San Francisco Coroner's Office now says this with conviction. The newspapers were blameless; their only crime was recycling, under tight deadlines, the information that was funneled to them. The attendant speculation that Cory died heartbroken because Cross had died before him was also wrong. Years before Cross died, there was a breakup, and Cory had taken on a new lover, the inscrutable Walter Hinton, another frustrated musician who got rich overnight as the result of the Cory/Cross song.

There was no blueprint for this book. Cory and Cross never wrote a memoir and left no diaries and few personal papers behind. News accounts of the pair were not to be trusted. In a rare televised interview, Cory even got the details wrong about how his lone hit song was discovered, first sung and developed. That is, if the accounts of Tony Bennett, Ralph Sharon and a bartender in Little Rock, Arkansas, are to be believed. Bennett and Sharon were there—Cory and Cross were not—and were in a better position to know.

Douglass Cross' death certificate was filed under the wrong name. His mother wrote a novel, partly drawn from her formative years, but it is out of print. For ten times what the novel originally cost, I was able to borrow a copy from a library in Sacramento.

I invited the San Francisco police to re-open the investigation into the death of George Cory, but they weren't interested. The original investigation into Cory's death was cursory, circumstantial and seemingly predetermined. Douglass Cross' nephew Ron Strowbridge—also a good friend of Cory's—was puzzled by the death at the time, but he lacked the wherewithal to pursue his doubts, and the passage of time had dimmed his curiosity by 2016.

There is no evidence that Cory and Cross did much songwriting after they moved from Brooklyn Heights to California. The residuals from their hit song were enough for them to live out the rest of their lives comfortably. Unfortunately, those lives were tragically short; neither of them reached sixty. Cross' heavy drinking precipitated his death. It was a family trait; his sister was a drinker and died from a drug overdose and his maternal grandfather was an imbiber who womanized and couldn't hold a job. Douglass Cross neglected to update a will that might have substantially changed how the benefits of the song have been passed down the line. Walter Hinton, Cory's best friend at the time of his death, was a contradiction: an opportunist who didn't care about money. Well, most of the time. Hinton gave away large chunks of his inherited rights to the song, first an extraordinary share to a lawyer who needed to be paid, later a lesser amount to a friend, yet for $250 he sued a group of senior citizens in Florida because they had thrown a three-dollar party and played a recording of Tony Bennett singing the Cory/Cross song.

Realizing he was seriously ill, Douglass Cross, without a lawyer, wrote a will (Appendix I) that left the bulk of his estate to his songwriting partner, George Cory. Cross intended to rewrite the will after he and Cory broke up, but never did. Cory, who died a few years after Cross, left the bulk of his estate to his new lover, Walter Hinton. Like Cross, Cory wrote a will (also Appendix I) without a lawyer.

Songwriting history is replete with songwriters who wrote one hit song but were never able to repeat their achievement (see Appendix II: Other One-Hit Wonders). Cory and Cross were scrambling to make a living before their song took off—but in the music business, just one hit song is often enough to dramatically change a songwriter's lifestyle, allowing him to live comfortably off royalties for years (and see Appendix III: The Richest Songs of All Time).

Some of the reporting for this book included trips around the many nooks and crannies of San Francisco. It's not a bad place to be for that sort of thing. The Tenderloin, Union Square, Chinatown, Russian Hill, Fisherman's Wharf, the Fillmore District, Nob Hill, they all have unique looks, even different smells, each with a distinct personality. Somewhere along the way, not far from where George Cory once lived, a man in a diner and I began talking about "I Left My Heart in San Francisco." He was learning something new. He had thought for all these years that Tony Bennett had written the song. Tony Bennett might have *sung* them all but he never wrote *any* song. But if that isn't an excuse for a book about George Cory and Douglass Cross, nothing is.

> Musicians and nightclub proprietors live complicated lives; it's advisable to check in advance to confirm engagements.
> —*The New Yorker*, April 29, 2013

1

The Puzzling Death of George Cory

In mid–March 1978, George Cory brought out an old manual typewriter at his apartment on Nob Hill in San Francisco. He was wealthy and unhealthy. Once scrambling to pay his bills, he had co-written one song and become well-fixed—wealthy enough to take around-the-world trips with his longtime lover and songwriting partner, Douglass Cross, and afford an expensive city on his terms. He was at a time in his life when he could live just about anywhere he wanted, and he did. By themselves, his rental residences around town could have been used by tour guides to show off the toniest neighborhoods. But Cory's glass was half-empty. He was a very sick man. Not many in his circle knew it, but he had cirrhosis of the liver and hardening of the arteries. Payment was due for decades of heavy drinking.[1]

An out-and-out bust as a songwriter for almost twenty years, Cory wrote the music for "I Left My Heart in San Francisco" while Douglass Cross contributed the magical lyrics. Tony Bennett recorded what they had wrought, and Cory's pumpkin turned into a landau. He and Cross, who wrote the song when they were living across the country, in Brooklyn Heights, really did miss the cable cars and the fog of San Francisco. They were eager to return to the city that was their muse.[2] Not long after they did, in the mid–1960s, Cory told a landlord that he had already earned millions of dollars from the residuals to the song.

"How many millions?" he was asked.

"Five," he said.[3]

But by 1978, though only in his fifties, Cory was closer to the end than the beginning. He got out the typewriter to write a will.[4]

By 1978, Cross was already gone. Three years before, at 54, he had drunk himself to death. Romantics were wont to say that Cross was depressed because his long amour with Cory had ended, and that may have been true—for whatever reason, Cross was drinking at least a fifth of whiskey a day in the final months of his life. He had a liver condition not unlike Cory's. Long before Cross' death, Cory had found new lovers, one of whom was the principal beneficiary of his estate. Cory and Cross had once lived under a conservatorship: Whoever died first, the other would inherit all of his lifetime rights to the song that had made them millionaires. Officially, that arrangement was voided when Cross wrote a will in the late 1960s, although nothing changed as far as Cory was concerned. He remained Cross' sole heir. Cory's will, drafted on that old typewriter in 1978, was necessitated by Cross' death and the emergence of the mysterious Walter Hinton, a sometime opera singer, in his life.[5]

Cory had fired one of his lawyers, who strongly disapproved of Hinton's *raison d'être*.[6] So Cory sat at a desk at 18 Pleasant Street, in one of San Francisco's poshest neighborhoods, and batted out what seemed to be a bulletproof four-page document. All of the herebys, aforementioneds and hereuntos seemed to be in place. There was a sprinkling of strikeovers

Pleasant Street on Nob Hill, two blocks from the Fairmont Hotel, in 2016. George Cory was found dead in his apartment building (foreground) in 1978 (author's photograph).

and whiteouts, but the changes here and there were authenticated by Cory's initials in the margins. The will was witnessed by three people, one more than required.

Cory's parents and his only sibling, a brother, had died. He allowed for four heirs: Lina Gastoni, Mr. and Mrs. Paul Morgenthaler and Walter Hinton. Gastoni, a San Francisco opera singer who was in her sixties, was left $1500. The Morgenthalers, who lived in Los Angeles, received $2500. "This," Cory wrote, "I leave to my fond uncle and his dear wife as but a token remembrance of their meaningful support and belief in me in times of trial." Paul Morgenthaler was Cory's mother's brother. The bulk of Cory's estate, including Cory's rights to the song, was left to Hinton, "my dear friend and business manager," Cory wrote. At 56, Hinton was a year younger than Cory. Hinton, too, had struggled as he kicked around the periphery of stardom, never coming close to being a household name. Now he was going to be a very rich man.

The will, dated March 15, 1978, was witnessed by San Franciscans Ernest V. Wade, a minister; his wife Agnes; and Mathilde Oppenheim. The Wades' address was 833 Fillmore Street, and more about that later.[7]

Lloyd Crenna, an attorney from suburban San Rafael who had once represented Cory, saw the will for the first time when I showed him a copy in August of 2016. Crenna's cousin was Richard Crenna, the film actor whose earlier credits dated to the popular Eve Arden radio show *Our Miss Brooks*. Lloyd and Richard Crenna's fathers were brothers.

"I have my doubts that George was thinking straight at the time he wrote the will," Crenna said. "He may have been influenced by others. Only two signatures are required for a will. For me, a will with more than two signatures smacks of someone being worried that the will might be challenged because of circumstances."

At the time Cory became a client, Crenna was fresh out of law school. He was working for a firm led by the picaresque Vincent Hallinan, whose flamboyance rivaled that of Melvin Belli in the true wheeler-dealer San Francisco tradition. In 1952, while serving a short prison term for contempt of court, Hallinan ran for president of the United States. Representing Henry Wallace's left-wing Progressive party, Hallinan polled 140,000 votes from a jail cell. If the newspaper headlines didn't find Hallinan, he would find them.[8] In 1975, Randolph Hearst, the publishing mogul, hired Hallinan to defend his daughter Patty after she had been apprehended by federal agents during her unfathomable sojourn with the Symbionese Liberation Army. It was Hallinan's idea to mount Hearst's defense around the theory that she had been "brainwashed" by the SLA, something known in psychiatric circles as the Stockholm Syndrome. The Hearst family replaced Hallinan and his son, Terry "Kayo" Hallinan, with F. Lee Bailey, whose strategy, it turned out, was not much different than Hallinan's.[9]

"The Hallinan firm had the reputation around San Francisco as the lawyers of last resort," Crenna said. "So a lot of characters walked through the door. If you had Vincent Hallinan arguing your case, his name mattered. He knew everybody, most of the judges. So I guess that's the way George Cory found us."

Walter Hinton, a well traveled singer who had appeared briefly with the San Francisco Symphony, was introduced by Cory to Crenna, who distrusted Hinton from the outset.

"He had a shifty look," Crenna said. "He couldn't hide his greediness. Right away, I knew he had an agenda."

There was the time when Cory was ill, necessitating that Crenna go over to the composer's flat on Pleasant Street so they could review and sign some legal papers. Hinton was also there, with a few others. Crenna needed Cory alone, to discuss their business, but Hinton and the rest of the crowd refused to leave. Crenna tried to impress upon Cory that they needed privacy, but finally the lawyer gave up and they finished the task, with Hinton looking over Cory's shoulder.

"I tried to get George away from Hinton," Crenna said while sitting in the living room of his San Rafael home. "This is what lawyers do for a client. But George was controlled by Hinton. It cost me a client. George found another lawyer. But I still think I tried to do the right thing. And here's a funny one: My wife's former husband was a George Cory. Same spelling, but not related. What are the chances of that?"

Cory and Cross had been together almost 25 years when they separated. "It was like a divorce," Crenna said.[10] Perhaps another song hit might have forestalled the breakup. Cross had a rural upbringing—his family had been among the first settlers in Lake County, California, in the mid-1800s—and he was always comfortable with the ranch life. By contrast, Cory thrived on the bling of the big city. For Cross, it was easier in the country than in San Francisco, which was slow in accepting gay and transgendered people. Cory and Cross had scarcely unpacked their bags upon their return to San Francisco in 1966, when there was a two-day riot at a cafeteria in the Tenderloin district, a disturbance that was later described as a watershed event for the gay movement. Plate glass windows were broken after a transgendered woman threw a cup of coffee into a policeman's face.[11] The San Francisco Board of Supervisors didn't elect an openly gay member until the ill-fated Harvey Milk took office in 1977. A year later, Milk and the mayor, George Moscone, were assassinated by Dan White, another supervisor, who had been supported in his election campaign by the city's policemen's union.[12]

Cory left Cross in Clearlake, a small town a hundred miles north, and moved to San Francisco. In effect, Cory was a bachelor again, and he began taking up with young gay men, who were impressed by his wealth and enthralled by his urbane ways. Between Manhattans, Cory's on-the-rocks drink of choice, he would tell tragicomic stories about his failures in New York before his song about San Francisco landed on Tony Bennett's doorstep.[13] One of Cory's favorite tales was the Thanksgiving when he and Cross were invited to Peggy Lee's Manhattan apartment for dinner. Lee was between two of her four marriages and wanted to be in the company of friends for the holiday. Before the evening was over, she and the two composers came to realize that they were all born in 1920—Cross and Lee in May, just three weeks apart, and Cory in August. As the early guests arrived, Lee told them that there was a big turkey in the oven. There was, but the rub was that she had forgotten to turn on the flame.

Hours went by, but everybody's glass was always filled, the show-biz chatter was ricocheting off the walls, and nobody complained. Sheepishly, a more than famished Cory at last asked about the status of the bird.

"Shouldn't we be smelling something?" he said.

"I'll go look," Lee said.

The turkey was still mostly frozen. For Thanksgiving, Plan B was going to kick in, whatever that was.

Cory would chortle as he finished the story and say: "Peggy never was a very good cook, anyway. The moral is, never go to Peggy Lee's for Thanksgiving."[14]

For a time, Cory lived at 1210 Lombard Street, a choice location on Russian Hill that had the San Francisco Bay, the Golden Gate Bridge and Alcatraz Island for a picture window. This was a block west from the part of Lombard that tour guides (mistakenly) call "the crookedest street in the world." The flat at 1210 has an interesting history. Billy Gaylord, the noted interior designer who worked for the Sherman House hotel and Dianne Feinstein before she became mayor, completed a ten-year lease and signed on for another ten years. Three years into the second lease, Gaylord, only forty but suffering from lymphoma, died at 1210 Lombard Street. The length of Yul Brynner's stay at 1210 was the opposite of Gaylord's—one night. Brynner signed a lease that was to run as long as his signature show, *The King and I*, ran in San Francisco. Inexplicably, the day after he moved in, Brynner was gone. He also stopped payment on his deposit check, leaving the owner of the flat, Rick Booth, with $7000 in bad paper. "At least it gave me a chance to clean out the closets," Booth philosophically says. Herb Caen, the snarky columnist for the *San Francisco Chronicle*, got wind of the dust-up and wrote: "All Brynner did was turn his back on the most breath-taking view in all of San Francisco." In 2015, Booth sold 1210 and the apartment next to it for more than four million dollars and returned to his roots in Salem, Oregon.

By 1977, Cory had moved to the apartment at 18 Pleasant Street, just two blocks from the Fairmont Hotel and the Venetian Room, where Tony Bennett had first sung "I Left My Heart in San Francisco" in public in December of 1961.

Pleasant Street is only a block long, a hilly one-way avenue tucked in between Jones and Taylor, two of San Francisco's major streets.[15] Pleasant Street was named after Mary Ellen Pleasant, the Georgia-born former slave who got fabulously rich and moved in 1852 to San Francisco, where she became known as "the mother of civil rights in California."[16]

The historic Grace Cathedral is not far from Pleasant Street. Cory's apartment was near the entrance to the street, close to Taylor. Tom Wolfe, who has been the head concierge at the Fairmont Hotel for more than twenty years, lives in the neighborhood. Every day he goes to work, Wolfe walks past the apartment where George Cory died. Wolfe, who has befriended Bennett during the singer's stays at the Fairmont over the years, never knew about Cory until I told him.[17]

At 624 Taylor Street, at the corner of Taylor and Post Street, is the Bohemian Club, an exclusive men's-only group that was founded in 1872. "It's the greatest men's party on earth," President Herbert Hoover once said of the Bohemians. Several former presidents have been linked to the Bohemian Club, along with Vaughn Walker, a former federal judge; Pete Wilson, former governor of California; Chris Matthews, a newscaster; Henry Kissinger; and Mickey Hart, once the drummer for the Grateful Dead. George Cory was not a Bohemian, but he knew many of the three thousand members and was welcome there.[18] Cory liked the Bohemian Club because its bartenders knew their way around a Manhattan on the rocks. The bar is arguably the longest in all of San Francisco. "Not many drink Manhattans anymore," Cory once said. "I shudder thinking of the time I will walk into a bar, order one and be told they don't know how to mix it. But I can't imagine that happening at the Bohemian."[19]

By the fall of 1977, Cory was telling Walter Hinton and other friends that he was concerned about his health. Cory had a degenerate heart, cirrhosis of the liver and lung disease. On October 28, 1977, Cory went to a drug store and picked up twenty Percodan tablets. Percodan is a dangerously addictive pain reliever.[20] Elvis Presley used it excessively. Jerry Lewis was hooked on it for thirteen years, once almost killing himself because of the side effects. Prince was an abuser of Percocet, a cousin of Percodan.[21]

According to Hinton, Cory failed to show up for an appointment with his attorney on April 7, 1978.[22] There are business acquaintances of Cory and a relative of Douglass Cross' who question anything Hinton reportedly said. In depositions taken when Cory's will was contested shortly after his death, Hinton, the principal heir, was caught time and again misstating facts. He testified incorrectly about where his mother was buried; he fabricated his education credentials; he claimed to have made certain singing appearances that didn't happen.[23] At any rate, Walter Hinton told police that he was concerned when Cory missed his date with the lawyer.[24] When Hinton couldn't reach Cory by phone on April 11, he called Ann Dunn, Cory's landlady. At 3:00 in the afternoon, Dunn and her nephew, Ken McKee, met Hinton at Cory's apartment and Dunn let them in with her passkey. They found Cory dead, lying on a faded blue brocade couch in the living room. He was wearing a bathrobe and stained underwear. Later, in a coroner's report, it was estimated that Cory had been dead for more than 48 hours. His body was in the early stages of postmortem decomposition and had begun to smell.[25]

Ronald Strowbridge, Douglass Cross' nephew, was close to his uncle as well as Cory (he called both of them "uncle"). Strowbridge, who lived in Lake County, more than a hundred miles from San Francisco, had a key to Cory's apartment. He said that his uncle and Cory had entrusted him with the key when they had signed their conservatorship.[26]

Richard Carpeneti, who was Hinton's attorney when the Cory will was being challenged, had never heard of Strowbridge and wasn't aware that he had a key to Cory's apartment. Carpeneti thought it was odd that Strowbridge, who was Cross' nephew and not related to Cory, would have a key to Cory's flat and Hinton wouldn't have a key. When I got too inquisitive about Hinton, Carpeneti cut me off and said: "I can't discuss Walter Hinton in great detail. Terms of the lawyer-client confidentiality agreement extend beyond the grave."[27]

On a coffee table near the body of Cory was a piece of paper which, the coroner's report noted, indicated that Cory "was taking his life." The police, who were called, kept the note to themselves.[28] In 2016, I made a request to see the note and was summarily turned down. Efforts to look at the note through San Francisco's mayor, Edwin M. Lee, were also unsuccessful.

"It would have been interesting," Lloyd Crenna said, "to compare that note with George's handwriting."[29] Strowbridge, Cross' nephew, questioned the validity of the note, and posited that Cory could have been coerced into writing it. A couple of days after Cory's death, Strowbridge went to the apartment on Pleasant Street. He was looking for seven oil paintings by Grace Carpenter Hudson, who was born in Northern California. Hudson knew the Pomo Indians as a child and devoted much of her long career to painting them. The Pomos also worked the Cross ranch when Douglas Cross' parents owned it. Douglass Cross' mother collected Hudson's works and left the seven paintings to her son, and after his death they were passed on to George Cory.

Strowbridge said Cory's apartment had been stripped by the time he got there. He said there was no sign of anything resembling food in the refrigerator. He said there were several empty half-gallon bottles of Gallo wine strewn about.

"George Cory was a connoisseur," Strowbridge said. "When he drank wine, it was the finest available. He could afford the best, and he drank the best. He wouldn't have been drinking a cheap wine like Gallo, especially in those quantities, unless somebody forced it on him."[30]

In 2016, I spoke with Jesse Stanton, of the San Francisco coroner's office, about Cory's death report. Stanton, who wasn't around in 1978, took the time to go over the report with a fine-tooth comb. He concluded that Cory wasn't a suicide, that he died from natural causes. This made many 38-year-old news accounts of the composer's deaths so much hooey. No matter what the cause of Cory's death, he wasn't a suicide.

"Where it says 'suicide, possible ingestion,' that's just a first-blush opinion," Stanton said. "There was an empty Percodan bottle on the premises, but it was purchased months before the day the body was found. So it doesn't necessarily follow that all of the pills in the bottle were consumed at the same time."[31]

The police at the death scene went up to the second floor of Cory's apartment, where they found an empty twenty-tablet bottle of Percodan. It was upside down, with the cap off. It was the Percodan that Cory had bought five and a half months before.[32]

The account of Cory's death in the *San Francisco Examiner* said that he "had swallowed poison."[33] But the toxicology report said that Cory's "blood [was] negative for common sedative-hypnotic drugs," and further that he tested negative for "morphine-type alkaloids and other common narcotics and dangerous drugs including Perdocan."[34]

I asked Stanton about the alleged suicide note. He said:

If you'll notice, the note "*indicated* [emphasis Stanton's] deceased was taking life." That's an interpretation of the note, and it might have just been a dark note. But since we no longer have the note, we have no way of knowing. Chances are the note didn't say suicide for sure. Take a look at the second page of the report. At the bottom, it says the death certificate was completed on May 12, a month after the body was found, and just below that it says: "Apparent mode of death, due to natural causes." That's the part of the report that is the most significant. The suicide notation on the first page? That's the result of an overly aggressive estimate of what was found at the scene.

Stanton went on to comment about Cory's health. "The cirrhosis alone, in its advanced stages, would have been enough to be fatal," he said.[35]

Talking to the police officers who had reported at 1210 Pleasant would have been useful. But the only officer who signed the coroner's register was "H. Elbert," badge number 812. This was less than forty years ago, so there was always the chance that Elbert might still be alive, but neither the San Francisco Police Department nor the San Francisco Police Officers Association could turn up the name.[36]

At the time, Tony Bennett mourned Cory's death. "I think he was frustrated, upset that his many songs, including many for Billie Holiday, were not more popular," Bennett said. "He was good to me.... He always came to my San Francisco openings."[37]

Bennett, however, only knew the songwriters in passing. He said that his accompanist, Ralph Sharon, knew them much better.[38] Rick Booth, who was Cory's landlord on Lombard Street, said that Cory once took him backstage, after one of Bennett's performances in San Francisco, and introduced him to the singer. Booth recalled that Cory hemmed and hawed, unable for a moment to recall Booth's name. Finally, a chagrined Cory gave up and said: "Tony, this is my landlord."[39]

This was in the early 1970s, the last time Bennett said he saw Cory.[40]

When the will was filed, six days after Cory's body was found, Hinton didn't anticipate any hitches. But on May 7, four of Cory's first cousins filed a protest. They were David Traver, his brothers Cory and Warren, and Winifred Hanson. They were all from the Davenport, Iowa, area. In court papers, the cousins argued that they were Corey's sole heirs because Corey's uncle, Paul Morgenthaler, "has disclaimed all interest in the decedent's estate."[41]

Without an appointment, Hinton walked into Richard Carpeneti's office on Post Street and asked if he could handle the case on a contingency, which meant Carpeneti would get a share of what Hinton got if Hinton prevailed in court. Hinton said that otherwise, he couldn't afford Carpeneti, who was a member of the family firm that included his father, a retired Superior Court judge and a former judicial advisor to Governor Ronald Reagan. Told that a contingency arrangement was out of the question, Hinton agreed to pay Carpeneti a hundred dollars an hour. The case dragged on and Hinton didn't sign the final declaration until ten years later. By that time, Hinton was strapped for cash and he and Carpeneti eventually worked out a contingency deal, which gave Carpeneti a whopping 40 percent of Hinton's song royalties. In time, that beat the hell out of a hundred dollars an hour.

The cousins' attorneys were well-prepared and didn't spare any cost. They hired a private investigator to shadow Hinton. They paid a premium to get the transcripts of the depositions typed up sooner than usual. They hardly cared about Cory's white Steinway baby grand piano; or Hinton's 1976 painting, entitled "Another World," a gift he had given to Cory; or a couple of Oriental rugs. It was the lucrative song rights they were after. By the summer of 1981, three years after Cory's death, a jury trial was imminent.[42] Carpeneti would be the defendant in a long legal battle of his own many years later. When he was in his late forties, his wife of only a few years sued for divorce. It was a messy affair, lasting through two trials that stretched across four years. At the end, after the wife, who was twenty years younger, had spent more than a hundred thousand dollars in legal fees, she got $1800 a month in child support, a flat amount of $54,000 in alimony, half of the proceeds from the sale of a house, and a Jaguar. Later, Carolyn Mundt Carpeneti bought a million-dollar home, became a high-priced political fund-raiser, bore a child out of wedlock to Willie Brown, then the mayor of San Francisco, and wrote a book about the mentally challenged son she had with Richard Carpeneti.[43]

As for the Hinton case, Carpeneti was in a quandary. He seemed to have an airtight document in Cory's will.[44] Other than Hinton, the Morgenthalers and Lina Gastoni, Cory wrote, "I have purposely made no provisions herein for any other person, whether claiming to be an heir of mine or not, and if any person, whether a beneficiary under this will and not mentioned herein, shall contest this will or object to the provisions thereof, or claim to be an heir of mine and as such assert a claim to my estate, or any part thereof; then to such person or persons I hereby give and bequeath the sum of one dollar, and no more in lieu of the provision which I have made or which I might have made herein for such person or persons."[45]

Carpeneti's ex-wife is envious of the deal her former husband cut with Hinton. "The interesting thing," Carolyn Carpeneti said, "is the amount of money Richard gets from the song. He was a genius to create such an annuity for himself."[46]

1. The Puzzling Death of George Cory

When interviewed in 2016, Carpeneti said that Hinton "was the strangest client I ever had." Hinton would answer a question one way one day, then change his answer the next time. Candor was not his bag, even in matters that were immaterial to the case. Carpeneti feared that if Hinton took the witness stand, he would wilt under a cross-examination. His credibility about everything could be called into question. There might be a real danger, in that event, that the cousins could take over the estate.[47]

In early August 1981, during a hearing in open court, the parties agreed to a compromise. The four cousins would receive $150,000, thirty thousand of which would be paid out to their legal team. The payments to the Morgenthalers and Lina Gastoni, a total of $4000, were made, and Walter Hinton was left with the rest. "The compromise and settlement of the will contest is just, fair and reasonable and is in the best interests of all persons interested in the estate," wrote John Ertola, a San Francisco Superior Court judge.[48]

Carpeneti was surprised that Cory's cousins settled for so little. "They had a chance to win the whole thing, with Hinton as an unreliable witness," Carpeneti said. "When they deposed him, they most certainly could see that he abused the truth right and left. And they must have known that the song rights were worth much, much more than what their clients settled for. It wasn't even close." Across the table from me in the fancy Olympic Club in downtown San Francisco, Carpeneti reached into his pocket and showed me two recent checks he had received. They represented just a partial payment for the song residuals, which had been signed over to him by Hinton all those years before.

Several years after Hinton's case with Cory's cousins had been settled, Carpeneti got a letter estimating that his contingency share of the song rights had come to about $1.5 million. Hinton's new lawyer said that, *ex post facto*, Carpeneti had now been overpaid for his work with Hinton, and that Carpeneti should relinquish his 40 percent rights to the residuals. I don't know if Karen Mitchell was Hinton's attorney then; she represented Hinton later on, not long before he died. Mitchell declined to discuss Hinton for this book.

"In one sense, they were right," Carpeneti said. "If you figured it out on an hourly basis, the million-dollar figure, whatever it was, came to more than what any lawyer in town might charge. But at the time, neither I nor Hinton knew what was ahead of us, in future royalties. They could have been anything. And I took a chance through the whole litigation, and deserved to be rewarded for that. Suppose the cousins had prevailed, and gotten the whole estate? I would have gotten forty percent of nothing."

Carpeneti hired one of the biggest law firms in San Francisco to represent him. They wrote Hinton's new lawyer a strong letter saying that anything that changed the *status quo* would be unacceptable, and that Carpeneti was prepared to go to court to argue his position.

"I never heard from Hinton's lawyer again," Carpeneti said.

Long before the legal tug-of-war ended, one provision in George Cory's will had already been satisfied. He wanted no funeral, no folderol, just a simple cremation and his ashes scattered at sea. He got his wish. There were no news accounts of the services. Not even the ubiquitous Herb Caen, of the *San Francisco Chronicle*, sniffed out something that would have been his kind of item. Walter Hinton rented a tugboat. With his lawyer, Richard Carpeneti, and about a dozen of Cory's friends, Hinton went out in the direction of the Golden Gate Bridge. Ten miles past the magnificent reddish-orange structure, arguably San Francisco's most iconic landmark, Hinton emptied the urn into the bay. Then Hinton, in his deep baritone, sang "I Left My Heart in San Francisco" acapella.[49] Some critics have found it odd that Douglass Cross' lyrics don't mention the bridge itself. The closest he came was when he mentioned his love waiting in San Francisco, a city alongside a blue and windy sea.[50]

Cross died in 1975 and was cremated. His remains were buried in a cemetery in Lake County, California, in the hinterlands. He is next to his parents, about a hundred miles north of San Francisco.[51] Thus it ended up the boonies for one, the briny for the other.

2

Walter K. Hinton

He might have been Walter *R.* Hinton, which seemed to be his name in 1940.[1] Or was he *Harry* Hinton, as a San Francisco newspaper identified him in 1978?[2] Walter Hinton was a professional singer who had trouble with his billing. In George Cory's will, written 27 days before he was found dead, it was Walter K. Hinton. Cory should have known. Although they didn't live together, he and Hinton had been a couple for several years, a pairing that had started only a few years after Cory's 25-year relationship with his songwriting partner, Douglass Cross, had ended.[3]

In Cory's will, Hinton was identified as his "dear friend and business manager."

On the phone from her home near Cologne, Germany, Daniela Schwarz chuckled. Schwarz—her friends call her "Lela"—was once a tenant of Hinton's, going back to the 1980s. She also became Hinton's friend.

"I can't imagine Walter being anybody's business manager," Schwarz said. "Walter never wanted to manage his own business affairs, let alone anyone else's. I was his tenant [in San Francisco] for about twenty years. Sometimes, he didn't even cash the rent checks. They just never cleared the bank, and he didn't seem to care. He wasn't money-motivated in the least, which is why I find it impossible to believe that he had anything to do with the death [of George Cory]."

When Cory was found dead at his apartment in 1978, the San Francisco coroner at first thought it was a suicide. Following toxicology results, the conclusion was accidental death. Some in Cory's circle suggest sinister possibilities.

When Walter Hinton was near death, at age 84 in 2005, twelve Dumpsters were to clear out the four-level flat he owned at 833 Fillmore Street. In sorting the detritus, checks written out to Hinton that totaled $300,000 were discovered.[4] Most of that money came from royalties that Hinton had inherited from Cory for the Cory/Douglass Cross song "I Left My Heart in San Francisco."[5]

"Walter," somebody said, "don't you want to endorse these?"

Many of them were so old that they probably wouldn't have been honored, anyway.

Walter, on his back in his bedroom, his once Olympian body eroded by time and illness to that of a dissipated old man, dismissed the idea with a dramatic wave.

"It's too late for any of that," he said.

His nephew, Ted Robinson, had come to San Francisco from Silver Spring, Maryland, to help Hinton in his final months.[6] Federal records indicate that Hinton's last residence was in Silver Spring.[7] Blame not the custodians for the error. The details of Hinton's life are a historical quagmire; Lela Schwarz, who became his friend as well as his tenant and knew him for more than thirty years, was told by Hinton that he was from Puerto Rico. Schwarz had heard enough of Hinton's fabrications to doubt that was true, but she also knew that getting the facts from him was impossible.[8] The truth was, he was from North Carolina.[9] Barbara Fluhrer Bauer, who wrote his obituary, didn't say where he was from. She wrote about some of his stage credits, as a singer,[10] but was not surprised when I told her that all of it didn't check out. "People in his profession do that all the time, don't they?" she said. "They embellish. I knew Walter for a long time, for many, many years, even before I wrote about his passing. I was very fond of him."[11] Richard Carpeneti, who represented Hinton when four of Cory's cousins contested Cory's will in court,[12] was aware of Hinton's reputation. Many of Hinton's friends and acquaintances said he was incapable of telling the truth about virtually anything. "He was a big liar," Lela Schwarz said, less than a minute after our interview began. Another friend of Hinton's once advised him: "Walter, none of us gives a damn whether you got a doctorate from Harvard or not." Someone else said that Hinton "lied just to lie, so why don't you just quit lying about it?" But Hinton's adagio with the truth was incurable.[13]

Walter Hinton's most preposterous lie, in my opinion, was repeatedly saying that he wrote "I Left My Heart in San Francisco." There's no evidence that Hinton wrote anything, yet he went on saying that he wrote the song that's always been credited to Cory (the music) and Cross (lyrics). When Hinton was asked why he was so wealthy, he would say: "Because of the residuals. I wrote that song, and the residuals just keep coming in. Those other guys [Cross and Cory] say they wrote it, but they got it from me."[14]

Cory once said that he borrowed elements of the 1930s Tommy Dorsey hit "On Treasure Island" for "I Left My Heart in San Francisco,"[15] but that's the only inkling that the San Francisco song wasn't an original. The history of the Cory/Cross song simply doesn't jibe with anything Hinton said. Too many people encountered the song before Cory ever met Hinton, which was in the early seventies. The song was published in 1954. Claramae Turner said that the song was written for her because of a friendship with Cory, but she never recorded it.[16] Tessie O'Shea said that Cory and Cross offered her the song when she met them one night in Greenwich Village in the 1950s.[17] Ralph Sharon, Tony Bennett's accompanist, said that Cory and Cross gave him the song in New York, probably in 1959, but at least before 1961.[18] Early in 1961, Cross offered the song to Tennessee Ernie Ford, who turned it down.[19] Bennett first sang the song at the end of 1961, at first informally in an nearly closed bar in Hot Springs, Arkansas, and on December 28 at the Venetian Room of San Francisco's Fairmont Hotel.[20] That was a lot of history for Hinton to rewrite.

The Reverend Dorsey Blake played devil's advocate. He delivered the eulogy at Hinton's memorial service in 2005. "How do we know," Blake said, "that Walter didn't know [George Cory] *before* 1954? There's no record of that, one way or another. Walter could have known both songwriters before 1954, given them the idea for the song, or even given them elements of the song, before that year, and they took it from there. Why did Cory leave most of his estate to Walter? Was it guilt he felt because Walter had had a big hand in the song? I don't think any of this is out of the question."[21]

Blake is a voice in the wilderness with this theory. There is too much evidence, albeit circumstantial, that Hinton didn't know Cory until the 1970s. Ron Strowbridge, Douglass Cross' nephew, was close to both his uncle and Cory—he called Cory "Uncle George"—and had never heard about Hinton until the 1970s. It seems unlikely, had the songwriters known Hinton as distantly as the 1950s, that they wouldn't have mentioned Hinton's name at least once, to someone, in a span of twenty years.[22]

Walter Hinton was born in Durham, North Carolina, in 1921.[23] Durham was a small town then; Duke University was in the future, and the population was about 50,000.[24] Martha Hinton, with her husband no longer around, had four children to support. Walter was the youngest. Martha worked as a steamer—putting creases in new clothes that were being prepared for the sales racks. Fanny Clive lived with the Hintons and cared for the children while the family's only breadwinner worked long hours at a steam press.[25]

Later on, Hinton said that his mother was an accomplished pianist, and for all anybody knows, she could very well have played the piano.

There's no law that says you can't be a steamer and a pianist at the same time. Not true was that Walter had a son—he didn't have any children—who became a renowned doctor in Pennsylvania and created a cure for syphilis. Not true that Hinton had once been a shipbuilder. Not true that Hinton had written scores for Hollywood films.

Hinton got a late start as a wannabe opera singer. At 37, he was one of 25 fledgling singers who were selected for the Merola Opera Program in San Francisco in 1959.[26] In 1960, he was a member of a West Coast company production of *Show Boat* that starred Joe E. Brown, Julie Wilson, Ruta Lee and Eddie Foy, Jr. Hinton played a doorman.[27] In 1967, he appeared at the War Memorial Opera House in San Francisco for three performances of *The Visitation,* an opera that starred Simon Estes. Hinton played a preacher.[28] Black opera singers had difficulty being accepted by the mainstream until the 1980s. Estes wasn't offered a contract by the New York Metropolitan Opera until he was 43, and the prima donna Leontyne Price received death threats when she began singing at The Met.[29] It was said after Hinton died that he had performed "opposite Leontyne Price" in *Aida,* but The Met and the San Francisco Opera Company have no record of that.[30] The male lead in *Aida* was written for a tenor; Hinton was a baritone. Many times when Hinton presented his educational credentials, they were questioned.[31] However, along the way, an occasional critic tossed a bouquet in Hinton's direction. "A well-produced voice, smooth rich voice with glowing top—outstanding flair for the lyric stage," wrote Greg Sargent in *New York* magazine; "Hinton's poignant singing brings tears to the eyes," said Paul Hertelendy, writing in the *Oakland Tribune.*[32]

In 1976, both Cory and Hinton performed at a Fourth of July celebration sponsored by the *San Francisco Chronicle* at Candlestick Park. During an hour-long musical show that preceded four hundred skyrockets being shot into the air, Hinton sang "Some Enchanted Evening" and then Cory, who had tagged along with Hinton but was not listed in the program, played "I Left My Heart in San Francisco" on the piano. Mayor George Moscone was supposed to make a speech, but he was tardy, too late to hear Hinton and Cory but in time for the pyrotechnics. "It's a little like singing in *Porgy and Bess* in Moscow," Hinton said afterwards. No one knew what that meant, or whether Hinton had ever been to Moscow.[33]

The Reverend Ernest R. Wade and his wife Agnes were intertwined with both George Cory and Walter Hinton. The details of the connection have been hard to ascertain. In 1978, when Cory wrote his will shortly before he died, the Wades were two of the three witnesses. It is unclear whether they were acquaintances of Cory's or possibly friends of Hinton's whom he recommended to Cory. They could have been both. At the time the Wades witnessed the will, they were living at 833 Fillmore Street. In the will, Hinton's address is listed as 2919 California Street.[34]

The property at 833 Fillmore is a Victorian home that was built in 1920. In 1982, the Wades turned over the house to Hinton.[35] "It's possible," said Will White, who bought 833 from Robinson for $1.6 million, "that the Wades could no longer afford the carrying charges on their residence."[36] Hinton was reasonably wealthy by then, since the residuals for "I Left My Heart in San Francisco" had been left to him by Cory fourteen years before.[37] Shashi Dalal, who knew Hinton through Dalal's affiliation with the Western Addison Senior Center in San Francisco, said Hinton would flash around check stubs from the residuals that came from the song. They amounted to several thousand dollars a month, Dalal said.[38]

Whether Ernest Wade was Hinton's pastor is also unclear. Both of the Wades died in the 1990s.[39] Even though he only knew Hinton casually, the Reverend Dorsey Blake gave his eulogy. Blake was a former professor at the University of Alabama and more recently a visiting associate professor of pastoral leadership and social transformation at the Pacific School of Religion in Berkeley, California.[40]

The property at 833 Fillmore, with more than five thousand square feet, consisted of a basement, two residential levels and an attic. Lela Schwarz, a rock singer from Germany, lived in either the attic or the basement for about twenty years. She was paying $600 a month rent when she moved in, and the same amount when she left. At one time, there were seven musicians and artists living in the units beneath her, and Hinton was living in the basement. Hinton was licensed to rent only two units at 833, but there were times when he was collecting rent for four units.

Schwarz self-recorded an album with her group, *Schizophrenia*. When I asked her if she played an instrument, she said: "I could play almost anything you put in my hands. But mostly I just sang." She is now a psychic healer living with her husband near Cologne, where she moved in 2010. She wouldn't have minded staying at 833 Fillmore, but White reconfigured the property so his mother-in-law could live with him and his family. She had also tired of living in San Francisco, a city that in her opinion had gone backwards on many levels. "It was no longer the city that I had first fallen in love with," she said.

Schwarz said that she kept her attic residence in good condition, but the same couldn't be said for the rest of the property. Hinton, who made few improvements downstairs, allowed Schwarz to make all the renovations she needed, and paid for the materials she used on the attic.

Hinton practiced voodoo. He was also affiliated with the Rosicrucian Order,[41] an international association of Christian mystics whose purpose, their followers say, is studying the laws of metaphysics, preaching the gospel and healing the sick.[42] Hinton usually had a collection of cats and dogs on Fillmore, and one day he brought in a goat. At the time, he was doing makeshift repairs on the back of the property, perhaps hoping to create a sub-basement and add a rental unit. The back porch was covered with a cheap piece of plywood, which had a cutout for a skylight that, Hinton believed, would make the new unit more attractive. There was a Rottweiler living next door who didn't get along with the goat. One day the Rottweiler got loose and chased the goat all over Hinton's backyard. The goat ran across the plywood, which couldn't hold him, and he fell into the basement.[43] Hinton had bought the goat for slaughter, a ritual that practitioners of Haitian voodoo perform every Easter Sunday. But word of the doomed goat leaked, and before Easter arrived a neighbor called the local American Society for the Prevention of Cruelty to Animals. It dispatched someone to Fillmore to rescue the goat.

The Hinton place got to be known in the neighborhood as "The Witch House." Inside and out, it was garishly painted purple, black, red and gold.[44] Although they were neighbors, there's no evidence that Hinton and Jim Jones, whose misguided Peoples Temple congregation had moved from Indiana to California's Redwood Valley to San Francisco's Fillmore district by 1970, ever met. Their approach to animals might have given them common ground. When he was young, Jones killed a cat as an experiment. He had hoped he could bring it back to life.

Of all of San Francisco, the Fillmore district was impacted the most by the hundreds of deaths at Jones' hands in Guyana. Most of the victims were black, and Fillmore was once the black hub of San Francisco. During the lengthy Jim Jones postmortem, the target of some of the finger-pointing by the white community extended to Steve Gavin, the city editor of the *San Francisco Chronicle*. Gavin fawned over Jones, attended services at the Peoples Temple and discouraged his reporters from doing any hard-hitting investigations that might have detoured Jones' manic path to the Armageddon in the jungle.[45] (Full disclosure: Years before Gavin landed in San Francisco, he wrote a popular Herb Caen-ish man-about-town column for the now-defunct *Baltimore News-American*. Frequently he prowled after-dark Baltimore in a tuxedo. On those nights, that made for a comical contrast, Gavin at his typewriter in full dress, surrounded mostly by ink-stained wretches in *dishabille*).

Hinton's friends frowned on a platonic relationship he had with a woman named Margaret Beale. Not many of those in Hinton's circle ever knew her last name. She was described as "a bag lady," "a fortune hunter," and worse. Some said that she dressed like "Aunt Jemima," the black icon for breakfast foods manufactured by Quaker Oats. Beale wore what looked like an apron, a kerchief around her neck and a babushka on her head. She was hardly attractive, and a large, pointy nose, something that might have led to a part in *Hansel and Gretel*, made her downright grotesque. Supposedly she stalked Hinton before he was finally smitten by her. They had sung together in the choir of the Third Baptist Church. "For a while, he was totally dependent on her," Lela Schwarz said. "Walter alienated a lot of his friends by continuing to see her." The day Schwarz was graduated from Psychic Horizons, a San Francisco school for meditation and healing, there was a party for her at 833 Fillmore Street and Beale was there. Hinton kept telling people that he had signed over some of his lucrative rights to "I Left My Heart in San Francisco" to Beale, and every time he told the

In an undated photo, Walter Hinton (left) is with Daniela "Lela" Schwarz (center) and Margaret Beale. Hinton inherited rights to the song after George Cory died in 1978. Hinton told friends that he gave a share of his residuals to Beale. Schwarz was a longtime tenant of Hinton's (courtesy Daniela "Lela" Schwarz).

story, her share grew. He started out at 7 percent, went up to 14 percent and finally he said her inheritance would be 21 percent. Hinton had already sacrificed 40 percent of his song rights to pay his former attorney, Richard Carpeneti.

The way Margaret Beale was described to me, she could have been what was once pejoratively known as a "fag hag." In another era, when it was mostly out of the question to admit homosexuality, gay men sometimes traveled with straight women in order to camouflage their true sexual preference. I first heard the term "fag hag" in the early 1960s, during a trip to the Mardi Gras in New Orleans. I met Tennessee Williams at a rowdy hotel party where he was accompanied by a woman; a few partygoers whispered to me that she was a fag hag.

Hinton often traveled to the Nevada entertainment meccas in Reno and Las Vegas, although he was not especially known as a gambler. The spectacular stage shows in the casinos had an appeal for him. He would have an occasional drink, but was never known as a drug user. Despite his bonhomie, he got into an occasional scuffle in San Francisco. Some acquaintances found his flamboyance repugnant. He was tall, a few inches above six feet, broad-backed and loved to talk. Some of his fanciful stories were hard to take. The night he was stabbed by a young gay man in a bar, he almost died. Fortunately the knife just missed both his heart and one of his lungs. Hinton was not armed and there were several witnesses, yet he declined to press charges.[46]

In May of 2000, a tenant named Craig Osterberg moved into 833 Fillmore. Not long afterward, Osterberg sued Hinton, Ted Robinson and a real estate management firm called Ramsey Properties. Osterberg was asking for $200,000, plus a million in punitive damages. Robinson, who was Hinton's nephew, was described as his conservator. The case was considered an illegal-eviction dispute by the time it dragged to an end five years later, but there were many other issues. Osterberg's suit cited these problems:

Lack of repairs to the unit.
Inadequate heat and ventilation.
No smoke detectors.
Construction and excavation without permits.
Presence of toxic materials, including mold buildup.
Four units in the building with permission from the city for only two.
No reimbursement for improvement materials.
Trespassing by owners.

Placed end to end, the documents filed by both sides would have stretched across the Golden Gate Bridge.[47] Left unexplained in this Everest of paperwork was why Osterberg continued to live in this allegedly uninhabitable place.

In May of 2005, approaching his 84th birthday and suffering from cancer, Hinton was declared an "incompetent person." Hinton was dying, and at first Robinson placed him in a nursing home, which didn't work out. Hinton's friends insisted that Robinson bring him back to Fillmore Street. "He died peacefully at home," Lela Schwarz said. "But he was only a shell of himself. He was a frail old man at the end."[48]

Hinton died on September 11.[49] The trial was scheduled for November 28. Osterberg had spent a thousand dollars to keep the case alive, and his lawyers were probably working on contingency. "[Osterberg] really loved Walter," Schwarz said. "But he was hooked on speed, and that habit made him crazy. When he did that, I got very mad at him. It ended a long, close friendship."[50]

Hinton had given a deposition in San Francisco before his health worsened. Robinson was deposed in Washington, D.C. Typically, Hinton rambled with his answers, and frequently had to be interrupted by Osterberg's lawyers to stay on track. Robinson, thirteen years younger than Hinton, was close-mouthed, and frequently gave one-word answers.[51]

It's unclear whether Hinton had many business dealings with Danny Tene, but he was linked in some way with Tene, who was one of the figures in what became known in newspaper headlines as the "Foxglove Deaths." From 1984 until 1993, six elderly men and one woman were found dead. Tene and other members of a Gypsy clan, who were enriched by the deceased's estates, were implicated. Some of the deaths may have been caused by digitalis, the heart drug that is derived from the foxglove flower.[52] The San Francisco police botched the investigation, and by the time the case reached trial, the accused plea-bargained their way down to lesser charges, such as fraud, and light sentences were meted out. Doug Schmidt was the attorney for one of the defendants, Mary Tene Steiner, who was Danny Tene's mother. Several years before, when he was a young lawyer of 32, Schmidt was the attorney for Dan White, who had assassinated George Moscone, the mayor of San Francisco, and Harvey Milk, a member of the city's board of supervisors.[53] Through clever jury screening—Milk was gay and there were no gay people on the jury—and emotional arguments about White's mental state, Schmidt turned the case around. The jury came back with a guilty verdict for manslaughter instead of double first-degree murder. White served less than five years. When he came back as a Man Without a City, he committed suicide less than two years after his release. At the time of the trial, Schmidt already owned six hundred acres of land in California, and the White case—the lawyer became synonymous with what was labeled "the Twinkie defense"— assured him a lifetime of fame.[54]

The only woman to die in the Gypsy case was Hope Victoria Beesley, a widow in her early eighties who was about fifty years older than Danny Tene. Beesley said she was coerced—or tricked—into signing a joint tenancy deed for her $400,000 home in the Sunset District of San Francisco, which meant that if she died, Tene would own the property free and clear. When Tene had what he wanted on paper, he left Beesley, who sued him in Superior Court. The proceedings began in the fall of 1990. In 1992, through her attorney, Beesley hired Fay Faron, a private investigator who ran the one-woman Rat Dog Dick Detective Agency. Beesley and Faron never got the chance to meet. A week after Faron accepted the assignment to shadow Tene, on the day after Thanksgiving, Beesley was found dead from what the coroner said was "cardiopulmonary arrest."[55] But the lawsuit continued, mainly at the behest of Barry Hughes, who had met Beesley on the telephone when she called his office at Pac Bell to complain about Tene's intimidating phone calls. Hughes, in his forties, eventually became Beesely's virtual caretaker, even doing her house cleaning and wash. By the time of Beesley's death, Hughes had become the executor of her estate.[56]

In February of 1993, three months after Beesley had died, and before the Gypsies had been indicted for the deaths of the elderly men, Walter K. Hinton told the court that he knew Danny Tene. "Hinton came in wearing a snappy hat, with his hair curled, the whole nine yards," said William Rozell III, who was working as a paralegal for Tene's attorney, Benjamin Kaplan, at the time. "He had a box of papers that was so disorganized that you didn't know what he was talking about. He had stuff written on napkins, all kinds of shit. By the time he had finished, you got the feeling that he might have been a loan shark."[57]

One of those scraps of paper in the box, Hinton testified, was a promissory note, supposedly signed by Tene and saying that Tene owed Hinton $90,000. Kaplan, acting on behalf of Tene, didn't believe Hinton. "He seemed like such an unseemly character," Kaplan said. "He even claimed that he had written 'I Left My Heart in San Francisco.'" Kaplan hired a private investigator to check it out. The PI came back with samples of Hinton's and Tene's signatures over the years. He did a slide presentation for the court, comparing signatures of Hinton and Tene that were written about the same time as the note. The court concluded that Tene's signature was a forgery, and looked more like Hinton's. They could have thrown the book at Hinton. Instead, he agreed to pay the accrued legal and court costs, which were an estimated $40,000. Hinton gambled $90,000 on a forged note, and lost $40,000.[58]

Fay Faron, who had been hired by Hope Victoria Beesley, was out of the private-investigator business in 2017 and living in New Orleans. When I told her about Hinton's scheme to bilk Tene, she said: "What a band of thieves! I've never heard of anyone trying a scam on a Gypsy. I would have guessed that the ninety thousand dollars was money that Tene scammed out of Hinton, and it probably was. Then Hinton forged the promissory note to make it easier for him to collect. That would fit with the personalities. Why else would Tene owe Hinton?"[59]

Beesley v. Tene didn't end until 1997, seven years after it began.[60] Hughes, the executor for Beesley's estate, persisted because there was supposed to be a hidden safe in the house, which might have contained cash and the dead woman's valuable jewelry. Even after Tene won in court and kept the house, the safe was never found.[61] Tene sold the house in 2009 for just over a million dollars.[62]

In 2017, I told Lela Schwarz, Hinton's friend and former tenant living in Cologne, Germany, about the Hinton-Tene connection. "The only person I know of who tried to take advantage of Walter was Margaret Beale," Schwarz said. "I believe Walter was incompetent near the end. That is why he was such an easy game for Margaret. She used that 'Aunt Jemima' look to take him in. [Margaret Beale] was white, but wanted everybody to think that she was black."[63]

Court records of Hinton's conservatorship began in early 2002 and didn't end until December 2006, more than a year after his death. The titles of the court proceedings alone take up seventeen pages.[64] "In California," said Arthur Park, a lawyer who represented one of Hinton's conservators early on, "a court asks for a conservatorship [akin to a guardianship] when a person has one or more cognitive deficits, and shows signs that they can't withstand undue influences on their affairs."[65]

Another lawyer who helped with Hinton's conservatorship was Debra Dolch. She said, without elaborating, that there were signs of "financial abuse."[66] At the end of the rainbow for someone was property worth more than a million dollars and song residuals that, over the years, would be worth many millions. As the conservatorship played out in court, a psychologist, on behalf of the court, interviewed Hinton. The results of that interview are considered confidential by the court.

Park's client was Lloyd Thomas, a retired sheriff's deputy who was a friend of Hinton's. They had met in the early 1960s, when Thomas worked as a doorman at the club where Hinton was singing.[67] Hinton had once said that he was thirteen when he became friends with Thomas, but that was another of his mostly harmless untruths. He was thirty years off in describing his friendship with Thomas.[68]

"It looked like [Debra Dolch] was going to do the right thing when she got involved in the conservatorship," said Park, who was Thomas' lawyer. "The thing turned into a big mess. When Hinton's relatives got involved, my client dropped out."[69]

The name of Ted Robinson, Hinton's nephew, first appears in the conservatorship on July 2, 2004, two years after it began.[70] "He came out of the woodwork," Park said.

"Do you think he was trying to take advantage of Hinton?" I asked.

"'Taking advantage' is a weak term," Park said.[71]

In June 2005, a few months before Hinton died, Robinson posted a bond of $539,000. This was to protect Hinton in the event something untoward happened to his estate. The court asked Robinson for more. The same day, he increased his bond to $744,000.[72]

Robinson was the seller of 833 Fillmore—the buyer, Will White, has corroborated that. Left behind was a baby grand piano. When I visited White at the vastly remodeled location, he said he was hoping that the baby grand piano left behind might have been a valuable collector's item, what George Cory and Douglass Cross used to write "I Left My Heart in San Francisco." He thought he might really have something.[73]

"I think I'm going to disappoint you," I said. "They wrote that song in Brooklyn Heights—what was it, about sixty years ago. I haven't found anything that says that when they moved to California, they took the piano with them."

Arthur Park said that Ted Robinson was Hinton's beneficiary,[74] and although Lloyd Thomas said that Hinton had made out a will, I couldn't find a record of one. Repeated interview requests to Robinson's attorney, Greer Smith, were fruitless. Somebody snoopier than me will have to find out how much of the song rights Robinson has retained. For sure, the lawyer Richard Carpeneti has 40 percent of what Cory left Hinton, but even Carpeneti doesn't know who his partners are. Did Hinton really give Margaret Beale 21 percent, as he said? If so, that would leave Robinson with 39 percent. The publisher of the song is Sony/ATV Music Publishing.

Walter Hinton's memorial service, on September 20, 2005, nine days after his death, was held at the Western Addition Senior Center in the San Francisco Tenderloin. About thirty people attended, including Lloyd Thomas. Lela Schwarz brought twenty pounds of potato salad. "It was a great memorial," Schwarz said. "A few people, including me, spoke about him. Everyone spoke well of him."[75]

Someone read part of the poem "Miss Me, But Let Me Go"[76] attributed to Edgar A. Guest.

Daniela "Lela" Schwarz said: "*Vater unser, der du bist im Himmel…*" That was The Lord's Prayer in German, her native tongue. Walter Hinton's ashes were put out to sea, beyond the Golden Gate Bridge. Schwarz and four others were on board.[77] The last of George Cory had been scattered in the same waters, almost in the same spot, about three decades before.

3

Westward, Ho

Douglass Cross came from sturdy stock. George Washington Hammack was the father of Douglass Cross' mother. Hammack's father, Brice Martin Hammack, was 24 years old when he left the farm life of St. Charles, Missouri, and went out to San Francisco in 1849. Almost a century later, it was a city Douglass Cross would fall in love with. Brice Hammack was engaged to be married when he left for San Francisco; he told his fiancée that he would return to marry her, and perhaps bring word that California would be a better place than the Midwest to rear their children.[1] News of the gold discoveries in Northern California was engulfing the country. The president, James Polk, told the U.S. Congress that rumors of all the gold in California were not greatly exaggerated. Victor John Fourgeaud wrote about San Francisco, the new Shangri-La. A couple thousand copies of Fourgeaud's come-hither treatise reached the Midwest via muleback. Thousands of sailors deserted ships in the San Francisco harbor to run off to the gold fields. So many reporters gave up their jobs that two of San Francisco's leading weeklies were forced to shut down. A city of only a thousand residents a few years before, San Francisco saw its population grow to a hundred thousand virtually overnight. School teachers, among the highest paid in the country, created a serious shortage of educators when they shucked their jobs and rushed off in search of gold.[2]

From San Francisco, Brice Hammack wrote his father, Martin Hammack, about the potential in California. He wrote his fiancée, Elizabeth Gray, that he was coming back to Missouri to marry her, but added that they wouldn't stay home for long. Gray, excited about their prospects, looked forward to the move. Her large family had been shaken by the death of her mother, hamstrung by the debts of her father.

Brice Martin Hammack, who had gone to California with his brother John, appeared to be in no hurry to get home. Having had a small amount of luck as prospectors, he and John stayed in Northern California for two years. Then they took a circuitous trip back to Missouri: By ship from San

Francisco to Panama; by land across Panama; by ship from Panama to New Orleans; and then a boat up the Mississippi River to St. Louis. Eighty-four hundred miles later, they had a party waiting for him, a party better described as a feast: Barbecued beef and other game; homemade gingerbread, a barrel of cider and enough hard liquor for the most diehard of the imbibers.

For his part, Brice Hammack did not return to Missouri empty-handed. He had gold rings for his fiancée and his sisters. Married on Christmas Day, 1852, Brice Hammack said that he and his bride were moving to Northern California. His parents, Martin and Eleanor Hammack, determined to keep the family together, made plans to sell their property and organize a large wagon train that would also go West with their son. The thirteen wagons were handmade in St. Louis, and the Hammack party, all 27 of them, not all of them related, left Missouri on April 15, 1853. They were among tens of thousands of Americans headed for gold country.

The Hammack party included at least one pregnant woman, and seven children between the ages of two and fifteen. Martin Hammack, a very fit 62, was the wagon master. He accompanied the party on horseback. They took the Santa Fe Trail, a trip of nine hundred miles, and Hammack's experience against the threats from Native Americans would be invaluable along the way. He had been a Native American scout, traveling between Missouri and Tennessee, prior to the War of 1812, and in 1832 fought for the United States during the fifteen-week Black Hawk Indian War around what is now Rock Island, Illinois.

The Hammacks traveled with oxen, horses and dairy cattle. While many of the other parties along the way were using horse-driven wagons, Martin Hammack favored oxen. He theorized that the powerful ox, while not as quick as a horse, was more durable and could cover more ground before it needed resting. The road was non-existent for the most part, and there were rivers and streams to cross. Sometimes there were ferries, but most times not. The Hammacks went through Kansas, Oklahoma and Colorado before reaching Santa Fe, New Mexico. Two in the party, one a Hammack cousin, died along the way, but there is no record Native Americans were involved. One of Hammack's horses was stolen, and a few cattle. Hammack himself disappeared from the encampment one night, but returned the next day, unharmed.

California had reached statehood in 1850. From New Mexico, it was on to the far reaches of Northern California for the Hammack group. Early in 1854, the Hammacks reached Shasta City. Martin's eight-year-old daughter never forgot the place. A man from a trading post gave her an opened tin, and she tasted peaches for the first time. They might have stayed, but Martin Hammack, talking to a few other settlers, heard them gush about an area about 150 miles to the south. It had fresh-water lakes, wild oats, deer, buffalo and other game, and was virtually uninhabited. The Hammacks pushed on, and arrived in what would be Lake County on April 14, 1854—a day short of the one-year anniversary of their departure from Missouri. Other than a few hunters and trappers, the Hammacks were probably the first whites to settle there. Elizabeth Gray Hammack, Brice Hammack's wife, was in her eighth month. The baby, Sara Eleanor, arrived on May 31, 1854, believed to be the first white child born in Lake County.

The Brice Hammacks had three more children. Their fourth-born, George Washington Hammack, came on December 15, 1864, six months after his father died.[3] George Washington Hammack was Mae Elizabeth Hammack's father—Mae Elizabeth Hammack Cross, the mother of the lyricist who would write the words for "I Left My Heart in San Francisco."

In 1920, Mae Cross gave birth to her first child, Harry Douglass Cross, Jr., who, under the name Douglass Cross, would become a famous songwriter because of only one song. After suffering several strokes, Mae Cross died at 77 in a Lakeport, California, hospital on October 14, 1967.[4] Douglass Cross' father had died eighteen years before, just a few days short of 67.[5]

Mae Elizabeth Hammack's mother, the former Minnie Jane Specht (records vary, and the spelling could have been Spect or Speck), would have four more children.[6]

At least two of them were peas in a pod. Mae Hammack and her brother Valentine, who was six years younger, knew early on what they wanted and were determined to get it. When he was a young boy, Valentine talked about being a soldier or a lawyer. He became both. He served overseas in the Army artillery corps during World War I, and afterward he worked his way through law school and ironically once practiced on Sutter Street in San Francisco. That is the street named after the gold prospector John Sutter. It was the possibility of finding gold—unfulfilled, it turned out—that brought Valentine's ancestors to Northern California.

Valentine and his older sister worked the family farm while they went to public schools in Lake County. At sixteen, Valentine took a job with a wholesale dry goods company in San Francisco, then joined the Army in 1917 when the U.S. entered the war. His fiancée, Helen Theis, whose father was an executive with Pacific Gas & Electric Co., waited patiently for his return. Valentine was discharged on March 17, 1919. A week later, he married Helen Theis, took a job with a wholesale supply company and began to study law. He was a U.S. assistant district attorney and in 1945, after the end of World War II, he was a special assistant to the attorney general in helping prosecute Japanese war criminals.[7]

From her early years, Mae Hammack aspired to be a nurse and a novelist and she became both. She studied nursing at St. Luke's Hospital Nursing School in San Francisco. She wrote several articles about her pioneering family, and in 1956, while her son was across the country in New York, trying to sell his songs, she self-published *Again to Earth*, a 423-page novel loosely based on her family adjusting to the challenges of an undeveloped land in California in the 1890s.[8] It is not difficult to deduce where some of the fictitious names came from. The book is a story about the Grey family. Mae Hammack's grandmother's maiden name was Elizabeth Gray[9]; the protagonist is a young girl named Liza Jane and another of the women is named Jane[10]; Mae Hammack Cross' mother's name was Minnie Jane.[11]

It is unclear when Mae Hammack met Harry Cross, but they were married in 1919, when she was 29 and he was 36. It is likely that they met when he was in San Francisco on business for the Boy Scouts of America. A few years before their marriage, Cross had been called from his base in Los Angeles to organize a scout council in San Francisco.[12] Eventually, Harry Cross left his job as a fundraiser for the Boy Scouts to continue in the same field, first with the University of Texas, then with the University of Oklahoma. At one time, he was a trustee with the Oklahoma school. Those jobs required a considerable amount of travel, and Mae Cross usually went with him.[13]

There is no indication that Mae Cross tried to get her novel published before she turned to a now-defunct vanity press in New York. Mae Cross was sixteen when the great San Francisco earthquake struck. This is the way she described an earthquake in her book (before this passage, saddened because the family had sold the ranch and was moving, a young Liza Jane Grey had prayed to God to end the world):

> Suddenly she was awakened. The air was filled with a heavy roar. The world was bathed in a vivid, weird light.
> The bed, the house, the whole world, began to tremble and shake. It bucked and heaved. The walls swayed and cracked. The brick chimney outside her room went tumbling down!
> Liza Jane sprang from her bed and was hurled back across it. Again she tried to rise and again she was hurled back!
> "My God," she cried, "the world IS coming to an END! God IS ending the world! He certainly IS! I sure did it this time!" Her face grew white. Her heart stopped, then started pounding like a locomotive on an uphill grade.

> A framed picture on the wall went clattering to the floor. Liza Jane wailed aloud, "It can't be true! Never would God listen to me and end the world!"
> The dresser left its place by the wide of the wall across the room and came jigging toward her like a playful elephant toward a peanut. The other vase joined its mate, and they blended their broken pieces together on the floor.
> The heaving and the shaking grew worse! Now it felt as though a huge giant had lifted the world in his hands and was shaking and rending it and hurling the shreds away.
> Her father's voice called up the stairs. "Don't be afraid," her father shouted. "It's an earthquake! Just lie still till it's over. Don't be afraid! I'll come to you as soon as I can get up there. It won't hurt you. Just lie still. It will soon stop."
> The small boys hushed their crying. Jack and Greg continued to talk. Jack shouted, "Liza Jane are you all right? Are you scared?"
> "N-N-NO, I'm not scared. I'm all right!" What a liar! And right on the verge of meeting your maker face to face! This is no earthquake!
> Even in the midst of her trepidation and fearful waiting for the final results, she was terrifically awed at the power her mistaken advice and demands had had upon the Lord.
> It was a dreadful earthquake. But Liza Jane had secret compunctions for quite some time. She was afraid she knew what might have brought the whole thing about, and while she was very careful for a long time in the way she talked to God, she couldn't help but be somewhat awesomely proud if her demands had had that much influence with the Almighty Lord.[14]

In 1910, when Mae Hammack Cross was twenty years old, her family sold off its land in Lake County. In 1920, four years after Douglass Cross, their first child, was born, Mae and Harry Cross bought a ranch that had once been owned by the Quigley family.[15]

A small section of Mae Cross' book that I particularly liked was about Liza Jane (who was also called Leesa) meeting Jack London, who was staying at a neighboring hotel:

> There were groups of people on the hotel porches, on the grounds, and out on the pier with its canopied landing that jutted out into the lake.
> Leesa looked searchingly as the horse came to a stop. "Oh, dear," she thought ruefully, "I hope Jack London isn't sitting on that porch. I don't want to meet him till I have on my blue organdy. Why, oh why, didn't I bring my graduation dress? The only really beautiful dress I possess. If this isn't the darndest luck; going to meet Jack London, and with nothing decent to wear!"
> Leesa's face was happily excited as she told the family of her visit. "And, Mama, I not only met Jack London and told him the Indian legend at his request, but I DANCED WITH HIM! And not only that"—Leesa giggled—"HE told Mrs. Eddy that I was the cutest little devil he had seen in a long time. AND THAT wasn't all— guess what?"
> Jane smiled at her excited daughter. "I can't imagine. What else?"
> Leesa Jane paused and looking around the porch at her brothers. Perhaps this wasn't exactly the time to tell the rest.

"What happened next, Leesa Jane?" George's question put an end to indecision.

"Oh, well, nothing much. He just kissed me goodnight on my cheek, when Mrs. Eddy said I should leave the clubhouse and go to bed because it was getting so late."

George was disappointed. "Huh, was that all?"

Greg gave a snort and said, "I bet the guy was drunk."

Leesa was disgusted. No use telling those boys anything thrilling. Bet she'd know next time not to tell big experiences like that, when that bunch of idiots were within hearing distance.[16]

The Indian story that Leesa told London was about a young warrior who was killed in battle with a tribal chief who had sought to prevent his marriage. The legend was that the red veins of ocher running down a mountainside represented the dead warrior's blood, and that the warrior's intended cried so much that her tears formed a lake. She then drowned in the lake.[17]

What isn't a legend is that Elizabeth Gray Hammack, the novelist's great-grandmother, had a Native American employee, a member of the Pomo tribe, who gave birth to a son. George Washington Hammack, Douglass Cross' grandfather, was born about the same time. Elizabeth Gray Hammack named the Native American newborn Benjamin Franklin Hammack. Officially, he was Chief Augustine's son. But not to the Hammacks. They called him Ben Hammack all his life.[18]

In 1959, then 69-year-old Mae Cross wrote: "We who have descended from these hardy, intrepid and indomitable pioneers have so much to be proud of. So much to be grateful for and to live for. We can only pray that the great spiritual force that brought our ancestors across the seas from other lands, that sustained them as worked and bled and died for liberty and in the pursuit of freedom and happiness, will be with their descendants until the brotherhood of all men arrives and peace and spiritual values rule the universe."[19]

4

Douglass Cross Writes a Will

Douglass Cross' liquor intake was up to a bottle a day. A fifth of whiskey, a bottle of vodka, Cross would drink whatever was handy. Cross could drink to excess without showing it. He rarely staggered, slurred his words, started a fight or behaved outlandishly. When he was still with George Cory, they drank together. When Cory left Cross in Clearlake, and tooled off for the bright lights and counter-culture nightlife of San Francisco, a hundred miles and light years away, Cross drank alone. Cross drank alone for four years, until 1974, when he got so sick that he was hospitalized. He never got out of that hospital.

By 1970, Cory and Cross were no longer partners in songwriting, or anything else.[1] The songwriting part of it, in truth, had been a façade for even longer than that. After they had left New York and come back to California, there was little writing. They made a virtual world tour, visiting Europe, the Far East and other lands, something they had always promised themselves they would do. As the 1970s creaked along, they saw each other once in a while; Cross would drive in to the city and stop by Cory's flat on Lombard Street, but he never stayed overnight and was never asked to. Cross knew about Walter Hinton at this point. When Cory didn't renew his lease at Lombard, and took up residence on Pleasant Street, on Nob Hill, Hinton was seen more, and Cross hardly at all.[2] Cross had written a will in 1968, leaving all of his considerable wealth to Cory while speaking about him in the tender terms he used when they were still together. Once in a while, Cross' nephew, Ron Strowbridge, who also lived in Clearlake, would discuss the will with his uncle. Strowbridge was just as close to Cory as he was to Cross; he called them "Uncle Doug" and "Uncle George." Cross and Strowbridge talked about Cross writing a new will. But Cross was still only fifty or so; there was no urgency. That's how it was always left. Cross didn't give it much chance, but maybe he didn't rule out that he and Cory might get back together again.

Now apart, Cory and Cross were left with all the memories: of meeting at the Presidio during their war-time duty in the 1940s; of sharing a place in San Francisco after their discharges, and telling themselves that they had a bright future as songwriters; of moving to New York, to get closer to Tin Pan Alley; of living in Brooklyn Heights, surrounded by other burgeoning talents like Arthur Miller and Jules Feiffer; of scrounging out a living, Cross as an editor at a small magazine, Cory as an itinerant piano player; of finding Ralph Sharon, Tony Bennett's righthand man, and giving him their song about San Francisco, which was either the best thing or the worst thing that ever happened to them; of moving back to California, Cross to be reunited with his mother, Cory to be close to the city that always felt like home; of at last realizing that they weren't going to squeeze the ship back into the bottle again.[3]

By 1974, the memories for Douglass Cross were cruel reminders of what had slipped away. His mother had died,[4] his lover had gone off and found someone else, and there were no more songs of his that anyone wanted to sing.[5] The songwriting world had changed, catching much of the old guard off-guard. Eric Clapton showed up at the Cow Palace near San Francisco, drunk or stoned or both, sold out the place and wisely stayed in the background so no one could tell. It was a night that should have cried out for refunds, but another guitarist took over the leads and thousands, many of them as spaced out as Clapton, still cheered.[6] The *hoi polloi* was listening to The Grateful Dead, not Cole Porter. Tony Bennett stayed with the music of the Jimmy Van Heusens, the Johnny Mercers and the Harold Arlens, and so did Sinatra, but they were the exceptions.[7] The songs Cory and Cross had tried to write at the end were as *passe* as the fox trot. San Francisco, hardly alone among cities, wasn't celebrating itself; it was toasting cynicism. *The Conversation*, Francis Ford Coppola's brilliant film, was pitch perfect for the times.[8]

The first part of 1968, Douglass Cross, in his late forties, might have been awash in thoughts about his mortality. He had been diagnosed with cirrhosis of the liver, but had ignored his doctor's stern advice and kept drinking. His problem with alcohol was not unlike his sister's but his capacity enabled him to endure the condition several years longer. Cross went to a family lawyer, Phil Crawford, to discuss a will. Crawford's father, Howard G. Crawford, had handled some of the affairs of Mae Cross, Douglass Cross' mother. Going back generations, there were few in the Crawford family who didn't cozy up to the law. Phil Crawford's brother was a lawyer, his grandfather was a lawyer. For almost a century, Lake County had never known a time when there wasn't at least one Crawford practicing law.

The Crawford family had settled in Northern California in the latter half of the 19th century,[9] not long after the Hammacks from Missouri—Mae Cross' kin—had followed a wagon trail to the unsettled area north of San Francisco. In the 1950s there was a scandal of sorts that touched the Crawfords. Thirty-one years after he had started his law practice, Howard Crawford ran afoul of the state authorities and was disbarred. But he continued to work out of his son Phil's office, was paid a modest salary—at least on the books—and handled clients. The state bar investigated this father-son firm, came down on the sham and while not suspending Phil Crawford's license, publicly reproved him (the equivalent of censure).[10]

"I see where they're still singing your song," Phil Crawford said to Cross.

"Yes," Cross said. "Tony Bennett will never let it go. It means too much to him."

"I heard Sarah Vaughan singing it the other day, on the radio."

"I had heard she's done the song. But I've never actually heard her sing it."

"Does that mean something to you, every time somebody different sings it?"

"It sure does. Somebody in New York keeps track of those things. A Catholic priest even recorded the song once. Did you ever hear of Father [Robert] White?"

"No."[11]

"I think he's out of New England. He did an album of songs, and ours was on it."[12]

(The strangest version of "I Left My Heart in San Francisco" was done by "Pancho the Parrot" on the Johnny Carson TV show in 1981. "Pancho," a double yellow-headed Amazon parrot from the San Diego Zoo, sang a few lines of the song, as well as strains from "It's Springtime in the Rockies" and "Bali Hai." Carson, while impressed, said: "But he still doesn't point to the sky, like Tony Bennett does.")[13]

Cross told Phil Crawford that his was a fairly straight-forward will. There was only one heir.

"I can do it for you," Crawford said. "But if you want to save the money, I can show you how to do it yourself. Just make sure you file it and have it witnessed by two people."[14]

4. Douglass Cross Writes a Will

On May 4, 1968, his 48th birthday, Cross took out a typewriter at his home in Clearlake and, using a model that Crawford had given him, drafted a two-and-a-half-page will. He wrote that both of his parents had died, and that his only surviving relative was his sister Shirley, who was living in Santa Rosa, California. Cross went out of the way to exclude his sister. "I have intentionally omitted [her]," he wrote. "She has been the beneficiary of considerable property from my estate and that of my mother during her lifetime."[15]

The first and middle names of Cross' sister may have been wrongly spelled throughout the will. It seems incongruous, because Cross was scrupulous in most ways, but census records show that she was born Sherley Mae Cross.[16] "Mae" instead of "May" makes more sense, since "Mae" is the way her mother spelled her name.

Upon first reading, I took the will at face value and thought Cross' intentions were a mite harsh. Later, I learned that Cross was being euphemistically practical. The former Shirley Cross, who was Shirley May Neilson in the will and once had been Shirley Strowbridge, was an alcoholic and a drug addict. She was Ron Strowbridge's mother and in her early forties when her older brother wrote the will. Douglass Cross died in 1975, and his sister would die a year later at 49. Perhaps what Cross was saying in the will, between the lines, was that he couldn't trust his sister with any of his estate. Cross had already seen his sister take much of their mother's money and fritter it away over her drug habits, and Shirley May Neilson's half-hearted attempts at rehabilitation had been for naught. Both her son and her brother were convinced that she was beyond help or redemption.[17]

In an emergency, Cross wrote, his desire was for his sister to be provided for. "It is my express wish," he wrote, "that my dear nephew, Ronald R. Strowbridge, at his sole discretion, but without lawful obligation to do so, provide to his mother, Shirley May Neilson, such financial assistance as he deems necessary in case of dire circumstances of his mother." A year later, that clause became moot when Strowbridge's mother was found dead under drug-related circumstances.

Referring to Cory as "my dear friend and business partner," Cross named him as executor of the will. In the event that Cory "fail to qualify" as executor, Cross wrote that Phil Crawford, his lawyer, would take over. Short of that, Cross gave Cory *carte blanche*: "I further authorize [Cory] either to continue the operation of any business belonging to my estate for such time and in such manner as my said executor may deem advisable and for the best interests of my estate, or to sell or liquidate the business at such time and on such terms as my said executor may deem advisable and for the best interests of my estate. Any such operation, sale, or liquidation by my said executor, in good faith, shall be at the risk of my estate and without liability on the part of my said executor for any resulting losses."

The most important paragraph in the will was this: "All of my estate at the time of my death, whether the same be real, personal or mixed, of whatever kind or character, and wheresoever the same may be situated, or in which I may have any interest or right of testamentary disposition, I give, devise and bequeath to my dear friend and business partner, George Cleveland Cory, Jr."

Cross made allowances should Cory die first. In that event, half of his estate would have gone to Ron Strowbridge, Cross' nephew, with the other half to be shared by Gertrude M. Cory, George Cory's mother, and Edward M. Cory, George Cory's brother. Both Gertrude and Edward Cory had died by the time George Cory died in 1978.

In pen, the date of the will was changed from May 4, 1968, to June 4. Cross' name was typed at the bottom, which is a good thing, because his signature, indicative of an unsteady hand, is illegible. The names of the witnesses are not typed in, but their signatures appear to be Frances L. Edwards, of Santa Rosa, California, and Lois M. Ricketts, of San Clemente, California.[18] Ron Strowbridge did not recognize either name.[19]

In late October 1974, Cross was dehydrated and had a high fever. It was difficult for the 24-year-old Strowbridge to lecture his uncle about drinking because Strowbridge liked to have a few drinks himself. Strowbridge called an ambulance and had Cross admitted to the Hacienda Convalescent Hospital in Petaluma, California. Strowbridge filled out the admission forms. Next to occupation he wrote "composer." Next to kind of business he put "music composing." Cross' condition was deteriorating on several levels: Besides suffering from Laennec's cirrhosis, caused in most cases by alcoholism and in this case incurable, Cross was also diagnosed with pulmonary emphysema, and after a few days at the hospital he also developed pneumonia.[20]

In the weeks and months that followed, Cross never got any better. On January 5, 1975, he and Ron Strowbridge, his nephew, talked about the will that was written about six years before. They agreed that it needed to be changed, but Cross, refusing to believe he was as sick as he was, said he would get to the revisions eventually. They didn't talk in any detail, but it's likely that George Cory would have been excluded, as Cross' sister had been, and Strowbridge would have been named as one of the principal heirs, instead of only an alternate.

"How is George doing?" Cross asked.

"He's doing OK," Strowbridge said. "I saw him a few weeks ago. It seemed like he was OK."

"Don't forget those paintings," Cross said.

"Paintings?" Strowbridge said.

"Don't you remember?" Cross said. "I told you about them one time. Those Native American things. They belonged to my mother."

"Yeah, yeah. I saw some of them when I was at George's. He's got some of them up. Who was the painter? I know it was somebody grandma liked a lot."

"Grace [Carpenter] Hudson. She painted almost nothing but Indians. My mother adored them. She had a lot of them. I gave most of them to George when he left. A half-dozen, maybe. You should have them."[21]

Two days later, Douglass Cross was dead. He died at 7:45 p.m. on January 7.[22] Ron Strowbridge was with him. The San Francisco-area newspapers carried full-length obituaries, but elsewhere there were only brief stories, if even that. In the *Chronicle*, it said that he died after "a long illness." A reporter interviewed Cory, who appeared to have been crying. "His lyrics," Cory said, "became more philosophical and at times openly sentimental. I badgered him about taking life so seriously, but who's to say I was right?"[23]

Unlike Cory, who three years later would write specifically in his will that his ashes be spread at sea, Cross left no burial instructions. Despite having left behind his sister, Cross was in the hands of his nephew, who had him cremated and buried the remains in the Hartley Cemetery in Lake County, next to the graves of his mother, who died in 1967, and his father, who died in 1949. A century before, some of Cross' ancestors were the first people ever buried in this cemetery. Douglass Cross' grave, like his father's, has a flat, minimalist marker that says:

Douglass Cross

1920–1975

Mae Cross' desire to be buried at her old ranch, the one she sold to Tennessee Ernie Ford, had gone by the wayside. Her headstone at the Hartley Cemetery is tall and much of the lettering has turned green. Under her name is an eleven-line poem that Gerald Manley Hopkins published in 1864. It reads in part: "And I have asked to be where no storms come…"[24]

Ron Strowbridge thought about Douglass Cross' will. Everything had been left to George Cory, although neither Cross nor his nephew wanted it that way. Strowbridge and his wife argued about whether he should attempt to contest the will. Strowbridge didn't have much money, but he scraped together a thousand dollars and went to Phil Crawford, the local attorney.

"The Crawfords had worked for my grandmother," Strowbridge said. "She liked using them, so I thought I was in good hands. But nothing ever came of it. I really don't think he attempted to do anything. I couldn't afford to spend any more money. It cost me my marriage."[25]

So now George Cory was double rich. He was listed as president and artistic director of the Cory Sound Company in San Francisco. His partner for a time was Lou Sinclair, whose real name was Lou Stumpe. Back in the 1950s, when Stumpe was doing a local TV show out of Santa Barbara called *Pacific Bandstand*, he was a summertime replacement for Dick Clark in Philadelphia on the wildly popular *American Bandstand*. Cory had met Stumpe when he worked at a radio station that featured classical music in San Francisco.[26]

"I don't think Cory Sound was much of a business," said one of Cory's friends. "It might have been set up mainly for tax purposes."[27]

In 2016, Strowbridge talked philosophically about the estate of his uncle's that had gotten away. Almost seventy, he was recovering from injuries suffered in a motorcycle accident, and colon surgery was not far off. He had been a policeman for ten years, leaving the force because he couldn't accept the marginal honesty of some colleagues.

"Who's to say what would have happened had I come by all that money of Uncle Doug's?" Strowbridge said. "I don't have much now. I live month to month, off what the government gives me. If I had become wealthy, maybe I would have blown the money anyway. Maybe I would have turned into a junkie, just like my mother."[28]

In his garage, in a tattered cardboard box, he's got a few copies of *Again to Earth*, his grandmother's 1956 *roman a clef*. In the first chapter, lamenting the deaths of so many Indians in Northern California, Mae Cross wrote: "Beyond the woods could be heard the angry roar of the lake, uncomfortable and protesting at so much turbulence. For days the storm had lashed and poured out its venom, and for days the lake had answered in an increasing roar."[29]

5

A Song Grows in Brooklyn

When George Cory joined the Army in September of 1942, almost a year after the U.S. entered World War II, he was assigned to the Presidio in Monterey, California. That was about three thousand miles from his birthplace in Syracuse, New York, but only 120 miles from Marin County, near San Francisco, where he had lived since he was ten years old.[1]

The Presidio, at full strength with 3500 troops, was a reception center for the Army's III Corps, a counter-offensive unit that fought in France and the Rhineland during World War II.[2]

Private Cory was not sent overseas. Before the Army, he had completed his undergraduate work as a music major at the University of California in Berkeley. Cory studied under Ernest Bloch, the Swiss-born composer and conductor who had become nationally known after his emigration to the U.S. in 1916. Bloch was once the director of the San Francisco Conservatory of Music.[3]

While Cory studied at Berkeley, Douglass Cross, at 21, had become the youngest to ever sing for the San Francisco Opera Company.[4] Opera in San Francisco dates back to the Gold Rush of the mid–1800s and fully took hold with the opening of the War Memorial Opera House in 1932.[5] The San Francisco Opera Company's founder, the Italian-born Gaetano Merola, died onstage at Stern Grove while conducting a performance of *Madama Butterfly* in 1953.[6]

Cross also worked as an actor, singer and artist for an Oakland radio station before Army duty landed him at the Presidio, where he met Cory in the fall of 1943.[7] Besides playing the organ at the chapel at the Presidio, Cory was entrusted with organizing musical variety shows for his fellow servicemen, and when Cross arrived he was added to the production team.[8] The two of them made plans to live together when the war ended, to work together writing songs. But at the time they thought all of this would happen in San Francisco, their adopted city. Cross was born in Englewood, New Jersey; his mother, a native Californian, had left the state to study nursing. Mae, as friends called her, and her husband Harry Cross, who was one of the original field commissioners for the fledgling Boy Scouts of America, were not on the East Coast for long. After the family returned to California, that was where they stayed.[9] Cory's parents, George Sr. and Gertrude, moved to Northern California from Chicago in the 1920s when young George and his older brother Edward, who was only a year older, were in grade school. The elder Cory was an office manager for a company that manufactured sign boards.[10]

In 1945, with the end of the war imminent, Cory and Cross mustered out of the military. Cory began playing the piano at clubs all over San Francisco and was musical director for a Gilbert and Sullivan repertory company. He lived with his parents and a younger brother, who had served in the Navy.[11] Cross landed a job as a writer, producer and announcer for the Office of War Information, which was on borrowed time.[12] The OWI, as it was known, began in 1942 as a wide-ranging propaganda arm of the U.S., but was rendered redundant by September of 1945.[13]

Half of Cory and Cross was out of work, and both were out of luck. Nothing they wrote was selling; they were scratching along with their other jobs. They were already at a crossroads, unsure of what path—pop music or classical—to take. They didn't have a lot of money, but they reasoned that they were too far from the heart and soul of the music business to make a dent. If they were to rouse the people who counted—recording artists, record executives—a move to New York was imperative. They landed not in Manhattan, where the living was expensive, but in Brooklyn Heights, which was close enough. If nothing else, they got to know Ralph Sharon, and that contact, by and large, would eventually turn them into millionaires. Sharon was the piano accompanist for Tony Bennett.[14]

Post-war Brooklyn Heights was a spirited mix of Italians, Irish and Jews. There was creativity on every corner. An undiscovered Arthur Miller, a recent graduate of the University of Michigan and newly married, was testing the Broadway waters. The poet W.H. Auden lived nearby. Thomas Wolfe, Norman Mailer, Truman Capote, Walt Whitman and Marilyn Monroe also lived there.[15] "It'd take a guy a lifetime to know Brooklyn t'roo an t'roo," Wolfe wrote. "An even den, yuh wouldn't know it all."[16]

It was in tree-lined Brooklyn Heights, in a ten-story apartment building on Montague Street, where a 29-year-old Miller wrote his first play.[17] *The Man Who Had All the Luck* opened two days before Thanksgiving, and closed the day after.[18] Like Cory and Cross, Miller kept trying.

5. A Song Grows in Brooklyn

For George Cory's music, Douglass Cross wrote wistful lyrics about a disconnected lover looking for a replacement, someone who resembles in some fashion the missing heartthrob.[19] They called it "I'll Look Around" and gave it to Mabel Mercer. It was their first big effort since leaving California. Mercer must have looked like the perfect launching pad for that tune. The English-born cabaret singer was already established in Europe before her permanent move to the U.S., where her popularity began to swell immediately in the late 1930s. She added "I'll Look Around" to her repertoire, but didn't always sing it. She concentrated on music by Arthur Schwartz and Howard Dietz, by Jerome Kern and Dorothy Fields and so many others with comparable heft.[20]

One night, however, when Mercer sang the Cory/Cross song at a club on New York's famed West 52nd Street, in the audience was Billie Holiday. She had been infatuated with Mercer's singing early on. One time, Holiday lingered so long listening to a Mercer set that she was almost fired for being late for her own show at a club across the street. In the spring of 1946, Cory and Cross were ecstatic—Holiday, inspired by her idol Mercer's version of the song, had agreed to record "I'll Look Around."[21] New York was suddenly beginning to look better. But Cory and Cross never did adjust to living and working there. "New York is a hard, ruthless city," Cross once said. "It lives on the edge of terror and catastrophe. New York is tired."[22]

Billie Holiday's first of several drug arrests came in 1947, but her heroin habit had begun before that. She needed money, and in 1946 agreed to take an ill-advised part in the only movie she ever made.[23] The script for *New Orleans* was misrepresented to her, and she played a singing maid surrounded by Louis Armstrong, Woody Herman, Kid Ory and other superstar musicians of the time. But for the music, the film is a waste.[24]

On April 9, before filming began on the movie, Holiday went to a New York studio to record for Decca, "Baby, I Don't Cry Over You," written by Morton Krouse, and "I'll Look Around." She brought along Jimmy Shirley, one of the original electric guitarists who had previously worked with Ella Fitzgerald. Krouse's song, part of a Decca retrospective by Holiday, was released in 1988, almost forty years after her death, and "I'll Look Around" was released in 2001, part of a fifty-song collection from Holiday's Decca days.[25] The most attention that was ever paid to "I'll Look Around" came when Nina Simone, the brilliant pianist and blues singer, included the song as part of an album called "Forbidden Fruit." It was released in June 1961, six months before Tony Bennett sang "I Left My Heart in San Francisco" at the Fairmont Hotel.[26]

In 1947, Cross wrote lyrics to another Cory melody. The words described a grief-stricken lover comparing his or her plight to being trapped in shadows, at the same time indefensible as a tree subjected to an electrical storm.[27] They called it "Deep Song," and Billie Holiday recorded it for Decca. Friends of Holiday's said it was one of her favorite songs, but it didn't have any traction in the stores. From 1952 through 1958, Holiday put out at least eleven albums, none of which included "Deep Song." It was, however, still around long after Cross and Cory had died.[28] The guitarist Kurt Rosenwinkel and his group included the song in an album they did for Verve in 2005.[29]

A couple of months after Cory died in 1978, Tony Bennett said: "I think [Cory] was frustrated that some of the songs he wrote for Billie Holiday were not more popular."[30]

Almost a decade before Cory and Cross began to work on "I Left My Heart in San Francisco," they went in another direction. Cory wrote "Four Songs in the Night," only one of which was lyricized by Cross. The other three were derived from poems written by Percy Bysshe Shelley, Lord Byron and Robert Adams. The Cory/Cross collaboration was called "Boat Song" and was written for Dame Maggie Teyte, the tiny English-born soprano, once known as "America's operatic sweetheart," who was reviving her career at the age of 57.[31] "Four Songs of the Night" was later recorded by Georgio Tozzi, the New York Metropolitan Opera star[32] (who did the singing for Rosano Brazzi in the film version of *South Pacific*).[33]

Cory continued to be attracted to melding good poetry with music. He once wrote a melody for "Music I Heard with You," from a 1916 Conrad Potter Aiken poem, and gave it to Eileen Farrell, the dramatic soprano whose fine operatic work was sometimes put aside for excursions into the pop field.[34]

Cory and Cross needed steady income, something that was going to pay the bills. Cory continued to work as a freelance piano player; Cross was hired as a recording director and also worked as an editor at a publication that would become *High Fidelity* magazine.[35] Cory also worked for four years as an assistant to Gian Carlo Menotti, the Italian opera composer who won Pulitzer Prizes in 1953 and 1955.[36]

A song called "On Treasure Island" was written by Edgar Leslie and Joe Burke[37] and was the first hit for Tommy Dorsey's orchestra (with a nineteen-year-old Edythe Wright on vocals) in 1935.[38] Wright, eight years younger than Dorsey, became the bandleader's lover and their romance led to the breakup of his long marriage.[39] Ironically, one of the many songs Wright sang with Dorsey was "San Francisco." Sung by Jeanette MacDonald in the 1936 movie of the same name, "San Francisco" became the city's official song until "I Left My Heart in San Francisco" came along. After some bitter in-fighting, the City of San Francisco diplomatically decided to honor both songs in 1984.[40]

Several years after Tony Bennett recorded "I Left My Heart in San Francisco" in 1962, Cory mentioned to Rick Booth, his landlord when he lived on Lombard Street in San Francisco, that "On Treasure Island" had been his inspiration. More than that, Cory suggested that he had even borrowed elements of the Burke-Leslie song in order to write the San Francisco song.[41]

"Nonsense," said Peter Mintun, a pianist and friend of Cory's. "I've listened to the Treasure Island song, and that melody is completely different from the other. There are a lot of songs that sound like other songs. There's 'Yours,' which was also called 'Quierme Mucho,' and 'Don't Cry for Me, Argentina,' from the Broadway show *Evita*. They might seem very, very similar, but they have different notes. I am a hundred percent positive that *no* songwriter would ever allude to *any* possibility of lifting an idea from any other song. George Cory was too bloated with his own success to admit anything of the sort."[42]

Dick Bright, who was conductor for the house band at the Fairmont Hotel for almost twenty years, wasn't so sure.

"One little comparison is the opening melody," Bright said. "Rhythmically, you actually sing 'I Left My Heart in San Francisco' right over the other song, but the melody is very different and the rest of the song is completely different. But comparing the two is an interesting exercise."[43]

Burke died in 1950, long before Bennett sang "I Left My Heart in San Francisco," and Leslie, who died in 1976, apparently never turned the Cory/Cross composition into an issue. If Cory had a guilty conscience, he kept it to himself. Booth said that he thought Peter Mintun might have also been aware of Cory's self-doubts,[44] but Mintun said that that was not the case.

Had there been validity to the connection between the two songs, the Cory/Cross song might have been subjected to more scrutiny in 2016 than a half-century ago. This is an era when musical plagiarism lawsuits seem to proliferate. In 2015, a federal jury, in a multi-million-dollar suit, found that Robin Thicke and Pharrell Williams, in writing Thicke's hit, the ironically titled "Blurred Lines," had copied material from the late Marvin Gaye. There was a seven-million-dollar award to Gaye's children which went to appeal.[45] More recently, two members of Led Zeppelin were challenged in court about the originality of "Stairway to Heaven," the band's signature hit and a song that was released more than forty years before. A jury took five hours to exonerate the defendants, who had argued that "the commonalities between [the songs in dispute] are generic elements in musical composition that go back decades and the core of the pieces in question are little more than a basic chord progression."[46]

Improbably, the lives of Gian Carlo Minotti, George Cory, Nina Simone, the New York contralto Marie Powers and the *wunderkind* poet Robert Horan kept crossing in the night. In 1928, when he was seventeen, Minotti's mother sent him to the Curtis Institute of Music, a new school, in Philadelphia. It was there where Minotti met and was smitten by the future composer Samuel Barber. It was a relationship that would last 54 years.[47]

Simone, who sang one of Cory's songs, insisted all her life that she had been passed over for admission to Curtis Institute, following an audition in the 1950s, because she was black. There is also evidence to the contrary, but the institute, without comment about alleged racism, gave Simone a *honoris causa* two days before she died in 2003.[48]

Horan, who was from Oakland, California, not far from where Cory—and for that matter, Cross—grew up, got to know Pauline Kael when she was an undergraduate at the University of California at Berkeley. Although five years her junior, Horan was already a published poet, including some verse that appeared in *The Yale Review* when he was fifteen.[49] Horan, once described as her "sometime lover," and Kael, just short of graduation, hitchhiked cross-country to New York, where they lived together for two or three years. Kael returned to California (she eventually became the estimable film critic at the *The New Yorker* for almost a quarter-century)[50] while Horan, now alone, was unable to eke out a living and sometimes lived out of Grand Central Station. One night, after attending a performance of the Metropolitan Opera, Gian Carlo Menotti and Samuel Barber found a disheveled Horan sleeping in the snow on a city street. They revived him and took him with them to Mt. Kisko, New York, where Menotti and Barber did much of their composing. Their home, which was called "The Capricorn," was a sometime respite for others in the arts, and Horan fit in perfectly.[51]

In 1948, Horan wrote "The Drowned Wife" for *Harper's* magazine, and Cory adapted the five-verse poem into a song.[52] Later, Cory adapted Oscar Wilde's *Requiescat* for Marie Powers. She had been previously cast by Menotti in *The Medium* on Broadway. Powers continued to work in New York, appearing in *Carousel* with Howard Keel and Barbara Cook, and *Becket* with Laurence Olivier and Anthony Quinn.[53]

Claramae Turner also did *The Medium* and *Carousel*. Before Marie Powers, Turner played the title role, Madame Flora, when *The Medium* had its world premiere at Columbia University in New York in 1946. In 1947 the production moved to Broadway, where Turner, having signed a contract with the Metropolitan Opera, was unable to repeat the role. So the part went to Marie Powers. In 1956, Turner was a co-star, with Shirley Jones and Gordon MacRae, in the film version of Rodgers and Hammerstein's *Carousel*. She would never make another movie, but is still remembered fondly for the way she delivered "You'll Never Walk Alone" and "June Is Bustin' Out All Over." Ed Sullivan asked her to sing "You'll Never Walk Alone" on his TV show.[54] Looking back on the film many years later, Shirley Jones said: "When I heard her sing, I said, 'Oh, no, I don't want to be in this movie with that woman.' She was extraordinary. Years later, I did Claramae's part in a summer theater production of that show. I said to myself, 'You're never going to do this part as well as she did.'"[55]

Turner started singing in her native California, and knew George Cory before they both went East. In San Francisco, she starred in several Cory productions of Gilbert and Sullivan operettas. As Cory and Cross began to write "I Left My Heart in San Francisco," they thought the song would be right for Turner. Like Cory, Cross knew Turner but not as well; though they had overlapped with the San Francisco Opera company. In 1953, the song went to Turner. She liked it, and began singing it as her encore at a number at recitals. But she didn't record it, other than for a version, with Cory playing the piano, for a 78 which was never released but has become a collector's item. Consequently, Tony Bennett had a clear path, eight years later. The San Francisco Opera Com-

"I Left My Heart in San Francisco" was written for Claramae Turner, an operatic contralto who was a friend of the songwriters. She sang the song at recitals, but never recorded it for the public (courtesy Joan Perry Ryan).

pany and Joan Perry Ryan, a good friend of Turner's, produced a testimonial video of Turner's life after she died, at the age of 92.[56] Turner's 1953 singing of the song is like night and day when compared to Bennett's versions. Turner's version is down tempo and naturally more operatic.

Although "I Left My Heart in San Francisco" sat around (with the exceptions of the few times Claramae Turner sang it) from the time it was polished and finished, in 1954, until Tony Bennett sang it at the Fairmont Hotel in December of 1961 and recorded it for Columbia Records in early 1962, it was hardly the first song that languished at the bottom of a composer's trunk. The record, for a dormant song that eventually became a hit, surely belongs to Irving Berlin's "God Bless America." Berlin wrote the song in 1918, thought better of it, and it wasn't sung in public until Kate Smith did it on her radio show in 1938.

Berlin, who was an Army sergeant at Camp Upton at Yaphank, Long Island, toward the end of World War I, was commissioned to write a show that would boost the troops' morale. Entitled *Yip! Yip! Yaphank*, it included songs such as "Kitchen Police," "Dream On, Little Soldier Boy" and "Mandy." He also wrote "God Bless America" for the show, but threw it out because the more he looked at it, he found it "just a little sticky, and I can't visualize soldiers marching to it." He wrote something called "We're On Our Way to France" and used that instead.

The show was such a rouser that it was moved to a Broadway theater. Berlin put the music for "God Bless America" into a thick file that included all the material that related to *Yip! Yip! Yaphank*. Then, in 1938, Ted Collins, who managed the radio star Kate Smith, came to Berlin asking whether he had any patriotic songs that might be appropriate for an Armistice Day program Smith was preparing. Berlin remembered "God Bless America," written twenty years before, and asked his secretary, Mynna Granat, to delve into

In October of 1953, Claramae Turner recorded the song for a now-defunct label, with George Cory accompanying her on the piano. The record was never released (courtesy Joan Perry Ryan).

the bulging *Yaphank* file. This wasn't easy; the song was there, but without a title page. Granat still found it, and Berlin rewrote a couple of lines, then Smith sang it before a live studio audience. The reaction was overwhelming; Berlin's publishing company was strapped to keep up with the demand for the sheet music.[57] "God Bless America" became Smith's signature song for the rest of her career. Thirty years after Smith's death in 1986, hockey teams, baseball teams, race tracks and other venues are still playing the Smith recording at their events.[58]

Berlin felt uneasy about cashing in on patriotism. He suggested to his business partner, Saul Bornstein, that they set up a "God Bless America Fund" and give all the immediate royalties to charity. Bornstein was a hard sell, but he finally went along. A committee that managed the fund settled on the Boy Scouts and the Girl Scouts as beneficiaries. Early on, the estimate was that both organizations received $250,000 from the song.[59]

Berlin would have gotten no argument from Harry Cross, Douglass Cross' father, about giving money to the Boy Scouts. In 1914, Harry Cross, a bachelor, was living in Los Angeles. He was one of the six original field commissioners for the Boy Scouts of America. In San Francisco's Chinatown, eight boys were playing in the yard of a Methodist church when they found a tattered copy of the Boy Scout Handbook. They wrote to National Boy Scout Headquarters in New York for information, and Cross was sent to San Francisco to sign them up. Thus Troop 3 was born.[60] While in San Francisco, Cross met a young woman who was studying nursing.[61] Her name was Mae Elizabeth Hammack, whose forebears, known as the Hammack party, had traveled the Santa Fe Trail, via covered wagons, from Missouri to Northern California in the 1850s.[62] Cross and Mae Hammack married. In 1920, four months after Harry Cross was named director of finance for the Boy Scouts, Douglass Cross was born.[63]

6

Woulda, Coulda, Shoulda

George Cory and Douglass Cross walked around New York for seven years with the sheet music for "I Left My Heart in San Francisco" in their pockets. They could find the Brill Building with their eyes closed. The Brill, at 1619 Broadway, was the *sui generis* of the music business, or, in a contrary opinion, "where the small-scale amusement industry nests like a pigeon" (A.J. Liebling). Liebling might have been envious that such a lucrative business should revolve around such a shabby locus. The Brill was where hopeful songwriters tried to sell their stuff. A songwriter would start at the top floor and work his way down. The more successful songwriters would have an office, if you wanted to call it that, at the Brill. Burt Bacharach said: "The offices were so small that there was just enough room for a desk, an old upright piano, and an air conditioner that didn't work in a window you could never open. When you finished a song, you would take it to a publisher and play it. If the publisher liked it, he would say, 'Go make a demo.' The publisher would pay for the demo and then it would be up to him to peddle the song to an artist who would record it. Some publishers knew a good song when they saw it, and some had no idea."[1]

Forget about getting somebody to sing and record their song, Cory and Cross couldn't even agree on the title. Cory thought it ought to be "When I Return to San Francisco." Cross favored "When I Came Home," but neither of them was sold on those titles. They showed the song to Claramae Turner, the operatic contralto and a friend of Cory's from their San Francisco days, and while she sang it a few times, at the end of her concerts, she never recorded it. Cory and Cross showed it to Tessie O'Shea, Great Britain's firebrand answer to Sophie Tucker, but she never recorded it, either. Then Cross introduced the song to Tennessee Ernie Ford, but it didn't resonate.[2] Tony Bennett recorded it early in 1962, the song developed a quick following among disc jockeys and the public, and then artists as diverse as Brenda Lee and Roger Williams were interested in piggybacking on what these two obscure songwriters had written.

When the Victor Feldman Quartet gathered in a studio in Los Angeles in 1962, they were the first of dozens of artists who thought that the song had an instrumental appeal. Instrumentally, Count Basie, Duke Ellington and even Liberace would follow Feldman.[3]

Feldman, originally from the Middlesex district not far from London, was a child prodigy on the drums. He played with the Glenn Miller Army Air Force Band when he was ten, was in pit bands for West End musicals not long after that, backed up British films and appeared on the BBC, all before he was twenty.[4] One of the groups he played for in England was the Ralph Sharon Sextet. Feldman had broadened his repertoire to the piano and the vibraphone, and his playing with Sharon was the first serious vibes work he had ever done.[5] Sharon, a young pianist, became Tony Bennett's accompanist and was the one who introduced him, in a career-changing moment in 1961, to the song about fog and cable cars.[6]

In 1953, Feldman went to New York, joined the musicians' union, but struggled to get steady work. He moved to Los Angeles, arriving with a $150 and a New York-to-London return air ticket in his pocket. He caught on with the Howard Rumsey All-Stars, who played at The Lighthouse, a dark, cramped, run-down jazz club handy to the sand and the Pacific Ocean at Hermosa Beach. Chet Baker, Gerry Mulligan and Miles Davis were playing there. Shelly Mann and Art Pepper were doing recording sessions there. "The Lighthouse," it was said, "was as far west as you could go for jazz without getting your feet wet."[7]

After eighteen months at The Lighthouse, Feldman signed on with the studios. He began to work with Henry Mancini, and was hired by Woody Herman. He went on to work with George Shearing, Miles Davis and Cannonball Adderley, and composed for Joni Mitchell and Steely Dan.[8]

The album Feldman recorded in 1962 was called "Victor Feldman: A Taste of Honey and A Taste of Bossa Nova."[9] It was done for Infinity Records, where Feldman's music seemed out of place; other artists in the Infinity stable included The Ring a Dings ("Snacky Poo"), Johnny Zorro ("Kangaroo Hop") and Penny Rae ("Chugga Lugga Choo Choo").[10] What was a serious jazz musician doing hanging out with material like that? Staying busy, that's what.

Feldman's album consisted of movie themes and songs associated with films, things like "Taste of Honey" and "Moon River." They placed

"I Left My Heart in San Francisco" as the second track on the A-side. Feldman, playing the piano, mixed and matched about ten musicians throughout the album, and used Nino Tempo (tenor sax), Bob Whitlock (bass) and Colin Bailey (drums) for the Cory/Cross number.[11] Three years later, Tempo, singing with his sister, April Stevens, won an Emmy for their recording of "Deep Purple."[12]

In "I Left My Heart in San Francisco," Tempo and Feldman take over. Tempo imbues the song with a haunting quality, giving it a wistfulness that somehow exceeds the longing that Bennett had instilled. The instrumental version is quite good, much better than I expected, perhaps because I wasn't aware of Feldman's wherewithal.[13] Johnny Guerin, once a drummer with Feldman, was right. "Victor," Guerin said, "will push you right out of the building."[14] On this recording, Nino Tempo was fairly good at doing that, too. Only he doesn't push, he escorts you, in a melancholy way. What helps—on this recording and for any musician who attacks the song instrumentally—is knowing the lyrics in your mind before you hear the unadorned notes. After all these years, it's impossible to absorb one component of the song without thinking of the other.

I told Tempo that I liked the Feldman Quartet doing the old San Francisco song, but he wasn't having any. When he heard it at first, he wasn't even sure it was him doing the sax work. "Maybe someone else did it, and they got me mixed up with him," he said. But the more he listened, the more he thought, regrettably, that it could have been him. "It's lackluster, if that's me," he said. "Normally, I wouldn't stick so close to the melody."

Tempo knew Victor Feldman well. "But I don't think there was even an arranger, or an arrangement for that," he said. "It might have just been a bunch of guys getting together and playing."[15]

In 1962, the same year as Victor Feldman's recording of "I Left My Heart in San Francisco," three singers recorded the song, starting with Frank Sinatra in September, Roberta Sherwood in October and George Chakiris in December.[16] Sinatra was recording for the Reprise label by then, and he surely knew, despite his egotism, that doing the song on the heels of Bennett was going to be next to impossible to top. Already, in a matter of months, this was known as a "Bennett song." A man of many grudges, Sinatra might have recorded the San Francisco song just to remind Columbia Records of what they were missing. Sinatra and Columbia had had a bitter parting, mainly due to Sinatra's virtual refusal to work with Mitch Miller, the Columbia boss in the pop world. Whatever the reason, Sinatra's "San Francisco" was abysmal, and withdrawn from the stores in a matter of weeks. Reprise issued the 45 RPM as the B-side with "The Look of Love," by Sammy Cahn and Jimmy Van Heusen. Reprise also needed a spell check: they listed "Carey" and Cross as the writers. Nelson Riddle did the arrangement, although he was still under contract to Capitol, and Neal Hefti directed what was listed as the "Frank Sinatra Orchestra."[17]

Roberta Sherwood came out with the song next. In the early 1960s, when I visited the Venetian Room at the Fairmont Hotel in San Francisco for the first time, Sherwood was there. I wish I could remember whether she sang the song. All I can remember is that she was very good. Almost fifty years old, she had gotten a late start professionally, forced to work in the 1950s because her husband was dying of cancer and she had three children to support.[18] Red Buttons saw Sherwood one night at a small club in Miami Beach, where she was working for $150 a week. Buttons told Walter Winchell, who saw her and gave her a plug in his widely syndicated column. Earl Wilson, another columnist, gave her a rave, and Irving Berlin came to hear her. Before long, Decca had signed her to a recording contract.[19] Her 45 in 1962 had "You Always Hurt the One Your Love" on the B-side.[20] After the record came out, she sang the song on Steve Allen's TV show.[21]

George Chakiris, who recorded the song for an album, *Memories Are Made of This*, in December of 1962, had won an Academy Award for supporting actor the year before, in the film adaptation of the Broadway show *West Side Story*.[22] Other songs on the Capitol album were "A Taste of Honey," "Moon River," "Witchcraft" and "Fever." Earlier in 1962, Chakiris had used "Once Upon a Time" as the B-side for "Maria," one of the evergreens in *West Side Story*. It was "Once Upon a Time" that was the A-side for Tony Bennett's "I Left My Heart in San Francisco."[23]

When George Cory gave the song to Claramae Turner, the chances of getting it recorded were remote. Not because Turner wasn't established. She was born in California, but by the mid-1950s, she had already been singing with the New York City Opera. She had leading roles in that company's *Hansel and Gretel*, *Oedipus Rex*, and *The Mikado*. She played Nettie Fowler in the film of Rodgers and Hammerstein's *Carousel*, singing "You'll Never Walk Alone" and "June Is Bustin' Out All Over." She did the Ed Sullivan TV show and performed Madame Flora in a TV production of *The Medium*, the opera she had done on the stage. But Turner didn't do that many recordings, if any, on her own. Naturally she participated in the various cast recordings of *Carousel*; she also sang on recordings done by Aaron Copland and Arturo Toscanini[24] and some of her work (*Samson and Delilah*) was made available to members of the short-lived Silvertone Record Club, which could be found in the Sears catalogue.[25] But she seldom ventured into the pop genre, which Cory was asking her to do. So from the outset, Cory and Cross chose the right church, but the wrong pew, for their song. Turner and Cory, playing the piano, put together a 78 RPM of the song in 1953. Its label was typewritten, and it was produced by a minor record company. It was never offered to the public. The last time Turner sang the song was in the 1970s, about forty years before her death, at the Stern Grove Festival near Golden Gate Park in San Francisco."[26]

One of the hangouts for George Cory and Douglass Cross during their Brooklyn Heights years was the Waverly Lounge at the seamy Hotel Earle in Greenwich Village. When Phyllis Diller, a rising comedian, stayed at the Earle, it had a linoleum floor in the lobby, guests paid $60 a week and washed their dishes in a small sink in the bathroom. "It was a joint either for people on the way up, or people on the way down," Diller said.[27]

The Earle, where Ernest Hemingway stayed in the 1920s and where the Welsh poet Dylan Thomas and his wife retreated after they were thrown out of their original hotel in the 1950s,[28] had a bar that featured Laurie Brewis, a piano player from London who had an encyclopedic memory for virtually every show tune ever written. Brewis was no secret; *The New Yorker* listed his playing schedule on a weekly basis. One critic called him "a fey version of Noel Coward."[29]

Tessie O'Shea was a regular visitor to the Waverly when she was in town. O'Shea was a Welsh singer and banjo player who billed herself as "Two Ton Tessie from Tennessee," even though she had never been to that state.[30] She trumpeted her girth; she admitted to weighing 217 pounds and measuring 49 inches at the chest and 54 inches at the hips.[31] "I've always been fat, but I'm limber," she said.[32]

One night in 1954, O'Shea was in the Waverly, listening to Brewis, when she was introduced to Cory and Cross. They had a copy of the recently completed "I Left My Heart in San Francisco" composition on them and showed it to her.

"It's pure nostalgia," Cross said. "We've tried to show the warmth and the openness of the [San Francisco] people that we left behind. Do you think you might be able to do something with it?"

O'Shea looked at the music, hummed some of it and told them that she would sing it when she got "back home."

Indeed, she sang the song in Britain several times. She had the chance to record it, well ahead of Tony Bennett, but never did. She added the song to one of her albums in 1973, eleven years after Bennett's recording.

The Cory/Cross songs didn't die for lack of salesmanship. Seldom was the time when they made the rounds without bringing some of their compositions with them. Early in 1961, before Ralph Sharon chanced upon the composition in his shirt drawer and showed it to Bennett, Cross conned his way into Tennessee Ernie Ford's office on Larkin Street in San Francisco. Cross was in California visiting his mother; Ford, who was in town to launch a TV show on KGO, had bought more than five hundred acres of the Cross family ranch in Clearlake several years before.[33] An outdoors type, Ford was pleased with the purchase. He spent some of the mornings fishing with his sons. "It was everything dad could have hoped for," said Jeffrey Buckner Ford, one of the sons. "Good hay ground, abundant water from the natural artesian springs underneath, fencing that was old [but still sturdy]." There was a tack room, full barn and the original stone home. Other than the Cross family, no one else had ever owned the layout.[34] The codicil to the sales agreement was that Mae Cross, the songwriter's mother, be buried on the land she had sold. That became academic when she died in 1967; she had left a will that ascribed her body to the University of California at Berkeley for medical research.[35]

With no appointment, Douglass Cross walked into the downtown San Francisco offices of BetFord Corporation, named after Tennessee Ernie and his first wife Betty. He had the composition of the San Francisco song, which was seven years old by then, in his inside jacket pocket.

"Douglass Cross is here," said Jim Loakes' secretary Bea,

Tessie O'Shea, a British star who won a Tony Award for a Broadway musical, facetiously called herself "Two Ton Tessie from Tennessee." She was offered "I Left My Heart in San Francisco" in 1954, but she didn't record it until 1973, eleven years after Tony Bennett's version came out (courtesy Steve Barclay).

as she buzzed the inner office. Loakes was Ford's personal manager and trusted friend. He had been both of those for more than ten years, and would remain in that job for almost forty more years.

"Does he have an appointment?" Loakes said.

"No," Bea said, "but he says it's very important."

"Well, send him in," Loakes said.

Loakes didn't recognize Cross, but asked him to sit down.

"My mother is Mae Cross," Cross said.

Again, Loakes was at a loss about whom he was talking to.

"She sold Mr. Ford the ranch," Cross said.

Loakes finally made the connection. This was Mae Cross' son. She had sold Ford the Clearlake property, and he had probably come about that. Maybe it had something to do with where his mother would be buried. That would certainly have been important.

But Cross went in another direction.

"I'm a big fan of Mr. Ford's," Cross said.

Loakes wondered if his visitor was ever going to get to the point.

Cross reached into his coat pocket and produced some sheet music.

"I'm a songwriter," Cross said.

"Oh, Christ," Loakes thought. "I've let a goddamn songwriter in here. Now he'll never leave."

Cross started to stammer.

"I thought it would be just great," he said. "Well, you know, they all thought it would be just great … for Mr. Ford."

Loakes took the arrangement and put it on his desk, without looking at it. Politely, he told Cross that Ford was offered much material, and they could only get to so much. He escorted Cross to the door and wished him well with his songs.

A week later, Ford was back in San Francisco, as was Jack Fascinato, his conductor.

"Douglass Cross, Mae Cross' son, was through here last week," Loakes said. "Mae Cross, the lady you bought Clearlake from. He's a songwriter, or at least he said he was. He left this."

Loakes handed Ford the composition.

"Let's see what it looks like," Ford said.

They went over to a piano. Fascinato played some, and Ford sang some.

"I don't know," Ford said.

"It's a love song," Fascinato said. "A love song to a city, but still a love song."

"Yeah, that's right," Ford said.

"It doesn't seem like your kind of song," Loakes said. "It's a little too ... a little too ... I don't know, it doesn't seem to feel like you."

Loakes called Cross and told him that while Ford looked at the song, and tried it out, he wasn't going to be able to do it. Maybe Cross was used to being rejected by this time, for dozens of the songs he and Cory wrote, but he must have thought he had come close with Ford.

By the end of the year, Bennett was singing the song at the Fairmont Hotel, and a few weeks after that, recording it for Columbia.

"Ernie, Jack, me, we all kicked ourselves," Loakes said. "The arrangement Tony used was almost the same one Cross showed me in my office. Who knew?"[36]

Five years later, Ford did an album called *My Favorite Things.* In the midst of songs such as "Red Roses for a Blue Lady," "Hello, Dolly!" and "Dear Heart" was "I Left My Heart in San Francisco."[37] There can only be speculation about what would have happened had Ford recorded it in 1961, ahead of Bennett. Maybe the song would have been lukewarmly received and been DOA. Maybe Bennett would have looked at it that night in Hot Springs, Arkansas, and decided it wasn't worth the risk in San Francisco a few days later. Maybe Ford's version would have clicked, and Bennett wouldn't have wanted to reach for his coattails. The music world has been inundated, since Edison,[38] with woulda, coulda, shoulda stories. In 1960, Roy Orbison went to Graceland, a copy in hand of a song he especially liked, and rang for Elvis Presley. The Everly Brothers had been offered the song, but since they had done some Orbison material the year before, they wanted to try other composers. A manservant came to the door and told Orbison that Elvis was sleeping in and couldn't be disturbed. So Orbison took the song, co-written with Joe Melson, and recorded it himself. "Only the Lonely (Know the Way I Feel)" went to number two on *Billboard*'s pop chart and became Orbison's first hit.[39]

Sometimes bad news can be good news. Harry Nilsson was asked to write a theme for *Midnight Cowboy*, which would go on to become the first X-rated film to win an Academy Award.[40] Nilsson submitted "I Guess the Lord Must Live in New York City," which was turned down. While Nilsson was rewriting, the producers went to Bob Dylan and asked him for a song. Dylan did "Lay Lady Lay," but he turned it in too late. Nilsson had already come back with an old Fred Neil song, "Everybody's Talkin'," and that song has been forever identified with the film. "Everybody's Talkin'," which did poorly the first time around, became a hit for Nilsson, and Dylan also had a hit with "Lay Lady Lay."[41]

Patti LuPone, the Broadway musical star, once did an entire one-woman show anchored around show tunes that she regrettably didn't sing. "The female lead always gets the romantic melodies," LuPone said. "[Those songs] are just too passive to me. I was always drawn to songs written for the second-banana female character or even the male lead."[42]

In the late 1960s, Peggy Lee's career was at a low-ebb when Mike Stoller and Jerry Leiber brought her their song "Is That All There Is?" The two writers had written "Hound Dog" and "Jailhouse Rock" for Elvis Presley, but in some ways they were just as much in the doldrums as Lee was. The songwriters had shopped the song around, and even let Leslie Uggams record it, but if Lee didn't know that, they weren't going to tell her. At one point, Stoller and Leiber had shot for the top, offering the song to Marlene Dietrich. At Dietrich's Park Avenue apartment, her musical director, Burt Bacharach, played the song, while Leiber did the best he could at singing it, after which, Dietrich snapped: "That song is about who I am, not what I do." Stoller and Leiber took that as a no. Lee, thinking the plaintive words had been written for her, and her only, won a Grammy for the song and never quit singing it.[43]

In the days when there were different sets of rules for singers, depending on whether they were black or white, black artists had to fend as best they could. "There was always an element of corruption in it," said George Avakian, who was an artists and repertory man for Columbia Records. Avakian referred to Billie Holiday and Fats Waller, who would be given a publisher's inferior songs in exchange for one song that looked like gold. The good song, the one that had *hit* written all over it, was known as the "push" song. "Some of the other songs," Avakian said, "were actually pretty good. [And] Fats was a master at making good records out of bad songs."

Two mainstays for Waller were "You're Not the Only Oyster in the Stew" and "You're Feet's Too Big." Other singers were not standing in line to cover those.[44]

7

The George Cory Ensemble

Here Today, Gone Tomorrow

In late December of 1961, almost to the day that Tony Bennett sang "I Left My Heart in San Francisco" for the first time, George Cory was joined by a diverse group of musicians in Rudy Van Gelder's recording studio in Englewood Cliffs, New Jersey.[1] By coincidence, Douglass Cross had been born in Englewood, 41 years before, though soon after his family moved back to the San Francisco Bay Area.

Until 1961, Cory had never been in Englewood Cliffs. He and Cross didn't live far away, in Brooklyn, but most of their work (Cory as a pianist and composer, Cross as a lyricist and magazine editor) had been in New York.[2]

In that New Jersey studio, Cory was playing the piano and had done the arrangements for the music they were about to record. I once asked Ron Strowbridge, Cross' nephew, if Cory was a good piano player. "He was more than that," Strowbridge said. "He was a *very* good piano player." Cory was versatile. While he might have been known in music circles as a pop composer, he had an operatic flair as well and was comfortable playing and writing classical compositions.[3] One of Cory's compositions, *Ballad for Voices and Orchestra*, had its premiere performance by the New York Philharmonic with Marie Powers as soloist.[4]

That December day in 1961, the guitarist Al Schackman joined the Cory quintet in the studio not far from the George Washington Bridge. Four years before, Schackman had met the jazz singer Nina Simone by chance in New Hope, Pennsylvania. She heard him play a set at a Holiday Inn and asked him to come around for tea. "Bring your guitar," she said. Schackman became her musical director, an association that would last until Simone's death in 2003.[5]

Earlier in 1961, Simone had recorded "I'll Look Around," a Cory/Cross song that dated to when they were in the Army during World War II and assigned to the Presidio, a military installation in Northern California. Billie Holiday had recorded "I'll Look Around" in 1946, but no one had covered the song until Simone, fifteen years later.[6]

"It was a lovely song," Schackman said. "I liked it the first time I heard it, and Nina took to it, which wasn't always the case. There were a lot of songs that came her way that she didn't like."

One night at the Village Gate, the legendary Greenwich Village club that had only been open a few years, Cory came around to introduce himself to Simone and Schackman. It was the start of a long, casual friendship. At the time, Simone was appearing at the Gate. According to one critic, she "blew the roof off" the club the night she recorded an album there.[7] Cory would also occasionally get together with Simone and Schackman at The Den at the Duane Hotel, at Madison Avenue and 37th Street. When Schackman saw Cory from time to time, it was not uncommon for the composer to have a drink in his hand. In 2016, when Schackman learned that Cory had been suffering from cirrhosis of the liver when he was found dead in his San Francisco apartment in 1978, he was not surprised. "The way I'm hearing it," I said, "he turned into a heavy drinker after he returned to California and began earning all that money from the San Francisco song."

"I think it was before then," Schackman said. "Right from the start, it looked like George knew how to drink."

Lenny Bruce, the raunchy comedian, was among the entertainers who appeared at the Duane in the 1950s. New York City was still enforcing a law that required live entertainers to take out cabaret cards before they could perform. Singers, musicians, comedians, they were all required to be photographed and fingerprinted. It was a practice that started during Prohibition, in the 1920s, and, depending on who the police commissioner was and which way the wind was blowing, the law was enforced in varying degrees.

Al Schackman said:

> "It was a sham. Hundreds of thousands of dollars was being funneled into the police retirement fund, which wasn't supposed to be the way it was at all. It affected a lot of people and their livelihoods. Some people couldn't get the cards and couldn't work. If you had a conviction, they could deny you the card. Billie Holiday couldn't get one. Charlie Parker was another one, and there was George Carlin. We tried to fight it. Nina was one of those who fought, and her lawyer, Maxwell Cohen, represented a lot of the people. George Cory was behind the fight, and I got to know him better as a result of being in the middle of all this."[8]

Some of the entertainers took the city to court. One litigant was Sally Rand, who had defied the censors with her fan dancing and bubble dances (dances where she used only balloons for a costume) at the Chicago World's Fair in 1933–34. Rand's racy dialogue could have been written by Mae West. "I haven't been out of work," she once said, "since the day I took off my pants."[9] In 1947, having been refused a cabaret card on grounds that her act at the Greenwich Village Inn was lewd, Rand sued and won. The judge ruled that the police commissioner, Arthur W. Wallander, was required to issue her a card. He said that a performer's act couldn't deprive an entertainer of a card until the act had been performed and evaluated. There is no record of Rand's card ever being revoked.[10]

Frank Sinatra was a strong opponent of the cabaret cards. "For many years," he said, "I have denied myself the privilege and enjoyment of playing before New York audiences in nightclubs because I have refused to submit to the demeaning requirements that New York has imposed on entertainers. It has been difficult for me to understand why the City of New York, which aspires to be the entertainment capital of the world, has continued to treat people who work in cabarets as second-class citizens."

In 1967, the New York City Council, by a 35–1 vote, abolished cabaret cards. "This is an overdue bill of rights [for entertainers]," said Michael J. Lazar, a council member who supported the change.[11]

Joining George Cory for that 1961 recording session in Englewood Cliffs was Peter Ind on bass. Ind, from England, played regularly on the *Queen Mary* when he was young. He came to New York in the 1950s and stayed for fifteen years. The tenor sax man was Frank Socolow, who had played with Artie Shaw and Gene Krupa. Rounding out the quintet on drums was Rudy Grant, a young musician from British Guyana, who would eventually move to England and go reggae.

They billed themselves as the "George Cory Ensemble." Englewood Cliffs had a studio that Prestige Records used after Bob Weinstock, at age twenty, had founded the jazz label at 47th Street and Sixth Avenue in Manhattan in 1949. The new location was closer to where Weinstock lived, in Tenafly. Incredibly, Weinstock attracted artists such as Miles Davis, Stan Getz, John Coltrane, Thelonious Monk and Sonny Rollins until he sold Prestige to Fantasy Records in 1972. Weinstock was known in the industry for cutting corners and getting away with it. He usually used recycled vinyl, which resulted in a small hiss on some of the recordings. Collectors nowadays pride themselves about having records with the hiss. Weinstock also believed in no rehearsals, no second takes. "Charts and rehearsals are the kiss of death," he once said. Weinstock felt that unrehearsed takes imbued the sound with the feel of a nightclub setting. When a take was unsatisfactory, Weinstock's engineers would erase the tape, and use the same tapes over and over for subsequent takes.[12]

The George Cory Ensemble supplied the backing for an album called *Let's Misbehave*. They got second billing on the album cover. The singer, improbably, was Billy Dee Williams, who had never recorded before (and never did afterwards, either). Billy Dee Williams had made his Broadway debut at seven (his mother was an elevator operator in the Lyceum Theatre, and when a producer needing a young boy as a walk-on in a play, he spotted young Billy Dee one day in the elevator). In 1961, as he continued to work on stage and in films, Williams had not yet reached the heights that the films *Brian's Song* and *Lady Sings the Blues* would take him.[13] He was singing at New York's Blue Angel, a club owned by Herb Jacoby, who had come from Paris to help launch the New York cabaret scene, and Max Gordon, who had been running the Village Vanguard and had loaned Jacoby $5000 when they became partners. His debt to Gordon notwithstanding, Jacoby lived up to his reputation as a snob when he said: "The Village Vanguard is a sewer. Max Gordon has about as much taste as a Vanguard hamburger."

At the time Williams was appearing at the Blue Angel, so was Dorothy Loudon, a fixture in the New York club *milieu* and a future star on Broadway in *Annie*, *Noises Off* and other shows. "In those days," Loudon said, "we didn't call it cabaret. It was saloons—or dumps, actually." Others who appeared at the Blue Angel during that era were the comedy team of Mike Nichols and Elaine May, Mort Sahl, Phyllis Diller and Carol Burnett.[14]

Williams said that through engagements at venues such as the Blue Angel, his agent was trying to mold him into what they called a *chanteur*, the male version of a chanteuse. Williams had trained as a singer and earlier in 1961 he was featured in the Broadway show *A Taste of Honey*, which starred Angela Lansbury and Joan Plowright.[15]

For the album, Williams sang the title song, "Let's Misbehave," along with "A Taste of Honey," "Life's a Holiday," "Warm Tonight" and several others. "Life's a Holiday" and "Warm Tonight" were written by Cory and Cross. (Another "Life's a Holiday," a completely different song, was written and sung by the pop singer Jerry Wallace in the 1960s.) Cory and Cross' songs were in rarified company. Other songwriters on the album included Frank Loesser, Harold Arlen, Johnny Mercer and Cole Porter, who wrote the title track.

Don Schlitten, who produced the album, allowed Williams and Cory to pick the songs. He had seen Williams on Broadway in *A Taste of Honey*.

Schlitten said: "George and Billy were well-rehearsed. There were some great players in the band. They seemed comfortable together, which made me feel good about doing stuff that was unusual and seemed challenging to Billy, so it all fitted just right. It was all recorded in just one day. It felt relaxed, although I would have liked more time. But all of the albums I was doing at the time were recorded in one day, so I knew how to work hard to make sure there were no complications."[16]

Cherry Red Records, a British label, reissued the album in 2014. Cherry Red, in announcing the re-release, said that "all" of the songs from the album were from Broadway shows. The truth is, some are, some aren't, but it's still an appetizing array.[17] Williams first met George Cory and Douglass Cross in the late 1950s in Brooklyn Heights, at Jules Feiffer's duplex apartment on State Street. Feiffer, a satirical cartoonist, was a future Pulitzer Prize winner, but long before that he worked—without pay but for possible recognition—at the *Village Voice*. Norton Juster lived upstairs from Feiffer. (Not yet a renowned architect, Juster had written a children's book called *The Phantom Tollbooth*. Feiffer drew a few sketches for the book. Nobody wanted to publish it until Feiffer mentioned it to his girlfriend, who knew someone in publishing. The book got published soon afterwards, and it has sold more than three million copies.)[18]

I asked Billy Dee Williams if the first edition of "Let's Misbehave" had sold at all.

"Let's put it this way," Williams chuckled. "It's a collectible."

Williams re-released the album more than fifty years later only because the topic came up while talking to someone in London, and one thing led to another. While Williams saw Cory a few times on the West Coast, Williams never worked with Cory after that recording. Williams himself didn't sing at all besides performances at the Playboy Club in Chicago and the Village Gate.

Al Schackman, the guitarist for the Cory Ensemble that one 1961 day in New Jersey, said that before the group assembled, he, Cory and Cross had gone over "I Left My Heart in San Francisco" together.

"I wasn't familiar with the song," Schackman said. "Nobody was. They had written it years before, but couldn't get anybody to do it. I thought it was pretty good. But why they didn't include it for the session after Billy Dee Williams got there, I just don't know. Since Tony [Bennett] hadn't recorded it yet, or even sung it before an audience, it didn't seem that important at the time."

By December of 2016, Schackman, age 83, was continuing to live in Wagon Mound, New Mexico, and was playing occasionally. We got to talking about songs with words that would still work if they were done instrumentally. At times, I've wondered how some songs would do if their words were taken out. I've always thought that "Stardust" was one of these songs, better as an instrumental, and Schackman, thinking for a moment, sort of agreed. I asked him about Cory/Cross' San Francisco song. Was Cory's music, by itself, good enough to carry the day?

"Let me think about it," Schackman said. He did better than that. A couple of weeks after our conversation, Schackman's group was playing locally. They did a medium-tempo jazz instrumental of "I Left My Heart in San Francisco."

"I thought it came out all right," Schackman said. "We didn't play it slow, like [Tony Bennett's] version."[19]

The song has been covered instrumentally at least 45 times. In 1963 alone (the year after Bennett first recorded it), it was covered without words eleven times, including versions by Ferrante & Teicher, the Charlie Byrd Trio, Dick Hyman and his orchestra, and Roger Williams.[20]

Of course, without Cross' poignant lyrics, the song wouldn't have had a chance in the beginning. Can anyone imagine Ernie Heckscher's Fairmont Hotel orchestra playing the song instrumentally, as part of Tony Bennett's overture, or playing it without words between a couple of his sets?

"The kind of songs you're looking for, songs that still sound great with their original lyrics excluded, well, there are just too many to list," Schackman said. Then, off the top of his head, he threw these songs at me: "September Song"; "How High the Moon"; "April in Paris"; "My Favorite Things"; and "Moonlight in Vermont."[21]

I might beg to differ with him about "September Song." Walter Huston's rendition (barely singing, mostly talking), in the 1938 Broadway show *Knickerbocker Holiday*, in no way suggests that the song could be bowdlerized. And Lotte Lenya's rendition (she was married twice to the "September Song" lyricist Kurt Weill) is, for many, superior to Huston's.

But I defer to Schackman. He's the musician.

In 1962, the year when Tony Bennett would record "I Left My Heart in San Francisco" and Douglass Cross' life would take a 180-degree turn, the lyricist's mother, Elizabeth Hammack "Mae" Cross, was living on a fifty-acre tract in Clearlake, California. That was a hundred miles north of San Francisco. She had sold almost five hundred acres to Tennessee Ernie Ford, a property that had been in the Cross family for three-quarters of a century. Ford was still active in show business, but glad to get away from Hollywood. "Hollywood," he said, "is for the birds and for the stars, and as my old grandpa would say, 'I'm not neither.' As an entertainer, I'm lucky enough to have made it, and I'm grateful to one and all for that, but nothing, absolutely nothing, could get me back down there."[22]

Mae Cross, who was born in 1890, had told her son that if he ever came back to California, they would build a house on the Clearlake property and live together. Mae Cross, who had trained as a nurse, had finally published a novel, the semi-biographical *Again to Earth*, in 1956. She started a second book, which was plotted around her family's wagon-train trip from Missouri to Northern California in the 1800s.[23]

Mae Cross traveled her property in Clearlake in a Jeep, with a .22-caliber rifle at the ready. She knew how to use it. One day, there was a visitor in another Jeep whom she didn't recognize. She called out, and when he didn't answer, and made a menacing gesture as he reached for something in his vehicle, she grabbed the rifle and needed only one shot to plug him in the shoulder. Police and an ambulance came, and the intruder was treated for a minor injury. Charges were filed, and Mae went before a judge at a preliminary hearing. She knew the judge, as she did many of the officials in Lake County, on a first-name basis.

"Did the injured party have a gun in his possession?" the judge asked.

"Yes, he did, your honor," Mae Cross' lawyer said.

"This sounds like a simple case of self-defense to me," the judge said. "Not only that, the injured party was trespassing. Case dismissed."

Another time, the roads leading to Mae Cross' home were badly in need of renovation. There were potholes every stretch of the way. She called the local roads department several times, asking them to do something. All she got was hollow promises. Finally, she called the head of the department.

"I'm fed up," she said. "When is something going to be done? Let's put it this way: If those roads aren't fixed soon, I'm going to run for your job. And you know how many friends I have around here. When they have that election, you'll be out of a job."

The roads were fixed.[24]

Mae Cross' husband, Harry, was seven years older than her. He died in 1949, just short of his 67th birthday.[25] In *Again to Earth*, Mae Cross is unable to disguise "Elizabeth Jane Grey," the heroine of the tale. Elizabeth Jane was a product of the turn of the 19th century; Mae Cross was born in 1890. Elizabeth Jane lived in Northern California. Elizabeth Jane wanted to be a journalist, but when the death of her mother and the desertion by her father dashed that goal, she settled for nursing and marrying responsibly, just as Mae Cross had done. Elizabeth Jane, Mae Cross wrote, was a "fiery, individualistic fighter" who grew up "despising the idea of a dull harp-playing heaven."[26] I asked Ron Strowbridge about the novel. The book is out of print, but he has several copies in a box in his garage. "That was my grandmother, to a tee," he said.[27]

The royalties from "I Left My Heart in San Francisco" were slow to come in, and when they did, they arrived in trickles. "Once Upon a Time," with the Cory/Cross song as the more popular flip side, began to sell, and when Bennett started promoting the San Francisco song, the entire 45 RPM took off. There was always a lag time before residuals kicked in, so Cory and Cross couldn't think about relocating back to Northern California yet.

Critic Gary Giddens said: "It was the kind of record that can float an entire career. It did not crown the charts; it just hung around forever.... The power of Bennett's perfect verse-and-single chorus on [the song] is derived not from an image of little cable cars climbing halfway to the stars, but from the uninterrupted emotional arc that builds gradually from an appealing melody [stroked by a hokey piano obbligato] to an ascension so juiced with its own fervor that when it's over you feel as though you've been on a trip, and it wasn't to San Francisco. Still, Bennett believes in—or makes us believe that he believes in—those little cable cars."[28]

In the midst of the burgeoning "I Left My Heart in San Francisco" euphoria, Bennett did a concert at Carnegie Hall. *In toto,* the list of bravura performances at the 126-year-old Carnegie Hall would reach the top of the Statue of Liberty and beyond. Generations of audiences that have gone to the great hall have heard them all—Enrico Caruso, Vladimir Horowitz, George Gershwin, Paul Robeson, Benny Goodman, Leonard Bernstein, Maria Callas, The Beatles, Leontyne Price, and Judy Garland more than once.[29] That list is vastly incomplete. Bennett's *tour de force* on June 9, 1962, rightfully belongs in that pantheon. The San Francisco record didn't gain traction for two more months.[30] "After that first time at Carnegie Hall, I finally had the feeling that my career was going to be a big success," Bennett said.[31]

Cory and Cross began to talk about heading west. They were optimistic that Bennett's recording of their song would be a stepladder to more hits. They couldn't have been more wrong. Bennett never tried another of their compositions, and other artists also were unimpressed. The industry has buckets of songwriters who couldn't replicate a good song (see Appendices). But for Cory and Cross *hubris* had set in. They disbelieved that this plight of the profession would also befall them.

There were plusses and minuses about going back to California.

Cross' mother had left him with an open invitation, and talked about building a new home on her Clearlake land. She liked Cory, thought he was a good companion for her son, and invited both of them to live with her. By 1965, they did all this, but it didn't last long. By the next decade, Cory and Cross would still be friends, but collaborators no more. By the middle of that decade, at ages when many songwriters might be reaching their prime, both of them would be dead.

Ron Strowbridge, Cross' nephew, called Cory "Uncle George."

Strowbridge noticed changes in Cross when his uncle returned to California. Stowbridge said:

> "Over the years, after he came back to California, Uncle George changed drastically. He was drinking a lot, but then Uncle Doug was, too. George made a lot of trips into San Francisco, where he could enjoy adulation from the song more, I suppose. The young studs started to go after him, and he liked that. You can imagine: He had a lot of money, and he was well-known, at least in his immediate circle he was. And these guys were chasing him, and he really liked it."[32]

More and more, for the excursions from Clearlake into San Francisco, Cross stayed back and Cory went alone. More so than his partner, Cross was repelled by the oppression of gay people in the city. In the late 1960s and early 1970s, the police of San Francisco were arresting about three thousand gay people a year. In New York City, they were arresting about sixty people a year.[33]

When Lloyd Crenna was a young lawyer, though already married and the father of young children, his family lived in the Castro district of San Francisco, where a disproportionate number of people were openly gay. Crenna was also George Cory's lawyer for a time in the 1970s.

"I don't have a homophobic bone in my body," Crenna said. "But at that time, with young kids, it was disconcerting to walk the streets of Castro and see young men passionately hugging and kissing in public, some of them with their shirts off."[34]

Many straight San Franciscans were conflicted. Gay people, despite the local authorities' resistance to their lifestyle, continued to move to San Francisco, as many as a hundred people per week, according to one estimate. Joseph Alioto, before he became mayor for two terms in 1968, seemed an unlikely *kemosabe* for Allen Ginsberg, the gay poet laureate for the Beat Generation. But there Alioto was one day, working for a fee of a dollar a year and posting bail for Ginsberg, a San Francisco resident who had been arrested at the Spoleto Festival in South Carolina for writing obscene poetry. One of Alioto's passions was poetry, but that didn't seem to be *raison d'etre* to attach his sail to Ginsberg's boat. By contrast, several years later, there was Alioto again, this time acquiring a reputation as the mayor who did the most to make life miserable for the city's gay residents.[35]

San Francisco newspapers were perplexed by the situation. As the population of gay people went past the 100,000 mark, the newspapers didn't know which side of the street they were on. The talented Armistead Maupin, who was gay, began writing a popular fictionalized series with a gay *leitmotif* in 1974. His "Tales of the City" was later picked up by the *San Francisco Chronicle* and eventually morphed into several books, three mini-series and a stage show. Mostly, Maupin enjoyed a free hand in developing his characters, but when one of them, played exquisitely by Olympia Dukakis in arguably the best role of her distinguished career, was a transgender, marijuana-growing landlady, editors at the newspaper advised that the author delay introducing her into the narrative. "We don't want to scare off the readers right away," one of the editors said. (Maupin only had to routinely tour the city for story lines; one night he went to a party that was to raise money for a man planning sex-change surgery. Sally Rand, at age seventy, did her signature fan dance and the Tommy Dorsey orchestra played. "This is a ball to end all balls," one person said.)[36]

In Clearlake, Cory, Doug and Mae Cross were compatible, but the two songwriters weren't writing songs anymore, now that the incentive had all but vanished. For Cory, the occasional trips to San Francisco weren't enough. He wanted to live there, and now he had money to live almost anywhere he wanted. Cross' mother suffered her first of three strokes in 1965. She recovered nicely, continued to dabble with her second novel, but that setback convinced Cross that he better not leave. After two more strokes, Mae Cross quit writing. "She pretty much gave up on everything," said Ron Strowbridge, her grandson. "She acted like she was ready to die."[37]

Mae Cross, age 77, died on October 14, 1967, in a Lakeport hospital.[38] Douglass Cross, her only son, perhaps began thinking about his mortality, and whether he needed a will.

8

"The Phantom"
Tony Bennett's Secret Weapon

One of the best things that ever happened to Tony Bennett, professionally, came on the day in 1957 when he hired Ralph Sharon.[1] It was Sharon who told Bennett to cozy up to jazz, at a time when Mitch Miller, the panjandrum at Columbia Records, was about to pigeonhole Bennett as a balladeer and not much else. It was Sharon who, on a late, quiet night in Arkansas, handed Bennett the sheet music for "I Left My Heart in San Francisco," which, when Bennett's career was at a crossroads, became the biggest hit of his life.[2]

Sharon's early contributions to Bennett's career were subtler, by leaps and bounds, than his later ones. Being faithful to jazz was a direction, a concept; singing the San Francisco song was, virtually overnight, capturing lightning in a very big bottle. Allegiance to jazz gave Bennett a focus, an anchor, when all else failed, when public tastes went fickle, when other avenues were turning to roadblocks. The San Francisco song stood above all else as a security blanket, and despite its enormous staying power and widespread international appeal, it is still just one song in the Bennett oeuvre. Ralph Sharon's advice about jazz was the long of it, his discovery of the San Francisco song the short of it. That synergy adds up to what has kept Bennett at the pinnacle for nearly seven decades.

Bennett, at 23, signed his first contract with Columbia Records in 1951. Mitch Miller, new on board in assembling talent for Columbia but given dictatorial power, had heard a demo record Bennett did of "Boulevard of Broken Dreams" and "Crazy Rhythm." Miller, however, had more of an insight into Bennett than that. The story was out that Bob Hope, who had gone to hear Pearl Bailey, had also stumbled upon a kid with promise. Hope had persuaded this upstart, who was christened Anthony Dominick Benedetto, to change his name a second time from Joe Bari to Tony Bennett.[3] Hope had enough proof that, as Shakespeare suggested, the name's the thing. Would Leslie Townes Hope have been half as funny?

After hearing the rechristened Tony Bennett for the first time, Hope cracked: "Well, I was getting tired of Bing Crosby, anyhow." At the time Bennett signed with Columbia, Mitch Miller was having one of his many serious feuds with Frank Sinatra, who would be gone, on his way to the Mercury label, within a year. The rift between Sinatra and Miller was irreparable.[4] Sinatra was up to his nostrils with the music Miller was giving him to record, novelty songs such as "The Hucklebuck," "Bim Bam Baby" and "Mama Will Bark."[5] For "Mama Will Bark," the background sound was dogs barking, and Sinatra co-sang it with Dagmar, the top-heavy, what-you-see-is-what-you-get television personality. During one recording session, Miller fooled around with the dials so much in the control booth that Sinatra yelled: "Mitch—out!" When Miller continued to mess with the dials, Sinatra turned to somebody riding shotgun and said: "Move him." Then he yelled to Miller: "Don't you ever come in the studio when I'm recording again."[6]

Looking back, Bennett surmised that one of the reasons Miller signed him was to prove to the industry that he didn't hold a grudge against Italian singers. Bennett could empathize with Sinatra. Many times, as Sinatra had, Bennett and Miller locked horns about the material Bennett would record. But the issues between Bennett and Miller were more entangled than that. Miller didn't put any of his artists on a pedestal, regardless of the hits they rolled out and the dollars they were ringing up for Columbia. Whenever Bennett questioned Miller about songs they would do, the goateed impresario would rhetorically say: "Am I going to have you put out a bad record?"

At the start, Bennett was respectful of Miller, who left no doubt about who was running the show. Bennett probably figured that if he wanted to stay with Columbia, he better dance, figuratively, to whatever tune Miller was playing. But sometimes Miller's demanding temperament was hard to accept. During a recording session for "In the Middle of an Island," a song Bennett was reluctantly doing, he stopped mid-song because his throat was bothering him. Miller thought Bennett had stopped because he didn't like the song. "Come on," he said, in front of a vocal group and four guitarists who were backing up Bennett, "just give me one take all the way through and we can all go home." Bennett thought he had been patient enough. He took off his jacket, tied it around his waist like a grass skirt, imitated a hula, and finished the take as Miller had ordered.

Bennett was a troubled performer in those days. He dropped his

8. "The Phantom"

manager, Ray Muscarella, because he thought his career was going in the wrong direction, and he continued to ward off blandishments from the Mafia, which in its inimitable way was renowned for poaching Italian singers. Bennett needed a rudder, someone like Ralph Sharon, and he found him.[7]

Sharon came out of London's East End, but his mother was an American who played the piano for theaters in New York that showed silent movies. She encouraged her son to study piano, and he did so grudgingly. But at age thirteen, young Sharon was smitten by the artistry of Fats Waller and Art Tatum. They inspired him to continue with his music lessons, and before long he began playing for local bands. These jobs led to his being hired in 1946 by Ted Heath,[8] the trombonist who led what was Great Britain's No. 1 band at the time.[9] Sharon was twenty years old. "Starting with Ted Heath, can you imagine?" Sharon liked to say. "I used to say that I worked my way down from there."

After two years with Heath, Sharon joined a band led by Frank Weir, whose accordionist was George Shearing.[10] "Ralph Sharon," Bennett would say many years later, "must be the only musician in the world who played piano *for* the great George Shearing."[11]

The Great Britain edition of *Down Beat* once named Sharon "Best Jazz Pianist in Britain." Sharon's mother was born in the U.S., and he was enamored with American jazz and musicians such as Dizzy Gillespie and Charlie Parker. When he was thirty, Sharon finally came stateside. "I grew up in the Tube during the Blitz [the London subways were places to hide during World War II bombings by the Germans]," Sharon said. "I wanted to go somewhere where I could see the sunlight."[12] In 1958, at the end of his first full year with Bennett, Sharon received his U.S. citizenship.[13]

Toward the end of 1957, Bennett's backup musicians were in a state of flux and he needed to make changes, fill vacancies. His guitarist, Chuck Wayne, took another job. Claude Thornhill played the piano for Bennett, but just briefly. Bennett scheduled an audition at the Nola Rehearsal Studio in midtown Manhattan to hire another pianist. He had heard about Sharon, and his office called the former Londoner.[14]

"The call came out of the blue," Sharon said. "I had never heard of Tony Bennett. He was in a different field completely. He was working in pop, and I was a strict jazzman. I was working with people like Chris Connor and Carmen McRae."[15]

History has buried the name of the first pianist at the audition, but apparently he was so-so. Sharon was next.[16]

He played a few things.

"I was entranced by his touch and delicacy," Bennett said years later.

Bennett sang a few things. Then they tried playing and singing together.

"This guy sounds pretty good," Sharon said to himself at the time.[17] Later, Bennett stated that he felt the same way, saying, "He just had to hit a few notes for me to know that he was the piano player for me," Bennett said. "He told me who he had played for [Connor, McRae, Johnny Hartman], and that's all I needed to know."

When they had finished, Bennett said: "How'd you like to come with me?"

"Come with you where?" Sharon said.

"Everywhere," Bennett said.

Sharon's contract was a handshake.[18]

They started out by doing a couple of club engagements together. Sharon still had a loose deal with Argo records, but when he told Bennett that it wouldn't take up much of his time, Bennett said that between the two of them, they ought to be able to work it out. One of their early trips took them to the Chez Paree in Chicago.[19] Opened in the 1930s, soon after the end of Prohibition, Chez Paree was a supper club, with a capacity of 650, that offered the *crème de la crème* of entertainment—Louis Armstrong, Billie Holiday, Bob Hope, Milton Berle, Sammy Davis, Jr., Jimmy Durante, Frank Sinatra; Chez Paree's marquee didn't miss many. For thirty years, it was *primo uno* in Chicago.[20]

Tony Bennett had yet to play there, however, and it was only by accident that he was booked in for the first time.[21] Nat King Cole, a supporter of President Dwight Eisenhower since he had spoken on the former general's behalf at the Republican National Convention in 1956,[22] had to cancel an engagement at Chez Paree because the White House called him to appear. Cole recommended Bennett as his replacement.[23] Sharon saw a trip to Chicago as a chance to squeeze in a recording session for Argo at the legendary Chess Records studio at 2120 South Michigan Avenue.[24]

Bennett, anxious to introduce himself to Midwest audiences, was on a bill that included Sophie Tucker, the Step Brothers and the husband-and-wife comedy duo of Phil Ford and Mimi Hines. Bennett and Tucker were so popular that their run was extended for a full month, during which they argued about billing. The dispute was resolved because the club had a double marquee—Tucker was placed on top one place, Bennett on the other, but Tucker persisted in giving Bennett a rough time. She claimed that he was taking too long for his section of the show, cutting into her time. One night she stood in the wings and said to his road manager: "Tell your friend to get off the stage." Bennett was able to tolerate the gaff because the room was selling out on a regular basis.[25]

The Chess studios were in their heyday then. Their eponymous blues label with Ahmad Jamal, Ramsey Lewis, James Moody and others was taking up hours of recording time, and Chess' Argo jazz subsidiary, with Chuck Berry at the forefront, was also flourishing.[26] The Chess brothers, Leonard and Philip, told Ralph Sharon that they could allow him a night session, but only if he promised to finish by 9 a.m. the next morning, since one of their major stars would be rolling in with a complement of musicians. That was a problem, because the last show at Chez Paree usually didn't finish until well past 3, but since it was a slow Monday night, management at the club promised that they could juggle the schedule so Bennett's last song would be finished by 1:30 or 2. The Ralph Sharon Quartet—Sharon, Candido Camero, Billy Exiner and Allan Mack—hustled over to Michigan Avenue as quickly as they could. They started at 2:38 a.m. and finished in less than three hours, well ahead of schedule. The Chess brothers required Sharon to log in the exact starting time, and afterwards he decided that *2:38 a.m.* was as good an album title as any. It was incredible how quickly and skillfully they worked, with one eye on the clock.[27] Included on the 28-minute recording is an eclectic mix of "Ol' Man River," "Teach Me Tonight," "How Long Has This Been Going On" and "Love Me or Leave Me." They must have sailed through most of them in one take. It's all instrumental but for one two-minute stretch at the fifteen-minute mark, when Bennett himself can be recognized doing a bit of scat. Those who bought the recording may have been surprised: The credit line simply says, "Ralph Sharon Quartet and Friend."

Columbia had already released two of Bennett's albums in 1958, and toward the end of the year, in time for Christmas, they came out with a third, called *Tony's Greatest Hits*. For the cover, Bennett chose a profile photo of him sitting on a tall red stool, microphone in hand. Unmistakably, it's a picture of him performing at Chez Paree.[28]

When Sharon joined Bennett, he went from the front man in quartets and sextets to a side man who modestly half-stood and bowed slightly when Bennett would introduce him at the end of a performance. People in the business began to good-naturedly refer to Sharon as "The Phantom."[29]

The nickname, and Sharon's new role, were no bother. "I rather liked that," Sharon said. "So all of a sudden, I became an accompanist and not a piano leader. That's not an inferior role, musically. Most people think that you're just in the background, but I don't think that at all."[30]

Sharon was shorter than Bennett, who is five feet, eight inches. When he was younger, Sharon wore wire glasses, a bowtie, a white shirt and a cardigan. He looked like he was going to an audition for the lead in *Goodbye, Mr. Chips*. Baldness came early, making him look older than he was, and he changed to dark suits and plain ties. Sharon hunched over the piano when he played, as though he was eyeballing every chord.[31]

Before Sharon died in 2015, Bennett said, "Hooking up with Ralph was one of the best career moves I've ever made. No one understands me more than he does, and we've become close as brothers. He is my idea of the perfect accompanist. He's a beautiful musician, and even more than most great players, he really knows how to perform with a singer or a soloist. He doesn't show off like a lot of other guys, playing lots of extra notes or fancy runs. After all, it's the emotion behind the music that's important. It takes a special person to support a performer and make him look good. Count Basie played that way, and Ralph has that same gift."[32]

Bennett compared Sharon with Bill Miller, who was Frank Sinatra's pianist, and Bobby Tucker, who worked with Billie Holiday and Billy Eckstine.

"They were very good musicians, but able to sublimate themselves to singers," Bennett said. "It's a real art, and it's rarely recognized."[33]

The list of Bennett's hit records began to mushroom, but he felt he was compromising himself by singing songs that only Mitch Miller liked. After getting comfortable with Sharon, and after more wrangling about material with Miller, Bennett went to Sharon for advice.

"He wants me to do one ballad after another," Bennett had said.

"Make sure you do some jazz," Sharon had said. "Why don't you do something with a jazz feeling? You can have six hits in a row, but if you keep doing the same thing over and over, the public will eventually stop buying your records."

Many years later, Bennett said: "Ralph knew how much I loved jazz. He knew that, really, I'm a jazz singer. In this commercial world, they put me in the traditional pop category because I'm white and Italian, which makes it tough to be seen as a jazz singer. But if you asked me what I was, once I'd learned how to sing, I'd say I was a jazz singer. And when I look back and review my recordings, I see that the best singing I do is when there's a great jazz artist around, like Stan Getz or Bill Evans, or when Ralph Sharon was playing piano for me."[34]

David Evanier, who wrote a warts-and-all biography about Bennett, without talking to the singer, says he's an "everything singer—no music is really alien to him."

While that might be true, the turn-around for Bennett, the ingredient that sustained him forever more, was his acceptance of Sharon's advice and his ongoing dedication to jazz.[35]

Right away, Bennett and Sharon knocked one out of the park. Late in 1957, Bennett released *The Beat of My Heart*, an album that included an incredible array of jazz musicians, including Nat "Cannonball" Adderley, Art Blakey, Chico Hamilton, Kai Winding, Herbie Mann and others. The cut included "Lullaby of Broadway," "Blues in the Night," "Let's Face the Music and Dance" and "Just One of Those Things."

Sharon, Bennett said, "was responsible for that [*The Beat of My Heart*] album. When we did that album, all of a sudden I acquired this whole new audience. Everybody said, 'Hey, wait a minute, this syrupy singer with strings can sing jazz…' The album showed that I wasn't just a ballad singer anymore."[36]

George Shearing, who worked with Sharon when they were just starting out in London, said that Sharon "was the musical foundation for Tony's singing."

John McDonough, the critic, said of Sharon: "He is sort of the other half of Tony's large body of work. He was the musical foundation for Tony's singing. Ralph had it all: sensitivity, touch, a well-grounded knowledge of musical theory, and a sense of loyalty. Tony was, indeed, very fortunate in having Ralph onstage with him. Ralph enhanced his singing and total performance."[37]

Sharon was a quiet man, a modest man, but not above an occasional practical joke. Before Bennett was to make an appearance at the Mogambo in Los Angeles, Sharon came across their drummer, Billy Exiner, crushing croutons in the club's kitchen. One of the songs Bennett was scheduled to sing later was "God Bless the Child," which had a line about crusts of bread. The impish Sharon suggested to Exiner that he take some croutons out of his pocket at that point and throw them on the stage. Exiner did that, and when Bennett didn't seem amused, Sharon felt that he had made an egregious mistake. But Judy Garland, who was in the audience, broke out with a loud laugh, and then so did the rest of the crowd. Bennett couldn't help but laugh, too, although he stared at Sharon in a way that said he might have been laughing on the outside, but not necessarily meaning it.

"I'm not bragging or anything," Sharon said, "but it's true that I got Tony into jazz. He found a whole new audience, and a whole new way to sing and phrase and to present himself. Now, he couldn't be without it. The great thing is that … jazz musicians really look up to him. People likes Miles Davis, Dizzy Gillespie and all the great players are very highly approving of what he does."[38]

When Sinatra, ten years older than Bennett, and Bennett were both singing, Alec Wilder risked a comparison: "There is a quality about Bennett that lets [the audience] in. Sinatra's singing mesmerizes you. In fact, [Sinatra] gets so symbolic sometimes that you can't make the relationship with him as a man, even though you may know him. Bennett's professionalism doesn't block you off. It even suggests that maybe you'll see him later at the beer parlor."[39]

A critic as perceptive as Whitney Baillet still found it difficult to categorize Bennett:

> [Bennett], a ceaseless experimenter, is an elusive singer. He can be a belter who reaches rocking fortissimos. He drives a ballad as intensely and intimately as Sinatra. He can be a lilting, glancing jazz singer. He can be a low-key, searching supperclub performer. He has gone through visual changes as well. He for a while affected a short haircut and was wont to come onstage with his shirt collar open and his jacket slung carefully over one shoulder. [But with] the disappearance of most of his hair—an occupational hazard that has likewise afflicted Bing Crosby and Sinatra—he wears a variety of stunningly accomplished transformations. He also keeps his jacket on, and is often seen onstage in a necktie.[40]

In James Kaplan's opinion, "Bennett had [and continues to have] the rare ability to bring joy to a song. Joy was an arrow Sinatra didn't quite have in his quiver."

Mitch Miller was right more than he was wrong about what songs to give Bennett at Columbia. Miller also gave Bennett strong arrangers, from Marty Manning on down, and after a while Manning did the work on virtually all of Bennett's mainstays, including "I Left My Heart in San Francisco." Bennett was cautious; he resisted songs that might be commercially right for him, because he didn't want to lock himself in to singing unwanted songs the rest of his life just because the public liked them. He cringed at singing the Hank Williams standard "Cold, Cold Heart" because he thought it was a cowboy song, and even rued the fact that it made the charts. He was different than Sinatra this way. Sinatra is identified with so many songs, but two undeniably near the top are "Strangers in the Night" and the patently autobiographical "My Way," yet Sinatra detested having to do them night after night. Part of his genius was that the audience never knew. Sinatra didn't need a set, a script and a movie camera to be an accomplished actor.[41]

Despite the successes that multiplied, the arrival of the 1960s did not bode well for Bennett, and he could sense it. Bennet said: "By the end of the fifties, the music of Elvis Presley, Chuck Berry and [the disc jockey] Alan Freed dominated the radio airwaves. Rock-and-roll music was being forced on the American public. I was fortunate that my string of hits in the fifties more than established me to make the kind of quality records I needed to make in order to assure that I'd be considered a lasting artist."[42]

Bennett's songs were no longer making the charts, but they were still earning money for Columbia, which was willing to give him the leeway he needed to co-exist with Mitch Miller.[43] He and Sinatra were the exceptions to the erosion of the old guard. Others were not as fortunate. Talents such as Nat King Cole, Frankie Laine, Dean Martin and Andy Williams found doors not as gaping as before. On the female side, Peggy Lee, Doris Day and others were beginning to see their popularity wane, and Columbia dropped Rosemary Clooney from its roster in 1958.[44]

Toward the end of 1961, George Cory and Douglass Cross, both in their early forties, were still shopping a song about San Francisco that they had written seven years previous. "I Left My Heart in San Francisco" found its way to Ralph Sharon by chance, and to Tony Bennett by accident. Bennett was headed for San Francisco for a week-long engagement culminating with New Year's Eve. Three nights before, he sang the song to an audience for the first time, and got some mild encouragement from a West Coast Columbia representative who was in the audience. It was recorded in New York early in 1962, and immediately began getting a lot of radio play even though Columbia wasn't pushing it. Many years later, Sharon said: "I always helped Tony pick his material. People are always sending me songs. They send Tony songs, too, and he shows them to me and says, 'See what you think of this.' The San Francisco song was the other way around, I showed it to him first. It took a while, other people began singing it, too, but it became a world-wide hit."[45]

Several times, Sinatra came along to record songs that Bennett had already sung. Sinatra also passed on songs that came to Bennett with Sinatra's fingerprints. Cy Coleman and Carolyn Leigh, who had written "Witchcraft" for Sinatra, also presented him with "The Best Is Yet to Come." But Sinatra let the latter song sit around for a year, and finally Columbia gave it to Bennett, who did a powerful rendition. Then Sinatra came along to cover it. "It was an act of sheer hubris for Sinatra to follow Bennett [on that song]," James Kaplan said, "but then, what was Frank if not the embodiment of hubris?"

Six months after "I Left My Heart in San Francisco" took off for the moon for Bennett, Sinatra inexplicably came along to record it. Of the event, Kaplan said: "[That] is something of a mystery, except that Sinatra was Sinatra and, though their relationship was fraught by Frank's domineering, he had been something of a mentor and certainly an inspiration to [the younger Bennett]. Sinatra might simply have felt it was his right to take a whack at it.... Sinatra was wrong. Bennett's version has stardust sprinkled on it, and Sinatra's, though he is singing well, simply doesn't.... For whatever reason, very likely embarrassment, Sinatra withdrew the single after it had been out for just two weeks."[46]

Sharon stayed with Bennett until 1966. Sharon's first wife Joyce preferred living in San Francisco instead of New York, and had asked him to get off the road. Bennett was able to temporarily re-locate Sharon and the other members of Sharon's trio to Los Angeles, where they worked at the Playboy Club and found time to do a couple of albums for Columbia.[47] While that was going on, Bennett took a fairly substantial non-singing part in a much-panned movie called *The Oscar*. Bennett's character, known as Hymie Kelly, said things that were written dramatic, but came off laughable. Peter Falk had been offered the part before Bennett, and was smart enough to turn it down. But Bennett wanted to broaden his appeal, whether it was Broadway or Hollywood. In *The Oscar*, he reminded one critic of an "incontinent basset hound." He never worked in another feature film again.[48]

About this time, Sharon moved to San Francisco to work for a new Playboy Club. Handy to Los Angeles, he was also able to work with Rosemary Clooney, Nancy Wilson, Robert Goulet and Florence Henderson. Unintentionally, Sharon missed out on Bennett's worst decade, the seventies. During that decade, Bennett's mother died, his marital life capsized, he took to drugs, his war with Columbia Records escalated, and he caught the interest of the Internal Revenue Service, which eventually hit him with a two-million-dollar tax bill. Bennett's work slowed down slightly, but not commensurate with the turmoil around him. Markedly, however, he went eleven years without recording an album.[49]

By 1980, Sharon had been divorced and remarried.[50] Linda Noone, his second wife, had worked for a theater-in-the-round in upstate New York which featured acts like Liberace, Bing Crosby, Robert Goulet and Connie Stevens, so she had a handle on how performers needed to travel to thrive.[51] At the time of Sharon's death, they had been married for 41 years.[52]

Bennett had gone through several pianists, including the veteran Torrie Zito, while Sharon was away, and in 1980, with another opening, he called Sharon, who agreed to make the move back to New York and go on the road. Bennett told Sharon he needed him, and Sharon was unable to resist. "It was a comfort to have him back," Bennett said.

Sharon never left Bennett again. Together in 1992 they did *Perfectly Frank,* an homage to Sinatra, which earned Bennett his first Grammy Award in thirty years. Sharon, at 79, announced his retirement from the music business in 2002.

It wasn't a bowl a cherries for the two of them all the time. Bennett was very particular about the way his drummers worked, and he would unload his gripes with late-night calls to Sharon, who uncomplainingly bore the cross as Bennett's sounding board. Sharon's well-being suffered, however, and he developed a heart condition. For a time, Sharon was less adventurous, mostly playing what Bennett wanted to hear. Bennett, according to Derek Boulton, who was once the singer's manager, sometimes destroyed Sharon's confidence. One night at the Fairmont Hotel, after a set had gone badly, Bennett laid all the blame on Sharon, who quietly took his beating.[53]

In the end, though, Bennett knew that he had a treasure at the piano. "I'm still inspired and guided by what Ralph Sharon told me so many years ago," Bennett said a couple of years ago. "He said to keep growing, and believe in what you do."[54]

Bennett, an accomplished painter, did a sketch of Sharon sitting at his piano. At the time of Sharon's death, the painting hung above Sharon's piano at his home.[55] Sharon might have retired, so to speak, but he was still playing at 91. He traveled between Boulder and Denver for club dates and recorded with his own trio, including albums of songs written by the great American songwriters, right on up to 2007.[56] For a time, he was a teatime regular at the old St. Julien Hotel in Boulder. One day, someone came up to him and said: "You've got the same name as a really famous pianist."

Sharon smiled. "So I hear," he said.[57]

Ralph Sharon, who gave Tony Bennett The Song and introduced him to The Knack, didn't push back from the piano for good until three months before his death.

9

"The middle of nowhere"

The sort of songs that Tony Bennett was singing in 1961 included "Toot, Toot, Tootsie (Goodbye)" and "I'm Coming, Virginia."[1] "Tootsie" was sung by Al Jolsen in 1927's *The Jazz Singer*, one of the first movies to move Hollywood into the sound era,[2] and "Virginia" was 35 years old and had been done by Bix Biederbicke and also the Paul Whiteman orchestra with Bing Crosby on vocals.[3] Both songs might have been issued on cylinders before they were put on discs. Bennett had been comfortable with golden oldies since he signed with Columbia Records in 1950[4] (he did "I Can't Give You Anything But Love" twice and "The Boulevard of Broken Dreams" in his first year),[5] but after a while it was not lost on him about what kind of retro material he was being fed. "Before ["I Left My Heart in San Francisco"], I was advised to try all sorts of tricks and gimmicks," Bennett said. "Songs were offered which were supposed to be surefire, but they weren't my style."[6]

Trying to reverse his downturn, Bennett had a brief fling with legitimate theater. He appeared in a touring production of *Silk Stockings* in Kansas City and *Guys and Dolls* in Chicago. But Broadway didn't call. Bennett approached Sid Bernstein, whom he had known from his salad days and who had just joined General Artists Corporation, one of the leading talent agencies. Bernstein shopped Bennett around, but came up empty. When Bernstein approached Felix Grossman, a promoter for acts at Carnegie Hall, he was told: "Sidney, I like you very much, but the man hasn't had a hit lately. Nobody will come." Moving on, Bernstein went to Bill Drummond, who was also in the concert business. "Sid, he's had nothing for years," Drummond said. "Forest Hills is twelve thousand seats. How are you going to fill it?" The music played on and on. "[Bennett] is a pain in the ass," Bernstein was told by Bill Gallagher at Columbia Records. "Get him off my back. He hasn't had a hit in years."[7]

Bennett wasn't the only singer who was caught in the rude awakenings of the late 1950s as rock-and-roll quickly took a foothold. Nat King

Cole, who had an assembly line of hits during the first half of the decade, suddenly cooled off. He refused to take the rock-and-roll route and clung to the middle-of-the-road material that had always worked for him. Other singers—Rosemary Clooney, Vic Damone and Perry Como were only a few—saw their popularity shrink. Clooney was dropped by Columbia. "What we have been witnessing," Arnold Shaw wrote, "is the demise of an entire generation of artists."[8]

Eventually, in 1962, Bennett did make it to Carnegie Hall, and found the top of the heap again by delivering a *tour de force* that was widely acclaimed. Bennett, taking a gamble, had to underwrite the rental of the building himself, and Bernstein and his future wife, Geri, turned into self-styled publicity dynamos in order to make the night happen.[9]

At Columbia, the early 1960s were a nervous time. Because of Mitch Miller, Columbia had never bought in to the rock-and-roll phenomenon. At a convention of disc jockeys in Kansas City, Miller lamented that much of the music being played on radio was directed at teenagers, and a lot of it, Miller maintained, was junk that barely qualified as music.[10] Substantively, Miller was right, and he had other plans for Columbia. In 1961, a nineteen-year-old whose real name was Robert Zimmerman left Minnesota for New York, sang one night at a Greenwich Village club and earned a review that said: "Bob Dylan is one of the most distinctive stylists to play in a Manhattan cabaret in months.... Mr. Dylan is vague about his antecedents and birthplace, but it matters less where he has been than where he is going..."[11] Miller signed Dylan to a Columbia contract before the *New York Times* printed another issue.[12]

It behooved all of the recording companies to continue sharing the pie, because the pie was growing exponentially. In 1955, the sale of records in the U.S. totaled $277 million. Five years later, that figure had mushroomed to six hundred million,[13] but the business was changing dramatically: In 1960, albums were outselling singles, three to one.[14]

Before Carnegie Hall, Bennett and Ralph Sharon, his accompanist, hit the road again. They started out in December of 1961 in Hot Springs, Arkansas, and ended up at the Fairmont Hotel in San Francisco. Sharon referred to Hot Springs as "the middle of nowhere."[15] Hot Springs, with a population of about 30,000, and not reachable by plane except by flying to Little Rock and going the final sixty miles by car, was sneaky fast. As local and state officials looked the other way, a town known mainly for its restorative waters became an illegal gambling mecca that was like a microcosm of Las Vegas. The hub of this activity was The Vapors, a theater, dance hall and restaurant on Park Avenue that was built in 1959 on a site previously occupied by a drive-in movie theater. It was run by Dane Harris, a former World War II pilot, and Owney "The Killer" Madden, the Englishman who owned The Cotton Club in New York.[16] Madden, a major underworld figure during Prohibition, had moved to Hot Springs after serving a stretch in Sing Sing and had married an Arkansas girl. Madden's next-door neighbor was John Ermey, the chief of police.

Gangsters had been swarming to Hot Springs since the 1920s. It was not uncommon to see Al Capone walking down the street, surrounded by bodyguards, and he had a permanent suite on the fourth floor of the Arlington Hotel. Bugs Moran, a rival of Capone's, stayed at the Majestic Hotel. Lucky Luciano was arrested in Hot Springs and extradited to New York to face penalties for his crimes.[17]

In 1964, the U.S. Justice Department said that the biggest illegal gambling operation in the country was in Hot Springs.[18] Prostitution, drugs and bookmaking went with the territory. The only legal gambling operation was Oaklawn Park, a horse-race track that was open only seven weeks a year. Public drinking was commonplace. Customers would leave a casino and walk the streets with drinks in hand, sometimes in glasses with the name of the casino on them, and move around the downtown area to other gambling dens. The casinos had a mutual agreement to return the glasses to the original establishments the next day.

A club like The Vapors could afford to pay an entertainer like Mickey Rooney—or Tony Bennett—$10,000 a week. Frankie Laine appeared in Hot Springs, as did the Maguire sisters, the Ames brothers, Liberace, Patti Page and the comedian Phyllis Diller. In broad daylight, The Vapors was bombed in 1963. A restaurant wall was torn out, exposing the large gaming room on the other side. There were no fatalities, but a dozen people were injured and several were hospitalized. No motive was found and no arrests were made.[19]

A young high school student had a front-row seat for all this nefarious activity. When Billy Blythe Clinton became President Clinton, he emphasized that he had been born in Hope, Arkansas, not Hot Springs. This was true, but it was also fact that he had moved the eighty miles south to Hot Springs in 1952 when he was five and didn't depart what was popularly known as "Sin City" until he left to study law twelve years later.[20]

"You couldn't live in Hot Springs without realizing that money and power controlled everything," said the author Shirley Abbott. "It was a place of fascinating contradictions."

Raymond Clinton, a brother to Bill Clinton's stepfather, sold cars for a living in Hot Springs and one of his regular customers was Owney Madden. Raymond Clinton knew Madden well enough that he called him by his first name.

One day, Madden paid for a car with a personal check.

"This check's no good, Owney," Raymond Clinton said. Clinton could get away with blunt talk in front of the short-tempered Madden. Many others couldn't.

"Sure, that check's good," Madden said. "I just put twenty thousand dollars in that account yesterday."

"That's not what I'm talking about," Clinton said. "You haven't signed it, and you haven't written in the amount."

In high school, Bill Clinton took up the tenor saxophone, and did well at it. He won state awards for his playing, and once, at a New Year's Eve dance at the Ambassador Hotel, a few visiting Jewish students from New York asked him to play "Hava Nagila." Not knowing it, he asked them to hum it. A minute later, he played a spirited version flawlessly, to enthusiastic applause.

Mostly, though, Clinton preferred what was known as progressive jazz, the kind that Dave Brubeck and his quartet popularized, the kind that Ralph Sharon, Tony Bennett's pianist, grew up with.[21] Sharon's real name was Schwalb—his parents were the Englishman Harry Abraham Schwalb and American-born Bella Shapiro—but he changed it to Sharon in 1946, when he was 23 and married for the first time.[22]

After Sharon moved from London to New York in 1953, he began playing at jazz clubs all over Manhattan. It was not unusual for George Cory and Douglass Cross, living in Brooklyn Heights, to frequent the same clubs, usually with copies of unpublished songs that they had written. This way, they got to know Sharon. By 1960, Cory and Cross had all but given up on "I Left My Heart in San Francisco." They had been showing it around for five or six years and couldn't get anybody to record it. Then, on the streets of Manhattan in early 1960, Cory and Cross bumped into Sharon. One of them had the sheet music for the San Francisco song stuffed in his pocket. Although Sharon kept seeing the two of them at jazz venues around town, he had only a vague sense of what they were doing. Cory and Cross told Sharon that they were writing children's songs that a few schools had agreed to use. Politely, Sharon listened. He was told that they were giving him a San Francisco song, but he was running late for an appointment and didn't pay attention. Sharon stuck the music in his pocket, told them he would look at it and perhaps show it to Bennett. By December of 1961, he had done neither. But while packing for Arkansas and San Francisco, Sharon looked over in his shirt drawer and saw a stack of sheet music. Had the Cory/Cross composition been any place but on top, it might not have caught Sharon's attention. The "San Francisco" in the title jumped off the page. Sharon reasoned that since Bennett was going to appear in San Francisco, and because he was always looking for fresh material, it might be a good idea to take this song along.[23]

Hands down, the two best hotels in Hot Springs were the Arlington and the Majestic. What was good enough for Al Capone and Bugs Moran was good enough for everybody. But a close third might have been the unfashionably named Velda Rose Motel, less than a year old and named after one of the daughters of Garland Anthony, the timber tycoon. Anthony owned a second motel in Hot Springs and named it after his two other daughters. Calling the Velda Rose a motel was a misnomer. It had ten floors and almost two hundred rooms. The Round Table Restaurant at the Velda Rose might have been reason enough for Bennett and Sharon to stay there; it had the reputation of serving some of the best food in a town filled with good southern cooking.[24]

It must have been disarming for Bennett to be dropped into a town and a state that wore segregation on its sleeve. The race riot in Elaine, Arkansas, where 257 African Americans were killed, was 42 years before,[25] but the National Guard blocking nine black students from attending a high school in Little Rock was as recent as 1957.[26] African Americans were not welcome at The Vapors and other downtown gambling clubs; Hot Springs had clubs called The Atmosphere and The Cameo for African Americans. Hot Springs also had separate municipal swimming pools, one for whites and one for blacks.[27]

Tony Bennett had been an active integrationist for a long time. Early on, one of his influences was Frank Sinatra, who as far back as 1945 had done a short film called *The House I Live In*, which championed racial tolerance.[28] Bennett, whose close friends in the entertainment business included Billy Eckstine and Count Basie,[29] embraced the causes of President Kennedy and Martin Luther King. When Sinatra organized a five-hour tribute to King at Carnegie Hall, Bennett and other stars chimed in and the show netted $50,000 for the Southern Christian Leadership Conference. King later wrote Bennett a personal note, thanking him for interrupting a busy performance schedule to be there.[30]

Late one night in Hot Springs, Bennett and Ralph Sharon finished their last show at The Vapors. Bennett didn't find out until many years later, during a visit to the Clinton White House, that the future president, as a teenager, had watched Bennett's show through a window. Hot Springs might have been a wide-open town, but Clinton was still too young to get in.[31] His mother Virginia, who was a nurse specializing in anesthesiology, liked to see the shows at The Vapors, but instead of the blackjack and slot-machine activity there, her passion was making two-dollar bets on horses at Oaklawn Park, the popular Hot Springs race track.[32] After the last show, Bennett and Ralph Sharon walked next door to the Black Orchid Lounge for a nightcap. The Black Orchid would become a topless strip club in a few years, and even featured female mud wrestling. Local newspaper reporters, as long as they promised they voted Democrat, were allowed to drink free. But in 1961 the Black Orchid was a romantic venue, favored by young adults and featuring soft jazz until 5 a.m.[33]

By the time Bennett and Sharon got to the Black Orchid, it was emptying quickly. The Reggie Cravens Quartet had played its final set of the night. Cravens was a Hot Springs fixture, a charismatic bass player who closed his eyes and swayed to the music as he played. His group usually played on Saturday nights in the large lobby of the Arlington Hotel, but this night they were appearing at the Black Orchid.[34]

By the time Bennett and Sharon got to the bar, there was no one in the room but C.B. Hudson, a 26-year-old bartender. A few of Hudson's

Ralph Sharon, Tony Bennett's accompanist, happened across the sheet music for "I Left My Heart in San Francisco" in his shirt drawer and showed it to Bennett in 1961. Above Sharon is Bennett's oil painting of his long-time pianist (courtesy Carmel Zucker).

close friends called him "Sonny." When he wasn't tending bar, he sold tickets on the horses at Oaklawn Park.[35] Sometimes Hudson, early in the day, would stand behind the bar and play cards with Earl Mazander, a municipal judge who once ran nineteen years for re-election without opposition. They played with their money on the bar, which was illegal in most places, including Hot Springs. When the Arkansas governor, Winthrop Rockefeller, closed down illegal gambling in the state in 1967, Mazander openly opposed him.[36]

Recognizing Bennett, Hudson was in no hurry to close up and go home.[37] Bennett's marriage to his first wife, Patricia, was on thin ice, and he talked briefly at the bar about that with Sharon, who was one of his regular sounding boards, personally as well as professionally. Tony and Patricia didn't separate for a few more years, and the divorce didn't go through until 1971. Officially, the reasons given were "adultery and desertion," but Bennett added another salient reason: "We fell out of love."[38]

For his part, Sharon had a song on his mind, not marital struggles. That sheet music, the composition that had kept his shirts company in a dresser drawer for about two years, was now in his pocket.

"I have this song," Sharon said. "A couple of guys in Brooklyn gave it to me once. You might want to take a look."

"What's it called?" Bennett asked.

C.B. Hudson might have been listening out of only one ear, but he wasn't missing a word.

"San Francisco something." Sharon had folded the composition in half and he pulled it out of the inside pocket of his suit coat.

"Here it is," Sharon said, "'I Left My Heart in San Francisco.' Not a bad title. I've really never looked at it, but it popped up when I was packing. Since we're going to be out there in a few days, I brought it along. We might need a song or two to fill out the show at the Fairmont [Hotel]."

Back in Brooklyn Heights, George Cory and Douglass Cross were still asleep. And here Ralph Sharon was traveling with their song. If they only knew.

Bennett looked at the four pages of music. He was mainly interested in the lyrics.

"Cable cars, fog," he said. "If it works anyplace, it would be San Francisco, wouldn't it?"

He swiveled on his bar stool and looked around the room. Up front, on the bandstand on one side of the dance floor, was the piano Charles Porter had been playing before he and the rest of the Reggie Cravens Quartet had called it a night.[39]

"Take a seat up there, Ralph," Bennett said, "let's give this a go."

Sharon sat down, spread the music in front of him, and played several notes. He played the music again, start to finish. Then he played it once more, and this time Bennett hummed along. Then Bennett indicated to Sharon what key they should use, told him he was ready, and Sharon played as Bennett sang.

For a first time, the words came easily.[40] Bennett liked every one of them. Bennett finished and Sharon said: "It might have a chance."

"Like I said, it sure as hell ought to work at the Fairmont," Bennett replied.

"I could do a quick chart after we get to San Francisco," Sharon said. "We've got a rehearsal with the house band at the hotel the second day we're there."

They went back to the bar to finish their drinks.

"Hey, Tony," C.B. Hudson said. "That's a really good song. If you ever put that on a record, I'll be first in line to buy one."[41]

Bennett and Sharon walked back to the Velda Rose Motel. They were still thinking about what to do with the song once they got to San Francisco.

"It's the kind of song that should help in that town," Bennett said. "San Francisco audiences can be tough, can't they? That's what they say. This song might warm them up a little."

"I've heard they can be demanding," Sharon replied. "Especially if you haven't been there before and they don't know you that well."

"Let's work with the guys at the Fairmont and try to put it together."

"I'll get on it. I'll fool around with it on the plane."

"I can't get over that bartender. He really liked it, didn't he?"[42]

10

December 28, 1961

Living together in Brooklyn in 1961, George Cory and Douglass Cross were stranded. Their overlapping career as songwriters was in stasis. They didn't like anything about living in New York, where they had moved in the mid-1940s to be closer to Tin Pan Alley. Their relocation had been well thought out, but the plan had foundered. Their grand plan had been to sell a few songs in New York, enough to shed the cloak of anonymity, and earn enough to afford another cross-country move. They both missed San Francisco (ergo, Cross' nostalgic lyrics for the melody Cory wrote).[1] Cross' widowed mother lived a hundred miles north of San Francisco, and he missed her, too.

One reason Cross disliked New York was that his sister, Shirley May Neilson, left California to work in advertising in Manhattan and, as her son told me, abused drug and drink, vices that would kill her by 1976. "Maybe it would have happened, anyway," said Ron Strowbridge, her son, who was living in Clearlake, California, in 2016. "You can find bad people, people who can lead you down the wrong path, anyplace. Maybe she didn't need bad people, maybe she just did it on her own. All I know is that when she came back to California from New York she was a changed person, none of it for the good."

When Shirley May Neilson died in bed of a drug overdose at 49, Strowbridge watched the medics carry her out. He was billed $90 for the body bag. Next to his mother in the bed was a man—Strowbridge was never interested in getting his name—who, the coroner estimated, had been dead for at least two days before Neilson's approximate time of death. Douglass Cross, who died a year before his sister, in 1975, wrote his last will in 1968. Even then, eight years before she died, Cross specifically stated that Shirley May Neilson be excluded from his small fortune. Cross feared that she would squander an inheritance on drugs. By the time he died, Douglass Cross was a drunkard. He was not, by all accounts, a drug user.[2]

10. December 28, 1961

Tony Bennett got to the Venetian Room, the Fairmont Hotel's lobby-level showplace, about a year before I did. The first night I was there, with my widowed Aunt Edna (my mother's older sister and one of my best friends) we saw Roberta Sherwood, the torch singer. Edna and I had gone to San Francisco, all the way from St. Louis, with a dual purpose: She was not opposed to remarrying, and it wouldn't have made me mad had I found a newspaper job in California. Neither happened, but we had a lot of fun trying. Over the years, I went back to the Venetian Room a number of times. I can remember Jack Jones, Bobby Short and Keely Smith, who was doing a single now that she and Louie Prima had split up. She seemed nervous and a bit off her game the night I was there, and the sophisticated San Francisco audience, accustomed to getting a top act after paying top dollar, was barely courteous. I felt sorry for her. Tony Bennett was right when he said he had heard that the Venetian could be a tough room to play.[3]

There was a mythical St. Gregory Hotel in a long-running TV series called *Hotel*, much of which was shot at the Fairmont. *Hotel* was fiction, and ran for several seasons. Material for more episodes could have been culled from the very history of the Fairmont itself.[4] The land at the corners of California and Mason Streets would have been turned into a mansion, not a hotel, if James Fair, the well-heeled silver prospector, hadn't died in 1894. Several years later, Fair's two daughters built a seven-story, six hundred-room hotel. But the opening, on April 18, 1906, was the same day as an early-morning earthquake that destroyed about 80 percent of the growing city and caused an estimated three thousand deaths. Instead of rebuilding, Fair's daughters traded what was left of the Fairmont for two office buildings—structures that had survived the earthquake—in the financial district. The new owners of the hotel hired Stanford White, a prominent New York architect, for the rebuilding project. Before White could get under way, he was fatally shot by Harry Thaw, whose wife, the chorus girl Evelyn Nesbit, had allegedly been sexually assaulted by White before the marriage, when she was sixteen years old.

The Fairmont owners then hired Julia Morgan, who had designed Hearst Castle for William Randolph Hearst, the publishing baron, in San Simeon, California. The Fairmont finally opened in 1907, a year to the day after the earthquake, and in 1908 Tessie Fair, one of James Fair's daughters, bought back the hotel. In 1929, George Smith, who owned the Mark Hopkins Hotel, across California Street from the Fairmont, bought the Fairmont and operated it until 1945, when Benjamin Swig, the real estate mogul, bought 54 percent of the hotel for two million dollars. That was the same year that delegates from forty nations, including new U.S. president Harry Truman, occupied the hotel for eleven weeks before they drafted the charter for the United Nations.

"All this hotel has really been is an apartment house for the very rich," said Swig, who oversaw a massive remodeling of the Fairmont that wasn't finished until 1950. The Venetian Room, which had been a dining room but was seldom open, became a nightclub in 1947. Swig started at the top. He booked Ethel Waters for opening night, and the stars just kept coming: Nat King Cole, Ella Fitzgerald, Edith Piaf, Sammy Davis, Jr., Lena Horne, Red Skelton, Marlene Dietrich, Joel Grey, Mel Torme, Peggy Lee and James Brown are a very incomplete list.

In 1961, a few months before Bennett came to town, the Fairmont became virtually a new hotel when Swig opened a section called the Fairmont Towers. It was 23 stories, loaded with suites instead of standard rooms. Not accidentally, many of them looked down on the Mark Hopkins, the competitor across the street, which had become threadbare and stuffy.[5]

On September 13, 1961, the road company of *Gypsy* did a performance in San Francisco. The musical had run for almost two years on Broadway, winning multiple Tony Awards, including one for its star, Ethel Merman.[6] Before *Gypsy* got to San Francisco, it was done in Chicago, where one night I saw the incredible Merman.

The curtain had not yet gone up as the orchestra played the overture. Everyone was seated while she slinked out of sight in the back of the theater. As the overture neared its conclusion, she came running up the aisle (I could have reached out and touched her from my aisle seat), bounded a few steps to the stage, turned around in full costume and shouted, in that bullhorn voice that never needed a boost from a microphone, "Hello, everybody!" Merman got a standing ovation before the show started.

Several members of the San Francisco cast were gay, and after the show on September 13 they took Merman to a neighborhood bar that was called the Tay-Bush because it was located at the intersection of Taylor and Bush Streets. Merman and her theatrical friends unwound, even put some coins in the juke box, until 3 a.m. on what had become the 14th.[7] There were three undercover policemen in the crowd of more than two hundred, and they weren't amused by the goings-on. At 3:15, just after Merman and her party had left, one of the cops went outside, walked to a phone booth, called his station house and said: "There are all kinds of men, kissing and dancing in there."

Within minutes, paddy wagons began lining up outside the Tay-Bush. The police broke into the bar, made dozens of arrests, and formed a procession with their captives back to headquarters, where more than a hundred customers were booked for being "visitors to a disorderly house." All of the charges were dropped but two, but one San Francisco newspaper ran the names and addresses of everyone involved, anyway. The owner of the Tay-Bush paid $400. "The only moral, if it's a question of morals," wrote the *San Francisco Chronicle*'s Herb Caen, the self-styled conscience of the city, "is don't be a poor one. Don't be a poor anything."[8]

Earlier in the year, San Francisco's mayor, George Christopher, who owned a dairy, was stopped by the union from hiring a black man to drive on one of his delivery routes.[9] This hardly seemed like a town that George Cory and Douglass Cross would enjoy coming back to.

In December, Bennett and his accompanist, Ralph Sharon, arrived several days before New Year's Eve. They had flown almost two thousand miles from Hot Springs, Arkansas. On the plane, Sharon had done a quick draft of the orchestration for "I Left My Heart in San Francisco." Their engagement began on a Thursday night, December 28, 1961, and ran right through New Year's Eve, on Sunday. The Venetian Room's capacity was 325, and the hotel had sold out New Year's Eve, but tickets had moved slowly for Bennett's other performances. The hotel expected that there might be a last-minute rush for the pre-New Year's nights. San Francisco was packed with holiday tourists and the hotel itself was sold out.[10]

Bennett and Sharon discussed where they might place Cory and Cross' song. They gave consideration to finishing the act with it, but Bennett said: "That might be risky. What if it lays an egg? I wouldn't want to leave them disappointed."

"It's got a better-than-average chance," Sharon said, "just because it's San Francisco."

There were certain long-standing songs, some of them hits, that Bennett included almost every time: "The Boulevard of Broken Dreams" (which took him back to 1950, his first year with Columbia Records); "Rags to Riches," one of his hits in 1953; "Sing You Sinners," which dated to the 1930s with several other performers; "Just in Time"; and "The Best Is Yet to Come," which he sang on a Columbia 45 RPM earlier in 1961.[11] Bennett also toyed with the idea of adding "Are You Lonesome Tonight?" which had been a 1961 hit for Elvis Presley.[12]

When Bennett's father died in 1936, at 41, his mother was left with three children to support. She kept her job as a seamstress in the garment district of Manhattan, and brought piecework home for extra money at night. Some of the dresses were cheaply made, and she rejected those and took them back the next day, without working on them. "She told me that she only did quality dresses," Bennett said. That policy was still embedded in his mind years later, when he would pass up some songs. "I always insisted," he said, "on singing nothing but great songs."[13]

The conductor of the house orchestra in the Venetian Room was Ernie Heckscher. In his mid-forties, Heckscher was a San Francisco mainstay. His Harvard-educated father was a poet who died, when he was 44 and his son eleven, in 1928. Heckscher played the banjo and guitar when he was young, worked on the RKO vaudeville circuit, went to Stanford and was drafted by the Army during World War II. In 1945, the war over, he went to Chicago and joined the band at the Blackstone Hotel as a piano player. A year later, he was back in California, at the Mark Hopkins Hotel, where he took over as the leader when the director of the orchestra was killed in an automobile accident. In 1948, Ben Swig invited Heckscher to move to his Fairmont Hotel, and he never worked anywhere else. After 36 years there, and with music tastes changing, he retired in 1984.[14]

By 1961, Heckscher and his orchestra had already recorded a couple of albums. *Billboard* called him the "Nabob of Nob Hill." Heckscher had been working steadily with a who's who of talent that included Mel Torme, Jack Jones, Harry Belafonte and whoever else Swig could bring to the hotel.[15]

Heckscher, Tony Bennett and Ralph Sharon had two rehearsals to work up their opening-night show. Heckscher complimented Sharon on his chart for "I Left My Heart in San Francisco." Bennett's accompanist was pressed for time in getting the arrangement ready. They didn't tinker much with George Cory's melody, and Bennett told me that they changed nary a word of Douglass Cross' sentimental lyrics.[16]

Many people staying in the hotel over the holidays began making Venetian Room reservations, and by late afternoon on December 28, Bennett's show was a sellout. "The Venetian Room," Bruce Bellingham once wrote, "is a good place to leave one's heart."[17] While Jon Akselsen and his girlfriend may have had different levels of amour rattling around in their heads, Akselsen was hopeful that all those Bennett love songs would work in his favor. He was an undergraduate at the University of Oregon, hardly able to afford a night at the luxe Fairmont, but the girl's father, a San Francisco stockbroker, got them the tickets to see Bennett. They had good seats, close to the Venetian Room's small stage. There were few bad seats in the room. Akselsen's father, an émigré from Norway, had survived the devastating San Francisco earthquake in 1906.

Akselsen and his date went to the Venetian Room with fake identification cards. Their waiter didn't notice. I asked Akselsen what he remembered most about December 28, 1961.

10. December 28, 1961

"Taking my girlfriend home, and making out for two hours in her driveway," he said.[18]

Lois and Maurice Rosano checked into the Fairmont Hotel on December 27, 1961. They were local, but they were spending two nights at the hotel to celebrate their tenth wedding anniversary. They had reservations for the Tony Bennett show in the Venetian Room, where they had seen Ella Fitzgerald a few years before. Their record collection included many 45s and 78s that Bennett had done. Lois Rosano looked around their hotel room after the bellman left. There was an automatic shoeshine machine in one corner. You wore your shoes, put them under brushes that would rotate madly when you pressed a button. They had never seen one before. Lois Rosano thought it was cute, and years later was surprised that she would remember such an incidental thing about their stay.[19]

Some of the crowd arrived early on December 28. The room had *Beaux-Arts* trappings, small, shaded gold-plated lamps halfway up the walls, and paintings of Italian scenes around the room. Julia Morgan had done a tasteful job. Some of the women were dressed in furs. Cigarette girls, wearing skimpy uniforms, their wares in large boxes connected by straps to the backs of their necks, moved among the crowd. The bow-tied waiters took drink orders. Mainly, it was a martini and manhattan crowd.[20]

Joseph Alioto and George Moscone came in. Alioto, in his midforties, was a wealthy antitrust lawyer who would become mayor of the city in 1968. Ben Swig, majority owner of the Fairmont, was among Alioto's backers; they feared that John Shelley, the incumbent mayor, could not win if he ran again. Shelley dropped out to pave the way for Alioto. Moscone, also a lawyer, had turned 32 just a month before Bennett sang. Moscone, who succeeded Alioto as mayor in 1976, was assassinated two years later by Dan White, a disgruntled former city supervisor, while he sat at his office desk. Both future mayors liked Bennett because he was a fellow *paisano* as well as an accomplished singer.

As Bennett moved through his repertoire, toward the new song, Ralph Sharon, at his piano, considered how propinquity had played such a part. "If I hadn't reached for that shirt in that drawer, the song would have just sat there," Sharon said.[21]

That night was a long time ago, and by 2016 details of Bennett's performance depended on whom you talked to. Lois Rosano thought that "I Left My Heart in San Francisco" was saved for last. Edwin Whitman, a young physician, recalled that Bennett sang the Cory/Cross song twice. Whitman remembered that Bennett sang the song one time with his jacket off, while sitting on the steps of the stage.

The Venetian Room at the Fairmont Hotel in San Francisco looked like this in the 1960s. It was there where Tony Bennett introduced "I Left My Heart in San Francisco" on December 28, 1961. Kay Thompson is the headliner on stage (San Francisco History Center, San Francisco Public Library).

Because of what Count Basie had once told him, Bennett saved the best songs for the back end of a performance. "Why open with a closer?" Basie said. "Start with a medium-tempo number, and give the audience a chance to settle in."

Recalling that advice, Bennett said: "If you wait, you can hit them with an up-tempo number later on, and it will be twice as effective."[22]

10. December 28, 1961

Bennett sang the San Francisco song. He had a good mind for lyrics and seldom muffed one. The crowd of more than three hundred stood and applauded. Many, wanting to hear the song again, shouted, "More!" A couple of West Coast representatives from Columbia Records were in the room. They looked at one another, pursed their lips and wondered if Bennett was on to something. They were going to go backstage to talk to Bennett, anyway, and now they really had something to talk about.[23] C.B. "Sonny" Hudson, that bartender in Arkansas, knew his onions.

Not many critics were there. Herb Caen, the *sui generis* of San Francisco newspaper columnists, would not catch up with the buzz until much later. A month later, John Bryan of the *San Francisco Examiner* wrote: "I thought the lyrics were pretty corny. But the people really liked it. He had to sing it again and again. And you know, after a while, the tune really begins to grow on you."[24]

Caen sort of felt the same way, once he heard the song. "At first, it wasn't for me," he said. "But then I was in Paris late one night, and I heard it again. Then it hit me. I got very homesick."[25]

Two days after Bennett first sang the song, Ivan Paul wrote a three-dot column that led off with a roundelay of mindless jokes that were really blatant plugs for restaurants about town. Halfway down, he got around to turgidly commenting about Bennett's performance: "Tony Bennett proved a miracle man in more ways than two. He packed the room on a customarily slow night just before New Year's, and was a positive revelation, a dynamic performer. He came up with a thrilling old tune, 'I Left My Heart in San Francisco,' that was a showstopper. This is a great performer with a controlled style and a twist of humor who had the mob in the Venetian arena huzzahing all over the place."[26]

A "thrilling old tune"? Well, maybe Ivan Paul had done his homework, and in that event, in a technical sense, he was correct. The song had been written seven years before Bennett sang it, and had kicked around with at least two singers—Claramae Turner, Tessie O'Shea—who didn't manage to get it recorded.

Backstage, one of the Columbia Records guys said: "The biggest hand you got was for that San Francisco song. You ought to go back to New York and tell Mitch [Miller]."

Miller, the powerful Columbia Records chieftain, called the shots on who got hired and what they sang. His star was on the wane, but he was still influential.

"Record it?" Bennett said. "Yeah, they liked it a lot, but I don't know.

Singing a San Francisco song for a San Francisco audience, it's pretty much like asking for applause."

"It still might be worth recording," the Columbia guy replied. "Say it only sells in San Francisco. That's still a pretty good-sized audience. A lot of people out here buy records."

"I'll tell Mitch, see what he thinks," Bennett said. "Don't get me wrong, I love the song. I loved it from the start, that night I first fooled with it in Arkansas. But Mitch knows me. He knows I never think about the commercial aspect when I consider a song. He's the other way. He always thinks first about how much it can sell, not the quality of the tune."

The next day, Ralph Sharon called George Cory and Douglass Cross and told them what happened.

"We didn't even know you had the song," Cross said.

"I had it all along," Sharon replied. "We just got around to it."

"Any chance Tony will record it?"

"We're going back to New York the first of the year. We'll see what Columbia wants to do."[27]

Back in New York, Mitch Miller was already thinking about what 1962 might bring for Bennett and the rest of the artists in the Columbia stable. Bennett didn't know it yet, but with an album about Broadway in mind, Miller already had a working list of songs at the ready: "Just in Time," "Put on a Happy Face" and "Strangers in Paradise" were a few. There was a musical that was opening on Broadway in March called *All American*, starring Ray Bolger. The book was written by Mel Brooks (at least Brooks wrote the first act; he reportedly lost interest after that), the score by Charles Strouse and Lee Adams. The best song in the show was expected to be "Once Upon a Time." Bennett had seen an advance copy of the song, and thought it might be a good fit. Because Columbia was signed to record the complete score, Miller thought that giving "Once Upon a Time" to Bennett for a 45 made sense. But Miller didn't have anything in mind for the B-side, and that's where the plot thickened.[28]

11

String Along with Mitch

In April of 1950, not long after he had been handed control of the pop-music division at Columbia Records, Mitch Miller signed a 23-year-old Tony Bennett to a recording contract. All Miller had to hear was Bennett's demo record of two songs, one of which was Al Dubin and Harry Warren's "Boulevard of Broken Dreams." Ray Muscarella, Bennett's manager, had sent the recordings to Miller,[1] who liked to boast: "In three seconds, I can tell a talent."[2]

In less than a month, Columbia released "Boulevard," and before the year was out, Bennett had also recorded "I Can't Give You Anything But Love," "Sing You Sinners," "I Wanna Be Loved" and a few others.[3] Bennett wasn't a one-man band at Columbia, but in the first 18 months its sales increased by 80 percent. Before Miller came aboard, Columbia languished in fourth place among the major record labels.[4]

Miller, the son of Russian immigrants, came from Rochester, New York. He was 38 when he was hired by Goddard Lieberson, who, two decades earlier, had been a fellow student at the Eastman School of Music.[5] Miller began playing the oboe in high school, and by 1935 he was playing in the pit orchestra for the Broadway production of *Porgy and Bess*. He played for the CBS Symphony in 1938, when it furnished the music for Orson Welles' controversial radio adaptation of *War of the Worlds*.[6]

Frank Sinatra and Rosemary Clooney were already with Columbia when Miller arrived. Although classically trained, Miller had an unquenchable liking for novelty songs and gimmicky sound effects, the kind of stuff that might be more identified with Spike Jones, the Hoosier Hotshots and groups of that ilk. Both Sinatra and Clooney took exception to some of the material Miller gave them. "These trick songs are coming out of my ears," Sinatra once said.[7]

At the time, Sinatra's career was at a nadir. He had borrowed money from Columbia (either $100,000 or $250,000 depending on the source) and his personal life was in disarray. Columbia dropped him in 1952, and he moved on to Capitol Records. Six years before he died, Miller reflected on those rough times: "The thing with Sinatra was that you always had to jump through hoops for him.... He'd flown in from the West Coast on his way to Spain to see [Ava Gardner], who was *schtupping* the bullfighter and he was furious. He came in at night with his Mafioso group, and he was furious. I played him the songs and he said, 'I'm not going to do that shit,' and walked out ... That was it for him. We loaned him a quarter of a million dollars to pay his taxes, and then he did *From Here to Eternity*, did his public penance and suddenly his records began to sell. Meanwhile, all the records he said I'd ruined his career with, he started making royalties on."[8]

Two of the songs Miller had picked out for Sinatra were "The Roving Kind" and "My Heart Cries for You." When Sinatra walked out on the recording session, the band was already being paid and Miller was determined to get those songs sung that night by somebody. He remembered there was a young singer hanging around Columbia, trying to get discovered and so poor that he slept in somebody's office. His name was Albert Cernik, and Miller found him, brought him into the studio and he sung the Sinatra songs cold. One song climbed to number two on the charts and the other reached number four. "But 'Al Cernik' won't do," Miller said. "My first name is Mitchell, so that's going to be your last name. And you seem like a decent guy." So Al Cernik became Guy Mitchell and he sang a few more hits for Columbia in the mid-1950s.[9]

Miller and Sinatra remained enemies, right to the end. Several years after Columbia had dropped Sinatra, and after his career had gotten back on track, Miller was at the Sands Hotel in Las Vegas when he ran into Joe E. Lewis in the lobby at about three in the morning. Sinatra, who had played Lewis in a movie about the entertainer's life,[10] was having a drink with Jack Entratter, who owned the hotel, and Lewis insisted that Miller go over and say hello.

"No, I'm not interested," Miller said.

Lewis knew all about the Sinatra/Miller feud. But he had been drinking, and took Miller by the arm and led him over anyway.

"I brought Mitch over," Lewis said to Sinatra, who was also drinking the night away. "Why don't you shake hands?"

Sinatra looked up at Miller and said: "Fuck you. Keep walking, creep."[11]

Clooney, a band singer before she signed with Columbia, had Sinatra and Manie Sachs, Miller's predecessor, for support, but now she was uneasy about working with somebody new, and especially someone with Miller's tyrannical reputation. Worse, Miller was telling her that she had made a mistake by marrying Jose Ferrer. Their sticky relationship came to a head when Miller told Clooney to sing "Come On-a My House," an Armenian folk song that Clooney thought was ridiculous.

"I thought the lyric ranged from incoherent to just plain silly," Clooney said. "I thought the tune sounded more like a drunken chant than an historic folk art form, and I hated the gimmicky arrangement. It was orchestrated for a jazzed-up harpsichord, of all things, with a kind of calypso rhythm."

When Miller asked her what she thought before they started, she said: "I don't think so. Do you think this song is a song that people will understand? Do you think that if they hear me sing this, that they'll realize that I'm a singer who can do other things, too?"

To that, Miller said: "If you don't want to sing this song, don't bother showing up at the session tomorrow, or ever again."[12]

Finally, she relented, and the song became a hit. For the umpteenth time, to the umpteenth singer under his control, Miller said: "If it was a bad song, do you think I'd ask you to sing it?"[13]

Johnny Mandel, who sometimes did arrangements for Doris Day's recordings, thought Miller did her a disservice with the material he picked out. Mandel said that Miller, his trademark goatee neat as a pin, would come storming into recording sessions smoking a long cigar, acting like a general and treating everyone else in the room like they were buck privates. Mandel got fed up with it all and walked out of a Doris Day session. He apologized to her before he left.[14]

Not all of the critiques of Miller's days at Columbia were brickbats. "They should build a statue to Mitch Miller at 57th and Broadway," said Jerry Wexler, who was instrumental in building Atlantic Records into a major label. "Before Mitch came alone, pop music was vestigial, strings-behind-potted-palms. He changed all that. He threw out the thirty-two-bar form, he used bastard instruments. He was the first great record producer in history. What they did at that church [Columbia's legendary recording studio on 30th Street] under his regime was some of the most incredible music ever made."[15]

But for every Jerry Wexler, there seems to be a legion of Johnny Mandels. "I think Mitch Miller set back the music business thirty or forty years, which is inexcusable for somebody who was as great a musician as he was," Mandel said.[16]

Tony Bennett was someplace in between. He could afford to stake out neutral ground on Miller because when Bennett first came through the door at Columbia, Sinatra was on his way out. Miller needed a Tony Bennett, a marquee singer to replace Sinatra. Although Sinatra's popularity was waning at the time Columbia dumped him, there were those who felt that Miller should have given Sinatra at least a measure of veto power in selecting songs. Miller heard this, and it probably occurred to him that if he had the same showdown with Bennett and lost, the front office might have concluded that Columbia had a Mitch Miller problem, not a singer problem. So in a little while, Bennett pushed the envelope with Miller and won. It was a compromise, but with the usually intransigent Miller, a compromise was as good as a win.

"Well, everybody puts [Miller] down," Bennett said in 2002. "I've always laughed at that, because I've not had a hate relationship. It was the age of my trying to compromise and make things work when you first start out."[17]

Clooney and Bennett talked over her problems with Miller. Bennett told her he regularly had to remind Miller that he was not going to sing songs he didn't like. Clooney was surprised to hear that Bennett could actually have confrontations with Miller and come away the winner.

In an early memoir, Bennett said: "Fortunately, Mitch and I came to an understanding. We were still doing four tunes per recording session at that time, so we worked out a deal. He picked two songs and I picked two songs. Of course, even then there were certain songs he'd come up with that I just couldn't do. But on the other hand, not everything that Mitch picked was a novelty. He often showed me that he still knew a thing or two about good songs. As a result, I had some great sessions with Mitch. But I always had the sword out, and I was always verbally dueling with him."[18]

By 1961, Miller's days with Columbia were numbered. He kept telling Goddard Lieberson that rock and roll was trash, and it's incalculable how much that hard-headed position cost the label. Columbia might have had Elvis Presley, Buddy Holly and others had it had not been for Miller's refusal to accept their brand of music. The decade-old departure of Sinatra, solely because he and Miller were incompatible, lingered with some of the people in the executive suite. Also, Miller was moving to other pastures, dividing his time and cutting himself thin. His string of sing-along albums were wildly successful. NBC, not CBS (who owned Columbia), had given Miller a TV show that was a long-running hit (CBS had been offered the show first, but thought it was too cornball to build an audience). It was hard for the public not to know who Mitch Miller was—he was everywhere, including being in demand as a product pitchman. One day, he popped up hawking Thom McAn Shoes.

There were those at Columbia who wondered how Miller could shoehorn all this activity into one life. One way to save time, Miller discovered, was to brown-bag his lunches, rather than joining the two-martini crowd all over town.[19] Lieberson, who had single-handedly accounted for Miller joining Columbia, hosted a retirement luncheon for Joe Higgins, a tireless worker on the company's financial side for decades. Just about anybody who was anybody stood up and spoke to Higgins' leaving. Finally, at one point, Lieberson wanted to give Miller a chance to speak.

"Is Mitch Miller still here?" Lieberson said from the dais. He didn't know that Miller had gone to the taping of his TV show.

"He had to leave," came a voice from the back of the room.

"I guess Mitch is singing along with someone else by now," Lieberson said, and everybody laughed.[20]

By the time Tony Bennett sang "I Left My Heart in San Francisco" at the Fairmont Hotel on December 28, 1961, Mitch Miller's job at Columbia Records had been filled twice. First the post went to Frank DeVol, an arranger-conductor-composer whose score for the 1959 Doris Day film *Pillow Talk* was nominated for an Academy Award.[21] But Lieberson quickly realized that DeVol, much in demand in Hollywood, would be spending a lot of time in California, so he moved on to thirty-ish Dave Kapralik, who only four years before had been unsure what kind of work he was out of. He had worked as a radio actor, carnival barker and shoe salesman, but caught Lieberson's eye after starting at Columbia as a trainee. After writing blurbs for Mitch Miller's 45s—and finding a sixteen-year-old Leslie Uggams, who would star on Miller's TV show—Kapralik was director of promotions at Columbia, a position that would lead to what had been Miller's job at the label.[22]

In 1961, before DeVol had officially taken over for Miller, and before Bennett took off for his appearances in Arkansas and San Francisco, Bennett had an idea for an album that would not require a full orchestra or even a quartet, just he with Ralph Sharon at the piano. Bennett had a load of songs in mind, including "I Didn't Know What Time It Was," "My Funny Valentine," "Street of Dreams" and "Happiness Is a Thing Called Joe." Bennett even thought up an apt title for the collection: *Tony Sings for Two*.[23]

Miller didn't like the idea. He didn't like it to the point where he wanted no part of it. Together, without Miller, Bennett and Sharon booked some recording time. They finished most of the songs in one take and in one afternoon they polished off sixteen songs, four more than what they needed. Part way through the session, Miller came in to see what they were doing. He couldn't believe the two of them were spending all this time on what he thought was cockamamie. Between songs, he asked Bennett to give up and spend his time on something more worthwhile. Bennett was undeterred. Miller turned to Frank Laico and said: "I'm leaving. I can't support this." *Tony Sings for Two*, Bennett said, "was one of my finest records ever."[24]

Although Miller didn't need Columbia's money anymore, not with the hefty income from his albums and the weekly TV show, he hung around until 1965. At first, he was given a year's leave of absence, with an office and a secretary. Early in 1962, it was Tony Bennett and Ralph Sharon who came to this office. They were fresh off the plane from San Francisco and they talked about the possibility of recording this new song that had rolled them in the aisles at the Venetian Room.

"I already heard," Miller said. "The sales guys from out there called."

"Maybe it's just a hometown song, but I don't know," Bennett said. "You know how it is with songs sometimes, you can't tell until you do them, and they get out there."

"Tell me about it. 'Cold, Cold Heart?'"

"Yeah, 'Cold, Cold Heart.'"

Over the years, any time Miller and Bennett collided over the choice of a song, Miller would mention "Cold, Cold Heart," the Hank Williams country song. When Miller wanted to record it, Bennett said that he had never heard of Williams and wasn't interested. But Bennett reluctantly did it, and it sold two million copies, became a crossover hit and reached the top of the *Billboard* charts. Williams called Bennett one day and jokingly said, "Hey, Tony, what's the big idea of ruining my song?"[25] Only 29, Williams was dead two years later.[26]

Miller told Bennett about "Once Upon a Time." There was a Broadway show, called *All American*, that was in rehearsals. It would star Ray Bolger. The songs, written by Charles Strouse and Lee Adams (who had had a Broadway hit with *Bye Bye Birdie* in 1960), included "Once Upon a Time." Columbia was signed up to record the whole show, with the original Broadway cast, but Miller thought it might be a good idea if Bennett did what he thought was the best song right away. Bennett looked at the sheet music for "Once Upon a Time" and liked it. You listen to the rendition from the show, sung in tandem by Bolger and his co-star, Eileen Herlie,[27] and you say to yourself, what a shame such a haunting song fell by the wayside because it was part of a show that flopped. It had a right to flop.

11. String Along with Mitch

Mitch Miller (left) with Dave Brubeck. When Bennett brought "I Left My Heart in San Francisco" to Miller at Columbia Records, he was told to go ahead and record it, but keep it on the B-side.

For one thing, Mel Brooks, who was then a joke writer trying his hand at a book musical for the first time, wrote the first act, gave up and the rest of the show was written by committee.[28] Bennett's version of "Once Upon a Time" was "trademark Bennett, with the song getting away from him more than once, like a plastic bag taken by the wind, but the elegiac tone so close to Bennett's sensibility that it works."[29]

They had nothing for the other side of "Once Upon a Time." Bennett kept suggesting "I Left My Heart in San Francisco." Finally, indifferently, resignedly, desperately, Miller said: "OK then. Do it and throw it in. But make sure it's the B-side."[30] In the days of the 45 RPM, the A-side of a record was usually the one that the label believed to be the better song. The song on the B-side was usually not promoted at all.[31]

Bennett asked Marty Manning to write the orchestration for the Cory/Cross song. "Marty was a wonderful arranger," Bennett said. "He was confident, but didn't have one iota of an ego. He promised me that when he did an arrangement, it would be perfect, and he lived up to that promise. Marty Manning did several of my biggest hits."[32]

Miller liked to fiddle with the words, even the titles, of many songs, and he won some and he lost some. Ben Weisman's "Let Me Go, Lover" started out as "Let Me Go, Devil." It was a song about a songwriter begging to be released from a drinking problem. By changing just a few words, it became a love song. "So many times," Miller said, "the writers would have the song, and it might work up to a point, but then maybe the bridge didn't quite make it. You'd lose people if you left it that way. But these writers [he had] were real craftsmen, I'd tell them what I'd need, they'd go off and a half-hour later come back with it, completely revamped."[33]

On January 23, 1962, Bennett, Manning and a 38-piece orchestra didn't arrive at the famous church-turned-recording studio at 207 East 30th Street, just off Third Avenue, until late at night.[34] In 1949, Columbia had converted the old Armenian Greek Orthodox Church into a building where Bob Dylan and Miles Davis did some of their best work; where Leonard Bernstein burnished the score for *West Side Story*; where Glenn Gould recorded *Goldberg Variations*; where Vladimir Horowitz worked most of the time. "I wouldn't record anywhere else," Davis said.[35]

The old church came to house a hundred-square-foot recording room. Columbia's technical maintenance team built a custom console inside an elevated, eight by fourteen control room. What started as an eight-channel capacity had been increased to twelve channels by 1962. Drapes on the walls, installed to purify the sound, reached all the way to the tall ceiling.

Engineers enjoyed working at East 30th Street because it was away from the hubbub at Columbia's main building, the "Black Rock," on East 52nd Street. "The day they knocked that studio down at East 30th Street was the saddest day of my life," said Frank Laico, who was the engineer the night Bennett recorded the San Francisco song. "That was the day I decided to get out of Columbia."

Mitch Miller was so enamored with the East 30th Street location that when he left Columbia, one of his last requests was not to disturb the trappings at the studio.

"Don't even paint it," Miller said. "There's too much leftover magic there, magic that shouldn't be disturbed."

But when Miller visited the studio in the 1970s, mainly just to reminisce, he didn't recognize the place.[36]

Uncharacteristically, Miller didn't tinker with the words or music of "I Left My Heart in San Francisco," With the exception of a larger orchestra, Bennett virtually duplicated the song he had sung at the hotel in San Francisco.

"I always had that sadness that my father died when I was very young," Bennett said. "That feeling might have subconsciously helped with doing the song. But what really helped was that I was singing a great song about a great city. We didn't know it yet, but that's the way it really was."[37]

There was ample room for all the musicians who came with Bennett on the night of January 23. The session didn't begin until a little after 10 p.m., because all of the musicians couldn't be gathered until then.

Laico once told an interviewer that Bennett was not enthusiastic about the song, but Miller was. I heard it the other way around, from multiple sources. At any rate, they did three songs first, then the San Francisco song, and by then it was a couple hours past midnight.

Some engineers placed a microphone above the entire orchestra, but Laico preferred a separate mike for each musical section. That way, the strings, the horns and the woodwinds would have separate tracks, as did the bass, the drums and the piano. To isolate the sound, Laico put a baffle around Bennett. He made it low enough so the singer could see the conductor. Laico had worked with Bennett long enough that he knew the right mike to use. In this case, it was a Neumann U49. Laico, a perfectionist, kept a log book with the best mike for each of Columbia's singers.

Singing three numbers before the San Francisco number probably helped Bennett. His voice was good and loose, but not tired, by 3 a.m. The first two takes, Laico said, were mainly to establish the right sound levels, and for everyone to get comfortable with the song.

As the night dragged on, Miller put on his hat and coat and said: "I gotta go. I got an appointment back at my office in just a few hours." He wasn't there for the take that counted.

Bennett and the orchestra swung into the third take. When it was done, everybody seemed pleased. Everyone but Laico.

"That's it," a weary Bennett said. "Let's not do any more."

"Tony," Laico said, "I think we're still looking for the one we need. We've gone this long, let's do one more."

Bennett shrugged, but he agreed. They did a fourth take.

"That's it," Laico said. "That's the one."

Laico stayed even later. He was left alone, but he knew that Mitch Miller would be expecting a rough mix of all the tracks the next day.

Miller was pleased with what he heard. Bennett had more than done justice to the song. Miller called Mike Figlio and told him to do the final mix. Figlio, who had been with Columbia for years, worked at a studio at 799 Seventh Avenue. Figlio enjoyed working with Laico, the consummate professional.

"Frank had a good habit of keeping different elements on separate tracks," Figlio said. "He would have the strings and horns together, and he'd keep the rhythm section grouped together."

Figlio sang a little, which meant that he didn't attempt to muffle Bennett's voice.

"It's the same with most mixers," Figlio said. "They subconsciously favor whatever their background was. If a mixer had been a drummer when he was younger, he'll give the drums a little boost. You just can't help it."

Figlio worked on the four songs from the session in the order in which they were done. The first song took longer, about an hour, because he needed to orient himself according to the sounds and balances. By the time he got to the fourth and final song on the reel, it took hardly any time at all. The recording didn't require much tweaking and he needed no equalization on the track. But he did run Bennett's voice and the strings through the building's renowned stairwell echo chamber, which started on the ground floor and ran all the way up to the top, or seventh, floor, where Figlio worked.[38]

"Once Upon a Time" was released, with "I Left My Heart in San Francisco" on the back side, on February 2, 1962. In the stores, Chubby Checker, twisting the night away, saw his record flying off the shelves; among the other best-sellers were "The Wanderer," by Dion without the Belmonts, and "Hey! Baby," by a singer who called himself Bruce Channel. Columbia and Bennett pumped "Once Upon a Time" for six weeks, but disc jockeys, responding to listeners, were playing, en masse, the flip side. Goddard Lieberson called Bennett and presciently said: "You're not going to stop hearing [about this song] for the rest of your life. As long as you keep singing, you'll be singing this song."[39]

Miller miscalculated regarding the A- and B-sides of the record, something that's not uncommon in the business. There are bags of stories from the 1950s about songs that started out on the B-side before they took off: Bill Haley's "Rock Around the Clock" ("Thirteen Women [and Only One Man in Town]" was the A-side); The Champs' "Tequila" ("Train to Nowhere"); Gene Vincent's "Be-Bop-a-Lula" ("Woman Love"); and the Righteous Brothers' "Unchained Melody" ("Hung on You").[40]

Conversely, if just one of the songs on a 45 was extraordinary, it didn't make any difference how mediocre the other song was. I had a friend, Gene Stevens, who grew up in New York with Bobby Darin when Darin was still Walden Robert Cossato. Stevens and Darin had a local band; Stevens was a singer and Darin played the drums.[41] Stevens told me a story about "Splish Splash."

After Darin went out on his own, and Stevens went into the publishing business, Darin had seven straight flop records before he wrote "Splish Splash" in eleven minutes and recorded it along with two other songs in ninety minutes.[42]

Darin called Stevens, thinking "Splish Splash" might be his breakout song. He sang it over the phone, acapella.

"That's just great," said Stevens, who was known to throw around compliments like they were manhole covers. "It's the best thing you've ever done."

"But we got a problem," Darin said. "We got nothing to go with it. We don't have a B-side."

"B-side?" Stevens said. "You could put anything on the B-side. It won't make any difference."

"There's another song we did the same day we did 'Splish Splash,'" Darin said. "'Judy Don't Be Moody.' That might work."

"That Judy song sounds awful," Stevens said. "But don't worry about it. Just get 'Splish Splash' out there."[43]

They released "Splish Splash" in May of 1958, and it sold more than a million copies, accounting for about a half a million dollars in revenue.[44]

Before long, "I Left My Heart in San Francisco" sold two million copies. At last count, it had sold more than fourteen million. At the start, the record remained on the charts for an unheard-of 25 months. On June 9, 1962, Bennett delivered a historic concert at Carnegie Hall, where he sang 44 songs, many of which were incorporated into an album. He sang the San Francisco song only once, although "they kept calling for more," said his sister, Mary Chiappa. "They were practically standing on their hands." On October 1, Bennett sang the song on national television as Johnny Carson made his debut on the *Tonight Show*. Bennett sang the song with Judy Garland on her show in 1963.[45]

Terry Teachout, the composer and critic, wrote:

> Following the introductory verse in which Cross' lyrics reference Paris, Rome and Manhattan, Bennett sings a single chorus, structuring it as an arc of steadily rising emotion that starts out quietly, then ascends to a climactic high G. The lyric is delivered with the unobtrusively clear diction that remains a hallmark of his style, and the phrasing is wonderfully free and expansive. Bennett's ability to sustain a very slow tempo is unrivaled. And though the last phrase of the song is colored with the near operatic drama that Bennett brings to most of his ballad performances, the overall tone of the performance is one of intimacy—and sincerity.[46]

Almost fifty years to the day that Bennett first recorded the song, he was asked for the zillionth time what made "I Left My Heart in San Fran-

Standing ovations are not uncommon for Tony Bennett—this one came in 2016 (Drew Altizer Photography).

cisco" so special. "There was a dream melody by George Cory," he said. "Like a lot of love songs, it's written out of longing and loneliness. [Cory and Cross] weren't happy in New York. It's not a city for everyone, and they really did miss San Francisco. Doug's lyrics are terrific. They tell a story, but let your heart and mind fill in the blanks."

Then Bennett began deconstructing the song, line by line. "'I've been terribly alone and forgotten in Manhattan.' Who hasn't felt forgotten in a strange city? 'To be where little cable cars climb halfway to the stars.' That's such a beguiling image to climb into. 'My love waits there in San Francisco.' That's songwriting brilliance. It touches your heart. Is it an old love you left behind? A new love you hope to find? A great song will let you put yourself inside it, to answer those questions for yourself, different answers for different times of your life."

Cory and Cross once told Bennett that they almost called the song "When I Return to San Francisco."

That might not have appealed to Bennett.

"I don't know how I would have reacted to that," he said. "'When I Return to San Francisco' sounds a little like you're reading an airplane ticket. But 'I Left My Heart…' You feel the love and longing, don't you?"

In 2016, Bennett published another memoir. Each chapter was an homage "to remarkable people who inspired" his life and career. There were 42 in all, and even a few pages of tribute to Astoria, Queens, where Bennett grew up. There were chapters about Pablo Picasso and John Singer Sargent, people Bennett never met but who "helped, influenced and steered me." There were chapters about both of Bennett's parents, and even a chapter about Sadie Vimmerstedt, the Youngstown, Ohio, woman who had mailed Johnny Mercer some of the lyrics he used to write "I Wanna Be Around," one of Bennett's hits in 1962. There was a chapter about Ralph Sharon, the longtime accompanist who had first shown Bennett the composition "I Left My Heart in San Francisco" in 1961.[47] There was no chapter about Mitch Miller.

12

The Battle of San Francisco

I met Wells Twombly at a baseball game in Los Angeles in the early 1960s. He was working for an area newspaper, and I was looking for a job on the West Coast. It was the beginning of a friendship that lasted until Twombly's early death, at 41, in 1977.[1] Twombly's final years were at the *San Francisco Examiner*, where, in a city brimming with exceptional newspaper columnists, he was nobody's second, not even Herb Caen. In 1974, when Twombly's original contract with the *Examiner* was running out, he went in to see Randy Hearst, managing editor of the paper and one of the heirs to the William Randolph Hearst publishing fortune.

Twombly looked somewhat like the British actor Jonathan Pryce, without the eye-catching misplaced eye. He knew this was a bad time for Hearst—his daughter Patty had been kidnapped by the Sybionese Liberation Army—but a contract was a contract, and he found himself in Hearst's office. Hearst laid out the morass he was in. Circulation at the *Examiner* was at a post–World War II low; advertising lineage was stagnant; Hearst had spent an obscene amount on private investigators and the like, trying to find his daughter; and a couple of million dollars in free food had been sent across the Bay, to Oakland, in a wrong-headed attempt to wrest Patty away from the Symbionese Liberation Army. Instead, the misguided venture led to a riot and two million dollars' worth of bad publicity.

As Twombly sat there, this might have been the first time that Hearst, in one breath, had recounted all of his albatrosses. At one point, Hearst seemed on the verge of tears. Hearst said: "What I'm trying to say, Wells, is that I've really got a bad case of the shorts. You're one of our best writers, your column is extremely popular, but I can't see how I can justify increasing your pay at this time. Why don't we do this? Your salary stays the same, but we'll allow you to *cheat* fifty dollars a week on your expense account."

Twombly, unlike many writers, had a personality that matched his writing style. Standing next to people, he could bowl them over with his sharp wit. His writing was quick, smart and irreverent, and he talked the same way. So he couldn't help himself—he looked at a despondent Hearst and smiled a wry smile.

"*Cheat* fifty bucks a week on expenses?" Twombly asked. "I've got sort of a problem with that."

"How's that?" Hearst said.

"I'm *already* doing that," Twombly replied.[2]

San Francisco's angst over the Symbionese Liberation Army was only one of the city's concerns. What Douglass Cross said about the town ("San Francisco has newness and vitality") when he and his partner, George Cory, moved from New York to California several years before,[3] rang hollow now. While denigrating New York, Cross had called San Francisco the land of milk and honey, but it seemed that almost as soon as the now-wealthy Cross and Cory were back in California, the city of their dreams took a wrong turn. Their love affair was to end and they both began to self-destruct through heavy drinking. They arrived at a San Francisco that was, step by step, losing its way. Acceptance of gay people was no better, perhaps even worse, than it had been when they last lived there, and beyond that the city was beset with other problems: the racially motivated Zebra killings would pile up by the dozens; the Zodiac killer would continue to brag about his murders via letters to San Francisco newspapers; Cesar Chavez, on behalf of the United Farm Workers, would lead a protest march from Union Square to Modesto, California[4]; there was a plot apparently afoot to kidnap Joseph Alioto, San Francisco's mayor; Gerald Ford, the new president, would almost be assassinated; and the Reverend Jim Jones' Peoples Temple, which got its start in Indiana, made a foothold in the Fillmore district,[5] only five blocks from where Walter Hinton, with money inherited from George Cory, would some day live.[6]

"By the early 1970s," David Talbot wrote, "the revolution was over in America, and San Francisco—its fallen capital—staggered on the edge of chaos. The city was overrun with false prophets and savage messiahs.... The sacraments of blood and guns replaced peace and love."[7]

Perhaps the San Francisco Board of Supervisors was looking for succor, an escape from what really mattered. For fifteen years, starting in 1969 and right on through the miasma of the 1970s and on into the 1980s, the supervisors wrung their hands and gnashed their teeth about what the city's official song should be. While gape-mouthed citizens questioned their leaders' priorities, Jim Lazarus, when he was deputy mayor, saw something strangely healthy about the unending dilemma, the much ado about just about nothing. "Having a competition over the official song is one of those 'only in San Francisco' issues," Lazarus said. "That makes us different than other cities around the world."[8] San Francisco was already different, and in the 1970s, most of the time, it was different for the wrong reasons.

Over the years, the supervisors considered only two songs—"I Left My Heart in San Francisco," the plaintive ballad that was first sung by Tony Bennett at the Venetian Room of San Francisco's Fairmont Hotel in December of 1961, and went on to two million in record sales in 1962, and "San Francisco," the cadenza that Jeanette MacDonald sang in Metro-Goldwyn-Mayer's 1936 movie blockbuster of the same name.

"San Francisco" had been the city's official song for many years, but in October of 1969, after the supervisors were shown a short film of Bennett singing "I Left My Heart," they unanimously voted for the George Cory-Douglass Cross composition as the new San Francisco song. Cory and Cross, who attended the meeting when the vote was taken, were ecstatic. "This is a very good moment for George Cory and me," Cross

Above and opposite: In a rare interview, Douglass Cross (left) and George Cory appeared on television in 1969 after the San Francisco Board of Supervisors voted "I Left My Heart in San Francisco" as the city's official song. Fifteen years later, the supervisors agreed that the Cory/Cross song would share honors with 1936 song "San Francisco" (courtesy of KPIX-TV San Francisco).

said. "If our song is a success, it is because it reflects in some small measure, perhaps, the history, the legend, the magic of this beautiful city that has fascinated the imagination of the world."[9] This wasn't a paid political announcement, but they were remarks that the Chamber of Commerce could have written.

Out in the streets, Cross' boosterism failed to resonate.

At city hall, the debate over the two songs went from festering to hysteria. Supporters of what was called the Jeanette MacDonald song, which was written by the team of Bronislaw Kaper, Walter Jurmann and Gus Kahn, refused to go away. One of the most resilient was Bob Grimes, a local trivia maven, a music historian, a collector of sheet music and a gadfly. As a boy, growing up in Texas, Grimes saw the movie *San Francisco*, starring Clark Gable, Spencer Tracy and MacDonald.[10] It was the biggest grossing film MGM released in 1936, and MacDonald and the song were so popular that she signed a two-movie contract with the studio at $125,000 a film.[11] Some critics thought MacDonald delivered a wooden performance. Years later, Judy Garland sang her audience into tears of laughter with her priceless parody of MacDonald. (MacDonald said she liked it. "I'm flattered that somebody like Judy would do such a thing.") Be that as it may, one critic of the film still said that "it is impossible to conceive of anyone [but MadDonald] in the part."[12]

The director of the picture was W.S. Van Dyke, sometimes known as "One-Take Woody Van Dyke."[13] In the film, MacDonald played a singer in 1906 San Francisco hoping to impress the swells on Nob Hill, but settled for a Barbary Coast music hall run by Gable's character, Blackie Norton. At her first rehearsal within the plot of the film, MacDonald sang "San Francisco" as though it were a ballad, and Gable, as Blackie Norton, shouted: "Whaddya think I'm running here? A funeral parlor? Heat it up! This is about San Francisco!"

With fortissimo, MacDonald sang the song five more times in the film. The showstopper came on the music hall stage, in feathers, ruffles and a sequined skirt. After MacDonald delivered the song in spirited fashion and started to walk off, an earthquake began to shake. The crowd scrambled to leave as the building was reduced to debris. The special effects were remarkable for the time.[14]

Bob Grimes saw the MGM film for the first time when he was fourteen. At the world premiere, in San Francisco, the portrayal of the earthquake was so graphic that several people who had been in the city in 1906 were sickened by the memory and left the theater. The film was shown every year, on the anniversary of the earthquake, at the Castro Theatre, and Grimes was usually there. This only reinforced his love of the MacDonald song and prompted him to say: "The Tony Bennett number is saccharine, soporific and focuses on people who are out of the city rather than its residents. There should be a vote by one and all and I vote for [the MacDonald song], which can be played as a rouser, a ballad, rinky-tinky, semi-symphonic, anything."[15]

Jeanette MacDonald, who sang the song "San Francisco" in the 1936 movie with the same name (courtesy of www.doctormacro.com).

Judy Garland first sang her parody of MacDonald's song at Carnegie Hall. As she sang the modified lyrics, Garland feigned a sigh for a MacDonald, singing in a music hall as the earthquake struck San Francisco.[16]

By 1974, Grimes was still crusading for the supervisors to reconsider the MacDonald song. He and Merla Zellerbach, a writer for the *San Francisco Chronicle*, and Zellerbach's husband, Fred Goerner, appeared

12. The Battle of San Francisco   117

on a radio trivia show, and afterward they discussed the merits of the 1936 song. Goerner, who had a radio show on KMPX, conducted an unscientific listeners' poll and the vote ran ten to one in favor of the song from the film. Then Zellerbach wrote an article in the *Chronicle*. "Should Grimes and company continue their banner-waving battle?" she wrote. "Or should we all let sleeping dogs lie?"[17]

George Cory, who had never met Grimes, called him at Patrick & Co. Office Supplies, where Grimes worked as a salesman. Grimes, who died in 2011, left behind papers that documented the exchange. Cory asked, "Who is behind you in all this?"

"Nobody. It's all my idea. Just my opinion," Grimes replied.

"You sure it's not MGM, trying to get new publicity for their old film?"

"There's nobody. I just feel that way about the other song, that's all."

"I'm going to have you investigated. I've traveled around the world, and everybody knows the song that Douglass Cross and I wrote. Our song's even been sung in Yugoslavia. Nobody knows the Jeanette MacDonald song. Her song was written as camp, and was never to be taken seriously."

"Well, a few people here in the city are taking it seriously. And they're the only ones who matter when it comes to picking a song. Don't get me wrong. What you wrote is a pretty little tune."

"You have no taste! Ours is a great song!"

"This isn't new. I was one of the original protesters when they named your song the official song in 1969."

"Who wants to be reminded of the 1906 earthquake? Do you know Gus Kahn's sister? She lives in San Francisco."

"I've never heard of her."

"You're probably speaking for her."

"Sorry, but I have to go. I have customers here in the store."

"I hope there's a good earthquake, and you're the first one to go!"

Later, Grimes got a call from Merla Zellerbach.

"I got a call from George Cory," she said.

"So did I," Grimes replied.

"He wasn't hostile or anything like that," Zellerbach said. "Except when he started talking about you. Then he asked me to retract the column. But what is there to retract?"

"What else did he say?" Grimes asked.

"He said that he was so upset about the whole thing that he got a nosebleed."[18]

Early in 1975, Cory finally met Grimes, at a benefit luncheon for the leukemia foundation. Douglass Cross, suffering from cirrhosis of the liver, had died the month before.[19] A few days after the luncheon, Cory wrote Grimes a long letter, sending copies to, among others, Joseph Alioto, the mayor; Dianne Feinstein, president of the board of supervisors; Tony Bennett; media members; and ASCAP (the American Society of Composers, Authors and Publishers), which collects royalties on behalf of its members. In his letter, Cory wrote:

> I have been persuaded to suggest that you put an immediate "cease and desist" restraint on your campaign to capitalize upon and to undermine in a tasteless and derogatory manner a valuable property which over the years we have carefully protected. In the past we have refused many lucrative offers from airlines and other commercial enterprises for the usage of our song, as well as attempting wherever possible to control inevitable and obvious parodies of the song, in order to maintain its image and integrity.... With the absorbing concern I have undergone throughout the recent illness and death of my collaborator Douglass Cross, and all the attendant tension it has brought upon me, I find it unfortunate to have to remind you of your personal indulgence. It is out of respect for the loss of my partner, who knew and loved The City and did much to enhance its image in the eyes of the world, that I react so strongly to your phony and fraudulent stand. We have sued more important opportunists than you—Steve Allen for one.

(Allen parodied the Cross-Cory composition with a song called "I Left My Nose in San Diego").

Cory went on to say that Hoagy Carmichael had said that "I Left My Heart in San Francisco" was just as much a part of the American fabric as "Battle Hymn of the Republic." Cory closed by saying that while "San Francisco" is "not performed at all in live performances, [Cory's song] has been recorded in every conceivable language—even Swahili."[20]

Cory, also suffering from cirrhosis, died in 1978. There was a preliminary report that he was a suicide, which is what was reported by several news outlets, but upon closer examination of the corner's report the death was attributed to natural causes (although a note that could have been a suicide note was found near the body, that note has disappeared. There are conspiracy theorists in San Francisco who believe that the cause was neither accidental nor suicide).[21]

In 1984, Warren Hinckle, a columnist for the *Chronicle*, went to Grimes' sixth-floor apartment in the Tenderloin district to research a piece he was writing about the British singer Gracie Fields. There was hardly room for Hinckle to get through the front door. Grimes' sheet-music collection had passed the 21,000 mark. The closets were so jammed with sheet music and albums of operas and Broadway shows that clothes were an afterthought.

12. The Battle of San Francisco

Grimes told Hinckle that probably more songs had been written about San Francisco than any other city (the zaniest being "The Only Pal I Ever Had Came from Frisco Town"). Grimes had put twenty of the San Francisco songs on a tape cassette, intentionally omitting "I Left My Heart in San Francisco." A meeting of the board of supervisors was scheduled for later in the week, and Grimes told Hinckley that momentum was building again for Jeanette MacDonald's "San Francisco" to be reinstalled as the official city song. It wasn't possible for George Cory to roll over in his grave; his ashes, at his request, had been scattered in the San Francisco Bay.[22]

All anyone had to do, to learn which way the wind was blowing, was spend five minutes with Quentin Kopp, one of the supervisors. Kopp said: "The Tony Bennett song is a nice tune, with romantic words, but it's hardly descriptive of a city that began with a gold rush [1849] and heroically survived a leveling earthquake [1906]. The Bennett song was capriciously adopted at the height of its popularity in the late 1960s, at a time when the hippie-love era apparently influenced our board of supervisors into memorializing a sugary sweet schmaltzy jingle. The Bennett song is a rhapsody for lovers, not a patriotic march to express the glorious traditions of San Francisco."[23]

When asked how he felt about the furor, Tony Bennett showed that he had more than one diplomatic bone in his body. "I learned from Richard Rodgers a long time ago that the public is the critic," Bennett said. "As far as the public is concerned, that's the tune."[24]

For the supervisors' meeting on May 3, Barnum & Bailey would have been an appropriate choreographer. Hundreds of people demonstrated outside the supervisors' chambers. There were an estimated five thousand milling in the Rotunda, and three hundred squeezed into the room where the vote was taken. Yvonne Jurmann, widow of one of the composers of the song "San Francisco," flew in from Los Angeles. "The whole world is so enthusiastic about my late husband's song," she said. Noah Griffin of KGO radio dressed in a tuxedo and sang "San Francisco." By most accounts, he was no Jeanette MacDonald. There was supposed to be a sing-off between Griffin and Bennett, which smacked of a mismatch, but Bennett, conceding nothing, was a no-show. Willie Kennedy, one of the supervisors, sang "I Left My Heart in San Francisco." A dozen first- and second-graders from the Chinese-American International School sang "San Francisco" in both Mandarin and English. Members of the Hastings College of Law's Rugby Club sang "I Left My Heart." They were booed. Carla Normand accompanied the Royal Society Jazz Orchestra and sang "San Francisco." The Gay Men's Chorus sang one song or the other. The soprano Pamela Brooks, descending a marble staircase, sang "San Francisco." An entrepreneurial vendor began selling bottles of Anchor Steam beer, before he was told that it was illegal to sell beer of any brand at City Hall. He gave away the beer that remained. Tony Bennett was in town for another reason: He was booked to sing as the city re-opened its renowned cable car system, after 18 months of renovation. Bennett proved sanguine once more; he stayed away from City Hall and hunkered down at his hotel.

Dianne Feinstein, the mayor, told the supervisors that she would veto any proposal that excluded the Bennett song. Bennett had helped Feinstein in her campaign to gussy up the cable cars.[25] Feinstein was at the peak of her powers. In 1983, there had been a recall attempt, helped along by the White Panther Party, which objected to Feinstein signing an anti-handgun law (later overturned by a state court), and the gay community, which felt deserted by the mayor because she supported an ordinance that would have precluded most partners of city employees from being covered by health insurance. The recall was a rout—80 percent of the vote favored keeping Feinstein in office. She was also up for re-election to a new four-year term later in the year, and there was such meager opposition that it turned into a landslide victory.[26]

George Cory (third from left) and Douglass Cross (third from right) visited the San Francisco City Pavilion at the Osaka Expo, a world's fair, in Japan in 1970 (courtesy Takashi Haruna).

Kopp proposed that San Francisco have two songs: the MacDonald song would be the official song, and Bennett's would be the official ballad. This Solomonic suggestion passed whole-heartedly and Feinstein promptly signed it into law.

"Everybody calls us a kooky city," Willie Kennedy said. "Why not have two songs?"[27]

Not everybody was thrilled with the compromise. Warren Hinckle, the columnist, usually saw things in black and white, and his middle name was Hyperbole. Generally, Hinckle was opposed to anything Dianne Feinstein was for, perhaps because she once poured a drink on top of his head. When the legendary author William Styron, in a review, trashed a book written by a friend of Hinckle's, Hinckle sent Styron a box of dog poop.[28] Hinckle argued that "I Left My Heart in San Francisco" deserved no recognition whatsoever. "The song is infantile drool," he said. "It is barely suited for elevator music. It is as much San Francisco as bathtub chablis."[29]

Overseas, there were counterpoints. "It's one of the most evocative city anthems ever recorded," Steve Turner wrote from England.[30]

In a rare TV interview, Cross was asked if he thought his song was "schmaltz."

He said: "No, I don't believe it's schmaltz. I believe it's sentimental, and that's not a bad word."[31]

Gerald Nachman revived the issue a quarter of a century later. He wrote that it was time to retire "San Francisco's worn-out official anthem, the gooey [Bennett song]." Nachman didn't favor retaining the Jeanette MacDonald song, either. He suggested that the city supervisors commission a famous composer to write an original song.

"Like the trouper he is," Nachman wrote of Tony Bennett, "he sings [his San Francisco song] everywhere because it's expected of him and he likes to please audiences. After fifty years, it has become iconic—but it's still cheesy.... [The song] hasn't gotten any better since 1961. Fifty years is long enough for us to wince and bear it."[32]

After Bob Grimes' death, much of his sheet music went to Michael Feinstein's Great American Songbook, a repository in Carmel, Indiana.[33] One of the songs in the Grimes collection was "San Francisco (Be Sure to Wear Flowers in Your Hair)." Don't laugh. The song was written by John Phillips of The Mamas & The Papas, recorded by Scott McKenzie in 1967, and was number one on the charts in Great Britain for a while.[34] It seems that there are many songs about San Francisco that have a way about them.

13

City Ditties

"New York, New York" was supposed to be Liza Minnelli's song. John Kander and Fred Ebb, who wrote the song, had also done the score for the incandescent *Cabaret*, the 1972 movie (from a Broadway hit) that led to an Oscar for Minnelli. "New York, New York" was written for the 1977 Martin Scorsese movie of the same name. The full name for the song is "Theme from 'New York New York.'" The film, which starred Robert De Niro alongside Minnelli, was widely ballyhooed—*Time* magazine even featured it on one of its covers. The movie was supposed to be so special, and the song so endemic to the film, that when De Niro heard the first version, he cold-watered it.[1]

De Niro, who played a saxophone player and bandleader in the film, was no musician, but he knew schmaltz when he heard it. He said that for a song to be so integral to the plot, it needed to be stronger. Scorsese was beside himself; De Niro was a star, but so were the songwriters in their own way, and now the director found himself in a position where he needed to ask Kander and Ebb to rewrite.

"We were kind of insulted," Kander said, "that an actor was telling us how to write a song."

The wily Scorsese was able to finesse De Niro's request, and the songwriters repaired to Ebb's house, where they redid the song in only 45 minutes. "We wrote the new song in a kind of rage," Ebb said. "But it turned out that De Niro was right."[2]

The rewrite that Minnelli sang in the film was a great song, at once an anthem and a love note to the city, but because the movie tanked, her recording of "New York, New York" failed to take off.[3] In 1978, Sinatra sang it during a charity appearance for Mercy Hospital at the Waldorf Astoria Hotel in New York. In September of that year, on opening night for several of his concerts at Radio City Music Hall, Sinatra sang an opening medley of New York songs that included the Kander/Ebb composition. Some of the other selections were "Autumn in New York" and "Sidewalks of New York." The reaction for "New York, New York" was so overwhelming—it dwarfed the other songs—that Sinatra said, "Man, that was big. We have to take it out of the overture." At subsequent performances, the New York overture remained, but "New York, New York" was saved for the closing song.[4]

Now Sinatra, and the people at Reprise Records, thought that the song might be in their future. There had been ongoing discussions about an omnibus album for 1979, a *beau coup* collection of songs that would encompass Sinatra's whole career. At first, Sinatra was reluctant to do "New York, New York"; he thought the song belonged to Minnelli and didn't want to tread on her material. Many years before, Sinatra had had no compunction about recording Tony Bennett's "I Left My Heart in San Francisco"; the Sinatra version was released several months after Bennett's, but it did poorly while Bennett's sold in the millions.[5]

On September 9, 1979, in a studio in Hollywood, California, Sinatra recorded much of what became *Trilogy: Past, Present, Future*, and "New York, New York" was included. *Trilogy* was problematic for most reviewers. Even an unabashed Sinatra-ophile like Jonathan Schwartz couldn't enthuse over the album, and when he was less than enthusiastic on the air, Sinatra used his clout to get him fired from WNEW radio in New York. Later, through his friend Nick Riggio, Tony Bennett launched a letter-writing campaign that restored Schwartz to his job.[6]

Despite *Trilogy*'s commercial and critical failure, Sinatra's version of "New York, New York" became a keeper. Sinatra was ecstatic about acquiring a replacement signature song for "My Way," a song he had grown to hate even though audiences wouldn't let him quit singing it. If he failed to sing "My Way" as a performance ended, the crowds would shout for the song and Sinatra would oblige them. He would grimace, sing the song and hope the audience didn't notice that he was forcing it.

So when "New York, New York" came along, Sinatra said: "This is one of the most exciting pieces of music of all my years."

James Kaplan, a Sinatra biographer, said: "The song meant so much to him on many levels. It described his own sense of triumph in what he had become."[7]

There are city songs about big towns, small towns, towns that don't even exist. Some of the songs are specific to the towns, but some are also so basic that while they have a town in the title, the name of another town could be substituted, and listeners wouldn't know the difference. Billy Joel wanted to write a song about his hometown, Levittown on Long Island, New York, but instead wrote a lyric that had a steel mill in it, then discovered that the town in the title—Allentown, Pennsylvania—didn't have a mill. The nearest town had a steel works, but the name of that town (Bethlehem, Pennsylvania) had a religious connotation, and Joel didn't want the Catholics complaining, so he left the steel mill in, as well as the name of the town (Allentown) without one. Good music isn't necessarily a history lesson. Joel still wrote a good song, unless you're a purist about steel mills.

I turned purist when I threw out "The Last Train to Clarksville," which had been on my list. I liked the melody, I liked the theme (anti-Vietnam war), I liked the story it told, I liked the group it was written for (The Monkees), but I was troubled by a geographical issue. The writers, Tommy Boyce and Bobby Hart, had never heard of Clarksville, Tennessee, which is not far from an Army installation and an Air Force base; hence it could have been worked in with the military polemic intact. But Hart, who's from Phoenix, was unfamiliar with Clarksville, Tennessee. He was thinking about an Arizona town he said was called "Clarksdale." But the actual name of the town was "Clarkdale." There is no "Clarksdale" in Arizona. Hart changed what he thought was "Clarksdale" to "Clarksville" on a whim, for the sake of euphony. There is no "Clarksville" in Arizona, either. So the whole title came from a mistake. Even after the song was released, there was trouble with the name of the town. There is a Monkees' video of the song that shows a town sign called "Clarkesville."[8]

So it goes. Even songs about states can be misleading. "Moonlight in Vermont" is a lovely standard, but you would have to look far and long in the state to find a sycamore, or a meadowlark, as the lyrics suggest. John Blackburn could have been winking as he wrote the words. Or maybe it was because Blackburn was from Ohio and never hung his hat in Vermont.[9]

For a book about "I Left My Heart in San Francisco," I've sacrilegiously put "New York, New York" at the top of the list of songs about U.S. cities. It's an unavoidably subjective exercise; please don't burn the book if not all the choices are bull's-eyes.

1. "New York, New York." For a time, the New York Yankees would play the Sinatra version after home games that the team won, and Minnelli's recording after losses. When this was brought to Minnelli's attention, she complained about second-class treatment. The Yankees dropped her song altogether and now use only Sinatra's. Fred Ebb, who died in 2004, must have been especially stung that Minnelli's version turned into a mere footnote everywhere. He and Minnelli were very close; when she married Jack Haley Jr., Ebb gave away the bride.[10]

2. "I Left My Heart in San Francisco." "A great city song," said Lou Curtiss, a San Diego music historian, "needs at least one line that's immediately memorable. That's what it takes."[11] Willis Conover, writing in *Billboard*, said that when Bennett sang this song for Vietnam soldiers and came to the line some of them teared up.[12] Douglass Cross had a bag of memorable lines.

3. "Chicago (That Toddlin' Town)." This 1922 composition by Fred Fisher includes the ironic line about a man dancing with his wife, which is what Lou Curtiss was talking about. The Cologne-born Fisher served in the German Navy and the French Foreign Legion before emigrating to the U.S. At 25, he learned how to play the piano in a Chicago saloon. The mention of the well-known State Street and Billy Sunday gave the song a definite Chicago feel. Sunday was a fiery evangelist ("I'll kick sin as long as I've got a foot, I'll fight it as long as I've got a fist, I'll butt it as long as I've got a head, and I'll bite it as long as I've got a tooth. And when I'm old, fistless, footless and toothless, I'll gum it till I go home to glory and it goes home to perdition").[13] Fisher had already strung some hits before he got to this song—"Dardanella" (lyrics), "Peg o' My Heart" (music) and "I'd Rather Be Blue" (music). Al Jolson sang the Chicago song early on. Frank Sinatra, playing Joe E. Lewis, sang it in *The Joker Is Wild*. When Tony Bennett sang it, he replaced Billy Sunday's name with Mart Faye, a Chicago disc jockey. In 1942, when he was 65, Fisher hung himself. His suicide note read: "No one is responsible for my death."[14]

4. "Do You Know the Way to San Jose." (Full disclosure: Burt Bacharach wrote a blurb for one of my books.) When Hal David, the lyricist for dozens of Burt Bacharach's songs (including "Raindrops Keep Fallin' on My Head," an Oscar winner), was in the Navy, he was stationed in San Jose, California. It was in 1968, long after World War II, when David finally decided to reminisce about San Jose with a song, but Dionne Warwick, who was singing much of the Bacharach/David material, didn't like it. There was a line in the song that especially turned her off. "It was a dumb song and I didn't want to sing it," Warwick said. Bacharach thought it was a song that would do well commercially, and urged her to reconsider. When David finally told Warwick about his San Jose military connection, she bought it. The song earned Warwick her first Grammy Award and made big bucks for all three of them. "I giggled all the way to the bank," said Warwick, who visited San Jose, for the first time, many years later.[15] Five years before "San Jose," Bacharach and David wrote a city song called "Twenty-Four Hours from Tulsa," which became an international favorite—it was even sung in Italian—when Gene Pitney sang it.[16]

5. "Kansas City." When I was in college, I had a classmate who was from Granite City, Illinois. This song, sung by Wilbert Harrison in 1959, was a fixture on every jukebox in our town. Every weekend, this guy would go home, and as he packed his suitcase he would be singing the Wilbertson song—he knew every word—but substituting the name of his town for Kansas City. It scanned nicely. Jerry Leiber (words) and Mike Stoller (music) wrote the song when they were both nineteen, and even though neither had ever been to Kansas City, Leiber was resourceful enough to throw a swinging Kansas City intersection, 12th Street and Vine, into the lyrics.[17] Talk about *kismet*: Leiber was from Baltimore and Stoller from New York, and they met in Los Angeles after their families had moved there. They wrote "Kansas City" in 1952, and it kicked around for seven years before Harrison recorded it. After that, the hits just kept coming for Leiber and Stoller: "Is That All There Is," "Hound Dog," "Stand by Me" and "Jailhouse Rock" are only a sampler.[18]

6. "My Kind of Town (Chicago Is)." I once saw the lyricist Sammy Cahn at a one-man show in San Francisco. At a Q&A with the audience, somebody asked, "When you write for a movie, which usually comes first, the words or the music?" Cahn smiled and said: "Neither. It's the phone call." The phone calls from moviemakers flooded Cahn with work. He wrote this song with Jimmy Van Heusen, one of Frank Sinatra's songwriting regulars and also a good friend. (Van Heusen had a pilot's license, and it was not unusual for him and Old Blue Eyes, after a few snifters, to get in a plane at the Palm Springs Airport and fly to Las Vegas.)[19] Sinatra liked this song enough to record it at least four times, and he used it in his 1964 movie *Robin and the 7 Hoods*. After the Union Stockyards closed in Chicago in 1971, Sinatra updated the lyrics by using "the Chicago Cubbies" instead. "My Kind of "Town" didn't win an Oscar ("Chim Chim Cher-ee," from *Mary Poppins*, got the award), but the Van Heusen/Cahn team, in only eight years, won with "All the Way," "High Hopes" and "Call Me Irresponsible."[20]

7. "I'm a Ding Dong Daddy From Dumas." Dumas, Texas, and Dumas, Arkansas, will have to step outside and settle whether Phil Baxter was writing about the Texas town or the Arkansas town when he wrote this novelty song in the late 1920s.[21] Since Baxter, a bandleader and pianist, was born in Texas and died there, my guess is that he was talking about Dumas, the town in the Texas panhandle, not far from Amarillo, which had a population of less than a thousand in those days.[22] But Dumas, Arkansas, will not concede, and even holds an annual festival called "Ding Dong Days."[23] Some heavy hitters immediately lined up to do the song:

Louis Armstrong, Phil Harris (who sang it with his orchestra on Jack Benny's radio show) and Benny Goodman (in the 1938 movie *Hollywood Hotel*). The song has been durable. The Osmonds sang it on national television.[24] In *The Honeymooners*, Art Carney, playing Ed Norton, said to Jackie Gleason's Ralph Kramden: "You ain't exactly no ding-dong daddy from Dumas."[25] When Bob Willis and his Texas Playboys recorded the song country style in 1937, Willis and Tommy Duncan (a teetotaler) turned the lyrics inside out. They included lines about a drug dealer selling morphine and cocaine, and drinking liquor by the shot glass.[26] Neither Texas nor Arkansas would want to claim that version.

8. "Meet Me in St. Louis." The urban legend is that Andrew B. Sterling, who wrote the lyrics for this song, attended the St. Louis World's Fair in 1904. One of the local beers was called "St. Louis," but locals called it "St. Looie." At the fair one night, in a beer garden, the thirty-year-old Sterling heard someone at the next table say, "Bring me another Looie, Looie," because the waiter's name was Looie.[27] Fair? Looie? Looie? Before the year was out, Sterling, who was from New York, teamed with the Philadelphia-born Kerry Mills to write the first two lines of the chorus. My favorite line is about the lights shining no place but St. Louis. In 1944, MGM released Vincent Minnelli's *Meet Me in St. Louis*, starring the future Mrs. Minnelli, Judy Garland.[28] What better song for this popular film than the Sterling/Mills composition?

9. "Do You Know What It Means to Miss New Orleans." Which of the following *never* recorded this song? Louis Armstrong, Billie Holiday, Frankie Laine, Fats Domino, Vaughn Monroe, Pete Fountain, Ricky Nelson, Al Hirt, Rosemary Clooney, Nat King Cole, or Jimmy Buffett? The song, written by Will Hudson, Eddie DeLange and Irving Mills (although it is likely that Mills was only the publisher), started out in the 1947 movie called *New Orleans*. Billie Holiday played a maid—her clenched teeth didn't show—and sang it with Louis Armstrong's band.[29] Hudson and DeLange headed their own swing band when they didn't write songs, and they wrote them by the cornucopia. One of their early singers was Frieda Lipschitz, barely seventeen, a high school dropout who later became Georgia Gibbs. DeLange died at the age of 45. Among his songs, with Hudson, were "Moonglow" and "String of Pearls." During a 41-week span, the *Your Hit Parade* radio show featured at least one DeLange song every week but one.[30] (Answer to the original question: Vaughn Monroe never recorded the song).

10. "East St. Louis Toodle-Oo." Duke Ellington pronounced it "toad-lo," after a jerky dance called the toda-lo. The song had no connection to

the town of East St. Louis; it was said that the name was suggested by the Brunswick Record Co., which released the song in 1926. Ellington, who was 27, wrote the blues instrumental with James "Bubber" Miley, who perfected the style of playing the trumpet and coronet with a rubber plunger that was really a bathroom implement.[31] The number became the theme song for the Ellington band until the 1940s, when he replaced it with "Take the 'A' Train." Miley, a heavy drinker and a serial no-show for recording sessions, was fired by Ellington in 1929. Three years later, ill with tuberculosis, he died at the age of 29.[32]

11. "Wichita Lineman." Billy Joel: "A song about an ordinary man thinking extraordinary thoughts."[33] Written by Jimmy Webb, this was a 1968 hit for Glen Campbell.[34]

12. "San Francisco." Bronislaw Kaper and Walter Jurmann wrote the music, and Gus Kahn contributed the lyrics; Jeanette MacDonald's rendition and an earthquake brought down the roof in *San Francisco*, the 1936 film.[35]

13. "Allentown." Written and sung by Billy Joel in 1982, this is a valentine to a Pennsylvania town down on its luck.[36]

14. "Gary, Indiana." Meredith Willson, who was from Iowa, wrote this song for *The Music Man*, the Broadway hit that opened in 1957 and was made into a movie in 1962. Eddie Hodges sang it onstage, Ron Howard in the film.[37]

15. "There's a Pawnshop on a Corner in Pittsburgh, Pennsylvania." Bob Merrill, who composed on toy xylophones that cost less than seven dollars, wrote this song and it became a hit for Guy Mitchell in 1952. Merrill committed suicide in 1998.[38]

16. "I Wish't I Was in Peoria." This 1925 song—music by Harry Woods, words by Billy Rose and Mort Dixon—rhymes the Illinois town with "morning gloria, toreadoria and Waldorf Astoria." Anybody with a banjo was eligible to sing it, including the Smothers Brothers.[39]

17. "Viva Las Vegas." This was written, by Mort Shuman and Doc Pomus, as the title song for the 1964 Elvis Presley movie.[40] Like many of Presley's films, the plot was a flimsy excuse for Elvis to sing and wiggle.[41]

18. "Lodi." John Fogerty, lead singer and guitarist for the Creedence Clearwater Revival band, stored song titles, and when he came to the California city of Lodi (low-die), seventy miles from where he grew up, he thought it was a cool name. Years later, in 1969, he wrote the song, something about "Oh! Lord, stuck in Lodi again."[42]

19. "Streets of Laredo." Derived from a 17th century British folk song, this song about a dying Texas cowboy has been revised many times. Marty

Robbins, Johnny Cash and Joan Baez are just a few of the artists who have recorded it.[43]

20. "Okee from Muskogee." During the Vietnam war, this retort to hippies and their ways was written in 1969 by the country singer Merle Haggard, an ex-convict, and his drummer, Roy Edward Burns. Using an Oklahoma city as a backdrop, Haggard railed against burning draft cards, smoking marijuana and using LSD.[44]

In 1965, three years after "I Left My Heart in San Francisco" had become a hit for Tony Bennett, he appeared on variety TV shows hosted by Dean Martin and Andy Williams. Both times he joined with the hosts to sing medleys of city songs.

For the Martin show, the two singers sat in rocking chairs, trading quips, high notes and low notes. Bennett appeared uncomfortable. The unpredictable Martin, capable of saying or doing anything and long-rumored to imbibe before and during his shows, fell out of his chair, landing off camera. He flipped his cigarette during one routine, and kept feeling around on a table for a drink that wasn't there. Bennett got more sheepish by the minute.

"What should we do?" Martin said.

"How about 'San Francisco?'" Bennett asked.

"How about 'Houston?'" suggested Martin, referring to one of his hits.

Bennett sang "Come Fly with Me," a Frank Sinatra standard. Then he quickly moved on to "My Kind of Town." Martin helped him finish that and picked it up with his "Houston."

"I Left My Heart in San Francisco," with Bennett, was next.

"Oh, yeah!" Martin said.

Then they did a duet of "I'll Take Manhattan."

When Bennett got to the line in "I Love Paris" about the city in winter, Martin interjected.

"When it does what?"

"When it drizzles," Bennett ad-libbed.

This was two show-business troupers at the top of their game.

"A Foggy Day in London Town" was still to come, after which Martin started "Way Down Yonder in New Orleans," and Bennett chimed in. The reprise of "Come Fly with Me" happily ended the routine.[45]

Bennett and Andy Williams were also seated for their roundelay. Bennett traded "Chicago (That Toddlin' Town)" with Williams' version of "My Kind of Town."

The tinkle of a piano could be heard in the background, with a few chords of "I Left My Heart in San Francisco."

"I know where we're going," Williams said.

"Where all the residuals are," Bennett said. Then he began singing a slow version of "San Francisco"—not his signature song, but the one popularized by Jeanette MacDonald in the movie.

"Thought I'd do the other one, didn't ya," Bennett said. Then he sang the "other one," too.

Williams helped him finish "I Left My Heart in San Francisco." Bennett stood, looked approvingly at Williams, and bowed in his direction as the audience applauded loudly.

From there, they both sang "Kansas City," with Williams sneaking in a couple of lines of "Everything's Up to Date in Kansas City" from *The Music Man*.

They traded songs again, Bennett doing "Way Down Yonder in New Orleans" opposite Williams' "Do You Know What It Means to Miss New Orleans." Their finale was "I'll Take Manhattan," but Bennett gave that a twist by cleverly singing "My kind of town, Manhattan is..."[46]

All that was missing was "Ding Dong Daddy from Dumas."

14

Suppositions

Suppose Ralph Sharon wore turtlenecks instead of dress shirts? Suppose Sharon kept his unwanted, unrecorded sheet music in the hall closet instead of in his shirt drawer? Suppose the music for "I Left My Heart in San Francisco" was not at the top of the stack? Suppose George Cory and Douglass Cross, who wrote the song, hadn't penciled in the title at the top of the page? The only reason the music caught Sharon's eye was because it was a San Francisco song with a San Francisco title, and he and Tony Bennett were starting a trip that would take them to San Francisco. After Irving Berlin finished writing "God Bless America," he didn't write the title on the first page, and years later his secretary had trouble finding the discarded music when Kate Smith came looking for a patriotic song.[1]

Suppose Bennett and Sharon went into a different bar late that 1961 night in Arkansas, and it was a bar without a piano? Suppose that even though they were in a bar with a piano, Sharon had left the music back at their hotel? Suppose Bennett, having sung the song to standing ovations at the Fairmont Hotel a week after Arkansas, hadn't persisted with Mitch Miller of Columbia Records to record it after he had returned to New York? Supposing Miller had still been the martinet he had been during his earlier years at Columbia? Instead, he was watching his control ooze away by 1962, and perhaps a little world-weary, Miller had softened his stance toward the label's artists. Had Miller not accepted that he was halfway out the door, Bennett might have found "I Left My Heart in San Francisco" on the C-side of an A-B 45.[2]

It is likely, had this chain of fortuitous events not dominoed into place, that "I Left My Heart in San Francisco" would have died in Brooklyn Heights, where Cory and Cross wrote it. The tattered composition was already close to eight years old before Bennett saw it. No one wanted to record it—not Claramae Turner, for whom it was written; not Tessie O'Shea, who returned to England with the music in the early 1950s but wouldn't incorporate it into an album until 1973[3]; not Tennessee Ernie

In 1971, Douglass Cross (left) and George Cory visited the opera singer Claramae Turner at her farm in Poughkeepsie, New York (from the Frank Hoffmann collection, courtesy Joan Perry Ryan).

Ford, who was looking for another "Sixteen Tons" instead of an ode to his adopted city[4]; not Mitch Miller, who thought Bennett's rendition was hokey and not capable of finding an audience east of Alcatraz.[5]

But soon after Bennett's recording was released, on February 2, 1962, a me-too phenomenon started. It might be one of the longest running phenomena on record, one that has abetted but not completely disappeared. The Song That Nobody Wanted quickly became The Song That Almost Everyone Coveted. From 1962 to 1963 alone, there were at least 29 other recordings of "I Left My Heart in San Francisco." Some of the artists were well known; some of them hardly anybody knew. Henry Jerome and his orchestra, whose popularity soared at the Hotel Edison in New York in the 1950s,[6] did the song in 1963. So did Jan Berry and Dean Torrence,[7] California high school pals who rode the waves with the Beach Boys' rhythms in the 1960s.[8]

One of the first covers of the Cory/Cross song to reach the shelves was Frank Sinatra's in September of 1962, seven months after Bennett's,

14. Suppositions

but it didn't stay there long.[9] There's been conjecture ever since about why the life of the Sinatra record was so brief, to the extent that copies of the 45 are collectors' items now. Nancy Sinatra, the singer's daughter, said that the recording was quickly pulled because her father, a friend and supporter of Bennett's, didn't want a repeat of "I'm Walking Behind You." In 1953, Eddie Fisher recorded "I'm Walking Behind You" for RCA Victor and it shot to the top of the charts. Later in the year, Capitol released a mildly popular cover by Sinatra, who then regretted doing the song because Fisher was a singer he held in high regard. Sinatra, his daughter theorized, realized that he might be doing the same thing to Bennett that he had done to Fisher and asked that his version of the San Francisco song be pulled.[10] (Actually, Fisher's recording was a cover, too; the original of "I'm Walking Behind You" had been done by the Welsh singer, Dorothy Squires, after the British bandleader, Billy Reid, wrote it especially for her.)[11]

As many as thirteen of the covers of "I Left My Heart in San Francisco" from 1962 to 1963 were instrumentals. Bennett was flattered that one of them appeared in an album called *This Time by Basie! Hits of the 50s and 60s*. Bennett had always admired Count Basie, and in 1958 he sang with the Basie orchestra at the Latin Casino near Philadelphia. There were technical problems recording their opening night, so a month later they re-recorded the songs in a studio and made an album out of it.[12] "Just in Time," "Without a Song," "Pennies from Heaven" and "Lullaby of Broadway" were just a few of the songs that soared with Bennett and Basie in tandem. Basie's 1963 album, without Bennett, included "I Left My Heart in San Francisco," "This Could Be the Start of Something Big" and "Nice 'n' Easy." The arrangements were done by Quincy Jones.[13]

Another 1963 instrumental of "I Left My Heart in San Francisco," by the Charlie Byrd Trio, was recorded live at the Village Gate in New York. But not all attempts at doing the song were successful. Had they still been around, Cory and Cross might have cringed at the versions that were delivered by Arthur Prysock and Luciano Pavarotti. A *ne plus ultra* among Italian tenors, Pavarotti sang the song in 1982's ill-advised *Yes, Giorgio*, the only movie he ever made. The film itself was savaged, but apart from that, one critic found Pavarotti's effort on the San Francisco song "excruciating"[14]; another said his interpretation was "sufficient to keep Tony Bennett in work for years."[15] In 1963, Prysock got inventive with the song, a wrong-headed approach in Will Friedwald's judgment: "Some of the ideas on Prysock's records are almost too corny for words, as in a series of songs that he introduces by reciting the verse, rather than singing it. This is so extreme that it is beyond any concept of camp."[16]

Some might argue, but Chet Baker may have been as good a singer as he was a trumpeter. At any rate, I would have liked to have heard him sing "I Left My Heart in San Francisco," just to see what he could have done with it. The song is a different animal than "My Funny Valentine" or "Embraceable You," some of the songs he had in the palm of his hand, but it is not far removed from "Moonlight in Vermont," another ballad made to order for Baker's soft, measured, tenor-contralto style. Instead of a vocal "I Left My Heart in San Francisco," in 1966, Baker played the flugelhorn to interpret the song on an album with The Carmel Strings.[17] (A personal aside: Maybe fifteen years after Baker's death in 1988, I was staying in Amsterdam at the Prins Hendrik, the hotel where he had taken his fatal fall.[18] I was staying on the third floor, and down the hall was Room C-20, which was now being called the Chet Baker Suite. It took a while, but the hotel finally got over the ignominy of Baker's death, named the room in his memory and also placed a plaque near the sidewalk where his body was found. My daughter Laura, on business in Berlin, took the weekend off and flew in to Amsterdam. The Prins Hendrik, heavily booked, gave her the only room available, the Chet Baker Suite. I was impressed. Laura, like most people born after 1960, had never heard of him.)

After peaking in 1963, interest in recording "I Left My Heart in San Francisco" remained brisk through 1966. But in 1967 only three singing versions were released, one by the great Sarah Vaughan, on the last album she ever did for Mercury.[19] Although the song was written for a woman—Cory and Cross wanted their friend, Claramae Turner, to record it—few female singers attempted to sing it after Sarah Vaughan. One of the last who could be taken seriously was Rosemary Clooney in 1995. She was 67 and had been in show business for fifty years when *Rosemary Clooney: Demi-Centennial* was released.[20] Clooney had had knee-replacement surgery but was still touring[21] and needn't have apologized for her voice. Many of her old reliables from yester-year were revisited in a sixteen-song collection, and "I Left My Heart in San Francisco," hardly a new song but a new song for her, made for a refreshing departure from the rest. Whereas Sinatra might have reneged on his recording of "I Left My Heart in San Francisco" because of not wanting to offend Bennett (the jury will always be out on this theory), by 1995 Clooney probably figured that Bennett had been singing the song for so many years (since 1962), her doing it wasn't going to make any difference. It was reasonable to conclude that by 1995, Bennett and the song were bulletproof, and without even trying, Bennett would drop intermittent recording hints that "I Left My Heart in San Francisco" was his, and it was foolhardy for anyone to encroach. After his single of the song in 1962, Bennett included it on a minimum of eight of his albums between 1962 and 1994 alone.[22]

In 1970, in order, the soul singer Bobby Womack sang "I Left My Heart in San Francisco," slept with his teenaged stepdaughter and was shot at by her mother. The stepdaughter later married one of Womack's brothers, who was also a singer. The mother's shot at Womack grazed his temple, and they divorced. She was the widow of Sam Cooke, who six years before had been fatally shot at a motel ("$3 and Up," said the sign out front) near the Los Angeles airport. Cooke's funeral was barely over when Womack took up with the widow, and they were married less than three months after that.[23] Other songs on[24] Womack's 1970 album were "Arkansas State Prison" and "Tried and Convicted."[25]

Who, if anybody, could have made a hit out of "I Left My Heart in San Francisco," had Tony Bennett not done it? My list only includes those who recorded the song. Here it is, in no particular order.

Dean Martin. The night Martin first sang it before a live audience at the Sands in Las Vegas, he started out by saying: "The next song I'm going to do is one I hate."[26] I guess he meant he hated it because he didn't find it before Bennett. The old ring-a-ding-ding of the residuals came out in him. It got to be, most of his career, that Martin couldn't perform without feigning drunkenness. Jerry Lewis said that Martin rarely drank when he worked, it just became his *shtick*; the amber liquid in his glass was really apple juice.[27] When Martin got to the chorus, he sang: "I left my heart in Fran Sancisco..." It always got a laugh, so he kept doing it. At the Villa Venice nightclub in Chicago at the end of 1962, when he, Frank Sinatra and Sammy Davis, Jr., came on separately, then returned to sing together and crack wise, Martin again intentionally butchered the name of the city. Their act that night was recorded, but the complete tapes were inexplicably forgotten until a German label released them in an album in 2003. Martin does a solo of "I Left My Heart in San Francisco."[28] Once he drops the patter between notes and just takes hold of the song, I can see where he might have had a hit had he hung out on Manhattan street corners, waiting for two obscure songwriters to come along. Bennett makes the song soar while Martin's is a different approach as he was never into soaring with much of his material. Bennett could be as romantic as the next guy, even Martin, but he picked his spots and went with the flow of the lyrics. Bennett never put a romantic label on everything, as the sexier Martin unavoidably did. For the San Francisco song, Bennett knew instinctively, without even discussing it, that the fulcrum for Cory and Cross was sentimentality. Martin's version, not surprisingly, is laid back. He sneaks up on the city, with a jaundiced eye even, whereas Bennett gives San Francisco a bear hug after just two bars, and never lets go. Neither way is wrong. Dean Martin's way wouldn't sound like Dean Martin if he did it differently.

Bobby Darin. Darin could put over a mediocre song. All of the truly great ones can. "Artificial Flowers," a mawkish song from a so-so Broadway musical called *Tenderloin,* was recorded by Darin and got as high as 20th on the *Billboard* list.[29] "If I Were a Carpenter" was a song that wouldn't have worked for many singers besides Darin.[30] It's not even on the first page of his oeuvre, yet it sold well. Darin recorded "I Left My Heart in San Francisco" during his Capitol years, from 1962 to 1965, but it was never released. Then in 1999, a quarter-century after Darin had died, Capitol came out with sixteen of his songs, one of them the Cory/Cross composition. Darin was in the wheelhouse of the rock-and-roll onslaught that Tony Bennett and the other pop singers feared. "I used to worry about that guy," Bennett reportedly said. "Until I found out he couldn't sing slow."[31] Which might be the reason why Darin let the San Francisco song sit on the shelf. It was too slow.

Buddy Greco. Don't panic. This is the last Italian on the list. Greco was a double threat. He could play the piano, which he started to study at age four, as well as sing. His friendship with Frank Sinatra was a boon. While Greco wasn't a card-carrying member of Sinatra's Rat Pack, he was at least on the alternates' list.[32] Sinatra was partly responsible for Greco being the answer to a trivia question: Who was the last person photographed with Marilyn Monroe a week before she died in 1962? There were Greco and Monroe, arm in arm, and Sinatra, looking disinterested, sitting in the background, reading a newspaper.[33] Those photos are sort of the back part of bookends for Greco. When he was just starting out, singing with the Benny Goodman band, a young Marilyn Monroe came around to audition. Goodman told her to find another line of work. Greco made an album in 1963, called *Soft and Gentle,* and the San Francisco song was one of the tracks.[34]

Brenda Lee. Even now, it's hard to recall what happened to an 18-year-old Brenda Lee in 1963 without missing something. On New Year's, the family house burned down and she lost her dog in the fire. A few months later, Patsy Cline, one of her best friends, was killed in a plane crash. (Lee named her second daughter, Julie, after Cline's daughter). Lee recorded about 25 songs for Decca Records, most of them on two albums. One of them was "I Left My Heart in San Francisco."[35] Some said that Lee's version rivaled Tony Bennett's,[36] and while that was a stretch, it is a better argument that Lee's rendition is the best ever by a female singer. Decca had signed Lee to a million-dollar contract. In 1962, for Lee's 18th birthday, Decca sent her a white Thunderbird convertible, which was her first car. Later, they deducted the cost of the car from her royalty checks. In the summer of 1963, Lee played Dorothy in a touring production of *The Wizard of Oz*. In Great Britain, *Melody Maker* magazine named Lee "Female Singer of the Year" after she got more than half the votes. In April, Lee married Ronnie Shacklett, whom she had met at a Jackie Wilson concert. In the fall, Lee told her manager, Dub Albritton, that she was expecting. His reaction: "You can't be pregnant! You're booked!"[37]

Mayer Hawthorne. Hawthorne is a soul singer who started out with a horn-rimmed, Buddy Holly look, plus a Pee Wee Herman bowtie. Hawthorne moved on to a fedora and Harry Potter glasses, only they were smoked. From Ann Arbor, Michigan, Andrew Mayer Cohen relocated to Los Angeles, changed his last name to the name of the street he used to live on, signed a record contract and has never looked back.[38] It's just a good thing he never lived on Lansky Avenue, otherwise he would go through life getting confused with the gangster. In 2010, Hawthorne sang a mesmerizing "I Left My Heart in San Francisco" to a skateboarding video.[39] I don't know if Hawthorne skateboards or not, but you don't see him on the video—it's three minutes of incredible skating in the vicinity of Fisherman's Wharf. The skating is a distraction from the fine music and the splendid, unobtrusive work of an unbilled pianist. Last time I looked, the video had gotten 1,423,950 views, probably more for the skating than the song, but you could argue either way. Hawthorne is not yet forty and hopeful about the future. He could be the next Tony Bennett, if he wanted to be, but few would roll the dice on the career choices Bennett made.

Johnny Mathis. Growing up on Post Street in San Francisco, Mathis had show-business breeding and was geographically likely to eventually sing "I Left My Heart in San Francisco." His father was in vaudeville. When young Johnny showed an interest in music, Clem Mathis dug deep and bought an upright piano for $25. Then he realized that there wasn't enough room to get his purchase through the front door. Clem's son was awakened one night to find his father dismantling the piano piece by piece, then reassembling it in the living room. The first song Clem taught his son was "My Blue Heaven." Johnny Mathis studied singing arduously, started college, and helped pay bills by singing in clubs around town. George Avakian, vacationing from his New York job with Columbia Records, saw

Mathis singing one night at Ann Dee's 440 Club in San Francisco and immediately sent this telegram to the home office: "SAW A NINETEEN YEAR OLD SINGER WHO CAN GO ALL THE WAY. SEND BLANK CONTRACTS."[40]

Mathis' first album was jazzy, and it got a lukewarm response, but Mitch Miller fixed that. Once Miller got him on the right track, away from jazz and into the pop format, Mathis at one point was outsold only by Elvis Presley and Frank Sinatra among the supernovas in the Columbia stable. The San Francisco song was one of the tracks on Mathis' *The Shadow of Your Smile* album in 1966. Almost every song he did on that was a grabber, including two from the Beatles ("Michelle" and "Yesterday"). Curiously, the Cory/Cross song was listed as "(I Left My Heart) In San Francisco."[41]

Julie London. The cover on Julie London's 1963 album, *The End of the World*, tries to make her look like a redhead.[42] All of London's album covers were inventive, which is to say, sexy. But she was more than a pretty face and an hourglass figure. She spent a lot of time as an actor, and was better than average, although the scripts ran from poor to poorer (in a cage with a man in a gorilla suit, getting a part opposite Gordon MacRae because she was one of the few actresses shorter than him, and co-starring with Robert Mitchum although she got only six minutes of screen time). It was her eventual second husband, after Jack Webb, who pushed her into a singing career. Bobby Troup, a musician and songwriter, heard her singing after she'd had a few drinks at a party, and it took a year and a half of cajoling before London finally listened to him. *The End of the World*, a 1963 release by Liberty, included "I Left My Heart in San Francisco." They also released the album in Japan, only they changed the title of the album to *I Left My Heart in San Francisco* and led off with the title song. She doesn't sing the song like someone who lacked confidence in her voice. The purr was natural, and Troup told her if she'd she keep her mouth close to the microphone, she'd be just fine.[43] She was more than fine.

Sammy Davis, Jr. Davis, the quintessential Triple Threat, also did impersonations, including those that no one else considered or dared to do. They ranged from the ridiculous Huckleberry Hound to the sublime Fred Astaire, and who else but Davis could pull off an Astaire, both singing and dancing? Davis did a fair Tony Bennett, too, without trying. "Sometimes," Will Friedwald said, "he sounds more like Tony Bennett than Sinatra does, [as though he's] anticipating Bennett's intimate meetings with [accompanists] Ralph Sharon and Bill Evans."[44] In 1964, it seemed like every day Davis woke up, he did an album. There were five, and Reprise's *Sammy Davis, Jr. Sings the Big Ones for Young Lovers* had "I Left My Heart in San Francisco" on it.⁴⁵ One critic said that the arrangement came with "a bass-intensive upgrade and heavy intonations."⁴⁶ Other numbers on the track were covers of "Kansas City," "Deep Purple," "Days of Wine and Roses," "Blue Velvet," and "Fools Rush In."⁴⁷ Some of the songs didn't match up with the album's title, not unusual for much of Davis' work. He was so versatile, had so many tools, that no one could pigeonhole him.

Dinah Washington. In just 18 years, Washington was married seven times, and another marriage, because the ceremony was performed offshore, was declared illegal. Drugs prescribed by her doctors were her undoing. She fought depression and weight problems. However, her failed marriages and lack of self-esteem never got in the way of her work. She could sing jazz, blues, pop and rhythm and blues, and she won a Grammy for the indelible "What a Difference a Day Makes." In 1963, she did four weeks in Las Vegas, two in Los Angeles⁴⁸ and recorded an album, *Dinah '63*, that included "I Left My Heart in San Francisco."⁴⁹ That July, she married for the last time, to a star professional football player named Dick "Night Train" Lane. In the fall, she did a recording session for Roulette Records and made a charity appearance at her new husband's alma mater in Texas.⁵⁰ In Detroit, where Lane played football,⁵¹ she was making Christmas holiday plans when she went to sleep alongside him one night and never woke up. She was 39. The coroner concluded that there had been an accidental overdose of lethal drugs, all prescribed.⁵² In her peak years, Washington earned as much as a $150,000 annually, but the IRS slapped her estate with a tax bill of almost a half-million.⁵³ When fans asked, she signed the jacket of that 1963 album "Dinah Washington Lane." Some of the tracks could have been strung together to tell her life story: "Rags to Riches," "Make Someone Happy," "What Kind of Fool Am I," "The Show Must Go On" and "Drown in My Tears."⁵⁴

15

Old Man River

On the second-to-last Friday of August 2016, an SUV took Tony Bennett, his wife Susan and her parents from the Fairmont Hotel on Nob Hill to the downtown waterfront park where the San Francisco Giants play baseball. There was a police escort, and nineteen Grammy Awards later, Bennett was still surprised that his party would rate this sort of movie-star attention. He thought they would just get the Fairmont doorman to flag them a cab in front of the hotel. Tony Bennett might be red carpet, but a big part of his mindset is still blue collar.

"Mr. Bennett," the chauffeur said when they were halfway there, "is the air-conditioning all right?"

"Perfect," Bennett said. "Thanks very much for asking."[1]

Thanks very much for asking. A longtime friend of Bennett's, who was also in the car, couldn't help but note another example of his unquenchable politeness.

The Giants might play an occasional doubleheader, but Bennett's appearance before 40,000 fans at sold-out AT&T Park was the middle piece of his weekend tripleheader in San Francisco, the city where, on December 28, 1961, he sang "I Left My Heart in San Francisco" in public for the first time. The 2016 festivities started at noon Friday, on the lawn in front of the venerable Fairmont, where there was a public unveiling of an eight-foot bronze-coated likeness of Bennett. After the ball game, there was a charity dinner back at the Fairmont in honor of Bennett, who sang for his supper by giving a small concert afterward. A nonagenarian since that August 3, Bennett was apparently being tested for stamina, and by all accounts he finished the gauntlet with energy to spare.[2] About a week later, having returned to New York, Bennett was on a plane to Italy, for a week-long vacation to the land of his forbears.[3] (Jerry Lewis, born five months before Bennett, also turned ninety in 2016. By contrast, Lewis, in Los Angeles to promote what is probably his last movie, was getting around in a wheelchair. He appeared frail, all the while razor-sharp with recollections and opinions.)[4]

But if there was one omission from an otherwise perfectly staged Tony Bennett weekend in San Francisco, it was that the names of George Cory and Douglass Cross were seldom mentioned, if at all. I paid fairly close attention, and asked a number of people who attended some if not all of the Bennett hullabaloo, and no one could recall Cory and Cross being cited. Maybe I'm too close to the subject matter, not an uncommon pitfall for a writer, but I feel that not recognizing the writers of Bennett's most famous song was an inexcusable oversight.

The day after the dinner where Bennett sang, I visited the Russian Hill district and 1210 Lombard Street, the flat that Cory once rented. A block up the street from Cory's old place, just over a crest, is a famously crooked street that has eight sharp turns on a forty-degree slope. The turns, called switchbacks, were built in the 1920s to allow traffic to descend the street.[5] The speed limit is five miles per hour. Online, three women from Virginia had rented 1210 Lombard just for the weekend; none of them knew the history of the location until I told them. Leaving Lombard, I lunched at a diner on Chestnut Street, where I chatted briefly with someone facing me in the adjoining booth. He had come from Los Angeles to scout movie locations.

"I always thought Tony Bennett wrote that San Francisco song," he said. Bennett has been a lot of things, but never a songwriter.

San Francisco street signs are rife with sub-headings denoting famous people and historic places and events. There was Isadora Duncan's name beneath the Taylor Street sign on a block around the corner from my Union Square hotel. The area in front of where the Giants play is called Willie Mays Plaza.[6] Farther south on Taylor, in the Tenderloin, there is an intersection at Turk with two sub-headed signs: One in honor of the Gene Compton Cafeteria, where there was a riot involving gay and transgendered people and the police in 1966; and another for Vicki Marlane, the transgender drag queen ("the girl with the liquid spine") who died from an AIDS-related illness in 2011.[7]

In truth, San Francisco hasn't given Cory and Cross much due since 1984, when the Board of Supervisors co-honored their composition along with a song from Jeanette MacDonald's 1936 film.[8] The *San Francisco Chronicle* covered the Tony Bennett weekend extensively. Early on, there was a long story about Bruce Wolfe, the 75-year-old California sculptor who did the million-dollar Bennett piece that stands in front of the hotel.[9] The writer, Sam Whiting, tossed in the names of Cory and Cross, but when he asked Bennett about the origin of the song, the singer said he couldn't remember who wrote it. In a phone interview that I had with

Bennett earlier, he said, "Ralph Sharon [his accompanist] knew those guys, I didn't," but when I related a few details from their troubled lives, it piqued his interest. He hadn't known that Cory and Cross never wrote another hit, and drank themselves to death.[10] Leah Garchik wrote a column about the unveiling celebration, and the names of Cory and Cross were not to be found.[11] In more than half a century, the only time the San Francisco newspapers wrote anything close to in depth about Cory and Cross was when they died. *Time* Magazine didn't run anything after Cross died; three years later, they ran one paragraph on Cory's death.[12]

It is not uncommon for cabaret singers to be unfamiliar with the writers whose material they sing. Frank Sinatra was a notable exception. He painted many a town with Jimmy Van Heusen, who wrote "All the Way," "Come Fly with Me," "My Kind of Town," and other Sinatra hits. What is more, Van Heusen—real name, Chester Edward Babcock—is buried in the Sinatra plot in a cemetery outside Palm Springs, California.[13] Non-stop, Sinatra was renowned for bringing those responsible for his songs out of the shadows. After a Sinatra concert in Philadelphia, Paul Willistein wrote: "Like a musicologist, Sinatra prefaces his songs by crediting the songwriters and the arranger. And his keen intellectualism where fine lyrics and melodies are concerned shows in the care with which he sings."[14]

The statue of Tony Bennett at the Fairmont Hotel was the idea of Willie Brown, a former San Francisco mayor, and Charlotte Shultz, the socialite wife of George Shultz, who was secretary of state during President Ronald Reagan's administration.[15] Charlotte Shultz said: "Tony and his song have been our ambassador around the world, encouraging people to come here. When we brought back the cable cars [1984], Tony was here. When we wanted to tell the world that San Francisco was back after the earthquake [1989], Tony was here. So it seemed to me that we should honor the person who has been a great ambassador to San Francisco."

In 1966, the year Cory and Cross, flush with royalties from their hit song, moved back to San Francisco from Brooklyn, Brown was a state assemblyman, on his way to bigger things. When the Society for Individual Rights, an organization trying to improve conditions for gay people, sought changes in California's anti-gay laws, Brown and a legislative colleague, John Burton, begged the question. Brown urged the society to "act as any other minority group would—discuss the issues, educate people. I see little likelihood of any change in the present California laws on the subject. Of one-hundred twenty members of the legislature, there are six or eight who would be willing to take a favorable stand [on changing the law]."[16]

San Francisco celebrated Tony Bennett's ninetieth birthday in August of 2016. Charlotte Shultz (left) and Dianne Feinstein, a U.S. senator and former mayor of the city, helped unveil a statue of Bennett in front of the Fairmont Hotel (Drew Altizer Photography).

At the Fairmont fifty years later, just down the street from the historic Grace Cathedral, somebody in front of the hotel pulled the cord on the blue cloth cover and Bennett looked out at the audience from the speakers' stand and signaled two thumbs up. It would have been churlish to do anything else, and it's fairly late in the game for Bennett to play the churl. Dressed in his favorite color, a blue sports coat and a dark blue tie, he stood next to Charlotte Shultz and said: "I can't believe what just happened. San Francisco will be in my heart forever. Thank you, everybody."

I thought that Wolfe didn't really capture Bennett's close-mouthed smile, but what do I know? As a collegiate film critic, I trashed *Separate Tables* and it went on to win seven Oscars.[17] For what it's worth, a San Francisco lawyer, sitting next to me at the unveiling and without being asked, commented that the face of the statue was half-Bennett, half-somebody else. Wolfe has done better with Margaret Thatcher, Arnold Palmer, George Shultz and Clint Eastwood.

All sorts of San Franciscans showed up, the *hoi polloi* as well as the swells. An elderly woman sat in the section reserved for the disabled. She had brought along her pet cat, who tried to sleep in a cushioned carry-all. The feline was the only one there who was bored. Before the ceremony, I met Robert Hawn, who lived three blocks away. He caught my attention because he was holding a Tony Bennett bobblehead. "They gave them away at a Giants game several years ago," Hawn said. "I hope to get Tony to sign it later." The Giants have been playing Bennett's recording of the song after every victory since they moved into their new downtown ball park in 2000. Midway through the 2016 season, somebody in the team's front office told me that they had played the Bennett song more than seven hundred times. Larry Baer, an owner of the Giants, spoke from the stage. Like Dianne Feinstein, the U.S. senator and former San Francisco mayor, and Nancy Pelosi, the minority leader in the U.S. House of Representatives, Baer had personal memories tied to the song, Bennett or both. "In 1992, they almost moved the Giants to Florida," Baer said. "It didn't happen, and at our opening day in 1993, Tony came out to sing at Candlestick Park. In 2010, 2012 and 2014, we won the World Series. Tony sang at least one post-season game every one of those seasons."

After ninety minutes of speeches, singing by the San Francisco Boys and Girls Chorus and music by the San Francisco Jazz Combo, Bennett retired to the suite named after him at the hotel, to rest up for the ball game that night. As the crowd broke up, it was impossible not to notice one Palmer Lamb, who had come to the affair on roller skates—three miles, up and down San Francisco's vaunted hills. I don't quite know how he did it. Maybe eating ice cream helps. He had a cup of vanilla in his hand, and he was dressed in two shades of yellow, a light yellow sleeveless shirt, and mustard-yellow pantaloons. He wore a sailor's hat and on his chest was a large heart that read "T O N Y." In all other respects, he seemed to have his wits about him.

At the ballpark, Willie Mays showed up for the pre-game testimonial to Bennett. They were both in New York in 1951; Mays was looking for base hits as a rookie for the former New York Giants (before they moved to San Francisco) and Bennett was looking for his first recording hit.[18] Cory and Cross were two or three years away from completing their "I Left My Heart in San Francisco" composition, and Bennett was eleven years away from recording it. During Mays' first season playing at the Polo Grounds, Bennett recorded "Because of You" and "Cold, Cold Heart."[19] Those hits saved Bennett from being dropped by Columbia Records. "Because of You" was one of those rare recordings that was being played all over the country in jukeboxes, before it was introduced by disc jockeys on radio.

After the unveiling ceremony at the Fairmont on August 19, I had two tasks that were only strolls away from the hotel. Across California Street was the Intercontinental Mark Hopkins Hotel, where I had been hearing that a plaque dedicated to Bennett on the front of the building, placed there many years before, had been stolen or misplaced. People at the hotel had been telling me that it couldn't have been stolen; there never was such a plaque. But several days before the unveiling, the *Chronicle* ran an old photo, showing Bennett, posing in a San Francisco fireman's hat, standing in front of a plaque that read: "The Mark Hopkins dedicates this plaza in gratitude to Tony Bennett for his devotion to San Francisco, May 20, 1977." In a biography of Bennett, it said that George Moscone, the mayor of San Francisco, had introduced Bennett to the crowd that day, and that afternoon the city also named a street in Golden Gate Heights, on the highest of the high hills in San Francisco, Tony Bennett Terrace.[20]

The first time I was ever in the Mark Hopkins was in the early 1960s, where, as fate would have it, I was left with the drink tab for Dan Dailey, the musical comedy star, and the singer Gene Austin ("My Blue Heaven"). But that's another story for another book. When I walked into the Mark Hopkins in 2016, the lobby-level nightclub, where Dailey and Austin destroyed my recently-graduated-from-college budget, was no longer there. Nor was anybody there who could shed light on the missing Tony

Bennett plaque in front of the hotel. So I moved on to Pleasant Street, a hilly one-way street, running only one block, that connected Jones and Taylor Streets.

On the way, I saw a woman going into an apartment building holding a half-dozen blue Tony Bennett balloons that had been left over from the unveiling.

"Nice balloons," I said. An innocent remark, honest, it just came out, but I was eligible to have my face slapped.

"We're having a Tony Bennett party here tonight," she said. "These will be perfect."

I asked her about Pleasant Street.

"Up to the corner, take a right, and then take your first left," she said.

I told her about 18 Pleasant Street, and she already knew that George Cory had died there, almost four decades before. Finally, after several days in San Francisco, I found someone not connected to the composers who knew of their existence.

The balloon woman even knew who lived at No. 18.

"Ask for Karen," she said. "She's nice. She'll let you in and show you the place."

"I don't know your name," I replied.. "Should I use your name?"

"Better not," and with that she disappeared into her building, careful to navigate the balloons through the front door.

Once I got to Pleasant Street, I wasn't paying attention, and walking too fast I found myself in the middle of the block, past No. 18. There was a moving van out in front, and a young woman was directing a couple of movers. She was moving to Los Angeles. I stopped to tell her what I was about. She hadn't known about Cory's death on this street.

"Eighteen is back there," she said, pointing to where Pleasant intersects with Taylor.

She volunteered an assessment of the neighborhood.

"A lot of weirdo's on this street. They ought to call it un-Pleasant Street." She got too busy with the movers to elaborate.

The street was named after a woman, not a state of mind. Mary Ellen Pleasant was a civil rights leader in the late 19th century, once called "the mother of civil rights in California." Born in Georgia, Pleasant bought and freed slaves, prospered through marriages and business acumen, and eventually owned a thirty-room mansion in San Francisco. There's also a park named after her in San Francisco.[21]

I went back to No. 18. There was a vestibule for three front doors in close proximity—Nos. 14, 16 and 18. Each one had a bright red door with a gold-plated knocker. I pressed on the intercom button at No. 18. The voice that answered didn't sound like a Karen.

"Sorry, but I'm having a meeting here now," he said cheerfully.

I told him why I was there. He knew that George Cory had lived there—and died there—a long time ago.

"I can't talk now, but slip your card through the mail slot," he said. "I'll try to get back to you. I'm interested." I left the card, but I never heard from him.

I left Pleasant Street and hoofed it back to the Fairmont Hotel. I wanted to peek inside the Venetian Room, where three hundred supporters of a local hospital were going to pay dearly to break bread with Bennett and hear him sing the next night.

My wife Pat was resting on a sofa in the lobby, chatting with some tourists. We got to talking about Bennett, and "I Left My Heart in San Francisco," and one of them remembered a parrot singing part of the song on a late-night TV show. She had a good memory. A bird named "Pancho the Parrot" had enthralled Johnny Carson in 1981.[22]

The Venetian Room was where Bennett first sang the Cory/Cross song publicly, on December 28, 1961. I had been there many times over the years; the last time to hear Bobby Short, the cabaret singer from New York.

Inside, the workers were setting up the room for the Bennett affair. There was something obviously missing from the room. The walls were bare. They used to be covered with paintings of scenes from Italy. I'm told that the paintings are still there, but they've been covered over with a second wall. The next night, it was mentioned to Paul Tormey, the new general manager of the Fairmont, that the paintings were still around. Tormey was hearing this for the first time. He promised that he would look into the possibilities.[23]

I didn't know what I was looking for inside the Venetian Room. Maybe the ghosts of Cory and Cross. Down the hall from the entrance to the room was a glass-enclosed tribute to Bennett: Copies of a couple of his paintings, photos of his family as he grew up in the borough of Queens in New York, a photo of him in an Army uniform during World War II. The only mention of Cory and Cross was their names on the cover of the sheet music for the song, published in 1954.

San Francisco hadn't had a good to-do over a song since 1984. That was the year the mayor, Dianne Feinstein, and the board of supervisors ended some bitter wrangling by compromising: The song "San Francisco" was designated the city's official song and "I Left My Heart in San Francisco" was honored as official ballad. But now, 32 years later, the issue was revived. A couple of weeks before the Bennett dinner at the Fairmont, a prominent member of the Calamari Club sent out emails to his fellow members, encouraging them to attend the charity affair. For decades, the Calamari Club has been an elite organization whose members are among the most prominent in the city. Sheldon M. Siegel once described the Calamari Club as a "fabled group of businessmen, politicians, labor leaders, lawyers and influence peddlers." The president of the Calamari Club is called the "kingfish."[24]

When Quentin Kopp, another member of the Calamari Club, got the membership email about the Bennett affair, he sprung into action. In 1984, Kopp opposed the Cory and Cross song and banded together with Warren Hinckle, an acerbic *Chronicle* columnist, and several others in support of the "San Francisco" song, which had been sung by Jeanette MacDonald in the 1936 movie. Hinckle referred to Tony Bennett as "an over-the-hill Italian croaker."

Kopp, who has been a Superior Court judge, a San Francisco supervisor and a state senator, couldn't let the pro-Bennett email pass. He sent out an email of his own to the Calamari Club list, calling the Cory/Cross composition "smarmy," and asked fellow Calamarians to stay away from the dinner.

"It was meant tongue in cheek," Kopp said. "I was just having a little fun with the thing."[25]

Noah Griffin agreed. Griffin is the San Francisco singer who founded the Cole Porter Society. He and Bennett were supposed to have what Griffin called a "sing-off" the 1984 day the Board of Supervisors was to vote on the songs, but Bennett, wisely, avoided the furor by staying back at his hotel. Griffin said Bennett's absence might have been due to what Hinckle wrote about him in his column.

"I thought [Kopp's] email was just a joke," Griffin said. "At least I took it that way."[26]

On the other hand, Richard Carpeneti, the lawyer who had represented Walter Hinton, George Cory's principal heir, in a challenge of the Cory will, was upset by Kopp's email and called him. "San Francisco's number one business is tourism, and the Bennett song is a perfect fit for that," Carpeneti said to me. "Why, after all these years, bring up that other song again?"[27]

I told Kopp that Cory was born in Syracuse, New York, which was also Kopp's hometown. Kopp hadn't known that.

"Syracuse, huh," he said. "If I had known he was a fellow Syracusan, I might have gone easier on him."[28]

15. *Old Man River* 149

On several levels, Carpeneti disapproved of Kopp's friendship with Hinckle, the newspaper columnist. In being outlandish, Hinckle worked overtime outdoing himself. His basset hound, Bentley, was known for peeing indoors, sometimes in the most fashionable bars around town. Hinckle and Bentley were known to loaf at a strip club in San Francisco's North Beach section. When police raided the club, Hinckle wrote that they were overdoing their duty. In his phone call with Kopp, about the merits of attending the Bennett dinner at the Fairmont, Carpeneti softened his objection when he was told that Hinckle was hospitalized, in grave condition. Hinckle died of complications from pneumonia several days after the dinner and Kopp spoke at his memorial.[29]

Kopp did not go to the Bennett dinner. Griffin and Carpeneti did. The timing was hardly right to ask for a re-vote on the two songs from 1984. Following the dinner, Bennett took to the small stage with the backing of a keyboard, bass, guitar and his longtime drummer, Harold Jones, who played despite having recently suffered a broken right foot in a fall. The 76-year-old Jones first worked with Bennett in the early 1970s when

In the same place where he first sang "I Left My Heart in San Francisco" publicly in 1961, a ninety-year-old Tony Bennett did an encore during a charity dinner at the Venetian Room of the Fairmont Hotel in San Francisco in 2016. Backing up Bennett on the bandstand were Tom Ranier on piano, Gray Sargent on guitar and Marshall Wood on bass. Harold Jones (not pictured) played drums (Drew Altizer Photography).

he was playing and Bennett was singing with Count Basie's orchestra. Jones was once called "the James Joyce of jazz."[30]

Bennett sang ten songs. As is his style, there was very little patter between numbers.[31] Long ago, when Jack Rollins was Bennett's manager, he repeatedly suggested that he put more humor in the act. "I'm getting four standing ovations without one-liners," a weary Bennett finally told Rollins. "So maybe I'm doing something right."

But Rollins was persistent, and one day the two of them were standing on Madison Avenue in Manhattan, unable to get a cab. Finally, a police car stopped. The driver recognized Bennett.

"Hey, how are you doin', Tony?" the cop said, as though he and Bennett had known one another since the flood.

"Fine," Bennett said. "Are you going uptown?"

"Yeah, hop in."

When the cop dropped them off, Rollins tried to use the incident as proof that Bennett had a sense of humor that he could transfer to his act.

"Now *this* is funny," Rollins said.[32]

Rollins would have approved the night of the benefit at the Fairmont, when Bennett said between songs: "As you probably already know, I've been working with Lady Gaga. I hope you buy the album we did together. She needs the money."[33]

He sang "I Left My Heart in San Francisco" by skipping the verse and starting with the chorus, something he has done with the song in recent years.[34]

In 2016, Bennett won his 19th Emmy, a trove that began with "I Left My Heart in San Francisco" 54 years before. His most recent studio album, the sixtieth, was called *The Silver Lining: The Songs of Jerome Kern.*

I called Rick Booth, who sold 1210 Lombard Street, where Cory rented, for more than four million dollars in 2015. I told him what the woman from Virginia said about the condition of the flat, thinking he would take it with a grain of salt. She said in so many words that the place needed to be "gutted." Booth sounded offended, as though he still owned the property. Booth, who had moved to Oregon, said that a former neighbor on Lombard had taken recent interior photos and he thought the developer who bought the property had done a nice job of renovating.

"It needs to be gutted?" Booth said. "I don't understand that."[35]

"I remember [Cory]," said a resident, who lived around the corner, on Larkin Street, and didn't want his name used. "He was a good neighbor. Quiet. He didn't say much, but was friendly. The neighborhood doesn't like what the developer is doing. He plans to make the building high, from

15. Old Man River

two floors to three, and that won't be any good for our views. Four lawyers are already involved."

Booth knew about all this, but he is just a distant observer now, rooting for his old neighbors while powerless to help them. He has some guilt, since his lucrative sale has in effect jeopardized the panoramic view of the San Francisco Bay from the backs of their properties.

Just east of the crooked part of Lombard, at 900, is an apartment that was used for exterior scenes in the film *Vertigo*. That was where the James Stewart character lived.[36]

I asked Booth if he had any special memories of Cory living at 1210 Lombard. Booth said,

> Not really. The nice thing was that we became casual friends. George took me to see Tony Bennett a couple of times. We went backstage one night, but George got addled, and couldn't remember my name. Finally he said, "Tony, this is my landlord," and I shook hands with Tony. I guess one of the things I remember most about Lombard Street had nothing to do with George. I was living in the adjoining unit, and one day a friend down the street called and told me to look outside. I asked what was going on. "There's a nude bicycle club," he said. "And there's about twenty of them pumping hard to get up the street. They're just about to your place."

Booth hurried to the front door. "They were going by, all right," he said. "What a sight. I got pictures of a few of them."[37]

Some things in San Francisco never change. On one of my early trips there, I can remember how startled I was to pick up one of their newspapers and see a listing in the entertainment section of "Hard Core Films." This was back in the early 1970s. Back at my hotel, after my informal walking tour of Lombard Street, I went through that day's *Chronicle* to see if there was anything in town to do that night. Among the entertainment listings was a bar on Castro Street. It was having its weekly underwear night. You can use your imagination. My imagination says that they made do without me.

It might have been August, and Bennett might have been ninety, going open throttle toward 91, but the year was only starting, relatively speaking. His new book, with a brief chapter about many of the memorable people he had met, grown up with and worked with in his life, came out at the end of the year. He appeared in the Thanksgiving Day Macy's parade, singing with Miss Piggy. In December, NBC broadcast a two-hour primetime special in his honor. (Their telecast around the time of his eightieth birthday won seven Emmy Awards.) At the parade, after Bennett and Miss Piggy had sung "Santa Claus Is Coming to Town" for a national TV audience, the float they were on lurched forward, and Bennett lost his balance. Miss Piggy caught him, and all was well.

As though Bennett needs new chapters to write, he said he is taking up jazz piano, taking lessons from Bill Charlap, his accompanist. "Doing that is the same way as it is with my painting," Bennett said. "I paint every day. Just by doing it every day, you get better."

In the next breath, he announced his open-ended retirement plans. "As long as my voice doesn't wobble and people like me," he said. "I'm going to keep singing until I die."[38]

Appendix I

Douglass Cross' Will (typographical inconsistencies retained)

Filed January 27, 1975
Lake County Superior Court
Lakeport, California
No. 6017

WILL OF DOUGLASS CROSS, also known as HARRY DOUGLASS CROSS, JR.

I, DOUGLASS CROSS, also known as HARRY DOUGLASS CROSS, JR., a resident of Lake County, California, declare that this is my Will.

FIRST: I revoke all Wills and Codicils that I have previously made.

SECOND: I am unmarried and have no children, both of my parents have predeceased me. I have one sister who is living on the date of this Will, to wit: SHIRLEY MAE NEILSON of Santa Rosa, California.

THIRD: I confirm to my dear friend and business partner, GEORGE CLEVELAND CORY, JR. His right of survivorship in and to any property, real or personal, or any cash that I may hold in joint tenancy with him at the date of my death, particularly my Long Valley home property in Lake County, California. I acknowledge that said joint tenancy property will go to the survivor of me, my friend and business partner GEORGE CLEVELAND CORY, JR. outside of probate and the disposition thereof as between GEORGE and myself will not be affected by the terms of this Will.

FOURTH: All of my estate at the time of my death, whether the same be real, personal or mixed, of whatever kind of character, and wheresoever the same may be situated or in which I may have any interest or right of testamentary disposition, I give, devise and bequeath to my dear friend and business partner, GEORGE CLEVELAND CORY, JR., if he survives me.

FIFTH: In the event that GEORGE CLEVELAND CORY, JR., does

not survive me and I shall die seised [sic] or possessed of real property in Long Valley, Lake County, California together with the household furnishings located therein to my dear nephew, RONALD R. STROWBRIDGE, if he survives me, and if he does not, to such children of my nephew RONALD who shall survive him in equal shares.

SIXTH: In the event that GEORGE CLEVELAND CORY, JR. shall not survive me, then I give, devise and bequeath an undivided one-half interest in and to all the rest, residue and remainder of my estate, whether the same be real, personal or mixed, of whatever kind or character, and wheresoever the same may situated, or in which I may have any interest or right of testamentary disposition to my dear nephew, RONALD R. STROWBRIDGE if he survives me, and if he does not to such children of my nephew RONALD who shall survive the said remainder of my estate, to GERTRUDE M. CORY, mother or [sic] my dear friend and business partner, GEORGE CLEVELAND CORY, JR. and to EDWARD M. CORY, brother of my dear friend and business partner, GEORGE CLEVELAND CORY JR. share and share alike but if either the said mother or said brother of my partner should predecease me, then the share of said predeceased person shall go instead to the survivor of those who shall survive me.

SEVENTH: It is my express wish that my dear nephew, RONALD R. STROWBRIDGE, at his sole discretion, but without lawful obligation to do so, provide to his mother SHIRLEY MAY NEILSON, such financial assistance as he deems necessary in case of dire circumstances of his mother.

EIGHTH: If in the event that my dear friend and business partner, GEORGE CLEVELAND CORY JR shall die under such circumstance that the order of death cannot be established by adequate proof, when I direct that it be conclusively presumed that he did not survive me and my estate is to be distributed and administered accordingly.

NINTH: I have intentionally omitted to provide in this Will anything directly for my sister, SHIRLEY MAY NEILSON of Santa Rosa, California, as she has been the beneficiary of considerable property from my estate and that of my mother during her life time and except as otherwise provided in this Will, I have intentionally omitted to provide herein for any of my heirs living at the date of my death. If any beneficiary under this Will shall in any manner contest or attack this Will or any of its provisions, then in such event any share of interest in my estate given to such contesting beneficiary under this Will is hereby revoked and shall be disposed of in the same manner provided herein as if such contesting beneficiary had predeceased me.

TENTH: I nominate my dear friend and business partner, GEORGE

CLEVELAND CORY, JR. as of this Will, to serve without bond. If my partner GEORGE shall for any reason fail to qualify or cease to act as Executor, I nominate and appoint my lawyer PHIL N. CRAWFORD of Lakeport, California. The term "my Executor" as used in this Will shall include any personal representative of my estate.

I authorize my Executor to sell, with or without notice, at either public or private sale, and to lease any property belonging to my estate, subject only to such confirmation of court as may be required by law.

I further authorize my Executor GEORGE CLEVELAND CORY, JR. either to continue the operation of any business belonging to my estate for such time and in such manner as my said Executor may deem advisable and for the best interests of my estate, or to sell or liquidate the business at such time on such terms as my said Executor may deem advisable and for the best interests of my estate. Any such operation, sale, or liquidation by my said Executor, in good faith, shall be at the risk of my estate and without liability on the part of said Executor for any resulting losses.

IN WITNESS WHEREOF, I have hereunto set my hand to this my LAST WILL AND TESTAMENT, consisting of three typewritten pages, this included, on the margin of each of which I have affixed my signature for greater security and better identification this 4th day of June 1968.

(Signature)
Douglass Cross

The foregoing instrument consisting of three typewritten pages, this included, was on the date thereof, by the said DOUGLASS CROSS, signed and published as, and declared to be, his LAST WILL AND TESTAMENT, in the presence of each other, have subscribed our names as witnesses thereto.

(Signature)
Frances L. Edwards residing at Carvel Drive, Santa Rosa, California

(Signature)
Lois M. Ricketts residing at San Clemente, California

George Cory's Will

Filed April 17, 1978
Superior Court of the State of California
For the City and County of San Francisco
No. 220580

I, George Cory, also known as George Cleveland Cory, Jr., a resident of San Francisco, State of California, over the age of eighteen (18) years, being of sound and disposing mind and memory and not acting under duress, menace, fraud ro [sic] the undue influence of any person whatsoever, do hereby make, publish and declare this to be my Last Will and Testament.

FIRST, I hereby revoke all former Wills and Codicils to Wills made by me.

SECOND, I have never been married and never been married [sic] and have never had children. My parents and one brother have predeceased me.

THIRD, I make the following specific gifts, provided each named beneficiary survives me and should any not survive me, then that particular gift shall lapse and become part of the residue of my estate:

$1,500.00 to LINA GASTONI
        1003 Lincoln Way
        San Francisco, California

$2,500 to MR. & MRS. PAUL K. MORGENTHALER
        And to the survivor of them
        526 North Plymouth Blvd.
        Los Angeles, California 90004

This I leave to my fond uncle and his dear wife as but a token remembrance of their meaningful support and belief in me in times of trial.

All of the estate at the time of my death, other then [sic] gifts aforementioned herewithin, I give, confirm, devise and bequeath to my dear friend and Business Manager, WALTER K. HINTON—2919 California Street, San Francisco, California 94115, his right survivorship in and to any property or any cash that I may hold, whether same be real, personal or mixed, of whatever kind of character, and wheresoever the same may be situated, or in which I may have an interest or right of testamentary disposition, if he survives me.

FOURTH: Depending upon the availability of funds and at the total discretion of the perpetual Trustee of same, WALTER K. HINTON, but without any legal obligation, it is my request that said Trustee maintain the GEORGE CORY MEMORIAL FOUNDATION, a scholarship fund.

FIFTH: I hereby nominate, constitute and appoint my dear friend and Business Manager, WALTER K. HINTON, as Executor and Trustee of this Will. If he should fail, refuse or be unable to act, or, once acting, he should fail, refuse or be unable to continue to act I nominate, constitute and appoint my friend LINA GASTONI as Alternate Executor.

SIXTH: I hereby give to my said Executor and Trustee, full, absolute and complete authority to sell, lease, mortgage and pledge the property in my estate and to exchange said property for other assets and to purchase other assets and generally to invest and reinvest the property in my estate as my Executor and Trustee may deem best, without obtaining an Order of court for any of said acts, subject however, to confirmation by court as provided by Law.

SEVENTH: I authorize my Executor and Trustee, on any preliminary or final distribution of the property of my estate, to partition, allot and distribute my estate in kind, including undivided interests in my estate or any part of it, or partly in cash or partly in kind or entirely in cash, in my Executor and Trustee's absolute absolute [sic] discretion. The value of the assets selected for distribution in kind shall be based on the value of such assets as of the date of distribution.

EIGHTH: I have purposely made no provisions herein for any other person, whether claiming to be an heir of mine or not, and if any person, whether a beneficiary under this Will or note mentioned herein, shall contest this Will or object to the provisions hereof, or claim to be an heir of mine and as such assert a claim to my estate, or any part thereof; then to such person or persons I hereby give and bequeath the sum of ONE ($1.00) DOLLAR, and no more in lieu of the provision which I have made or which I might have made herein for such person or persons. If my estate or any portion thereof should become undisposed or by reasons of the provisions of this Article, then I give, devise and bequeath such undisposed of portion or portions in accordance with the terms of this Will and to the persons named as beneficiaries herein, exclusive, however, of the person or persons contesting or objecting and to all intents and purposes as if such person or persons so contesting or objecting has predeceased me.

NINTH: I direct that there be no funeral at the time of my death and that my remains be cremated and scattered at sea; and empower my Executor and Trustee to determine each and every aspect of the said final disposition of my remains. I am working on a musical program to be produced six months following my death. I expect to leave more detailed instructions concerning the same as a Codicil to this Will, and I instruct my Executor and Trustee to see to it that instructions I may make for this program are followed.

IN WITNESS WHEREOF, I have hereunto set my hand to this my LAST WILL AND TESTAMENT, consisting of four, (4) typewritten pages, this included on the margin of each of which I have affixed my signature for greater security and better identification this 15 day of March 1978 A.D.

(Signature)
GEORGE CORY (aka GEORGE CLEVELAND CORY, JR.)

The foregoing instrument was on this date thereof, signed, published and declared by GEORGE CORY, the Testator therein named, as and for his Last Will and Testament, in the presence of us who, at his request, in his presence and in the presence of each other, have hereunto subscribed our names as witnesses thereto. Each of us observed the signing of this Will by GEORGE CORY and by each other subscribing witness and knows that each signature is the true signature of the person whose name was so signed.

Each of us is now more than eighteen (18), years of age and a competent witness and resides at the address set forth after each of our names.

We are acquainted with GEORGE CORY. At this time, he is over the age of eighteen (18) years, and to the best of our knowledge, he is of sound mind and is not acting under duress, menace, fraud, misrepresentation or undue influence.

Executed this 15th day of March 1978, at San Francisco, California

Agnes V. Wade (signature) residing at 833 Fillmore St., S.F.

Rev. Ernest R. Wade D.D. (signature) residing at 833 Fillmore St., S.F.

Mathilde H. Oppenheim (signature) 405 Davis Court, San Francisco, Ca. 94111

Appendix II

Other One-Hit Wonders

Jim Lowe's only hit recording was "The Green Door," a 1956 novelty song that he didn't write (words by Marvin Moore, music by Bob Davie). What Lowe did write, before that, was "Gambler's Guitar."[1] In 1953, Lowe and Rusty Draper, a guitar-playing country singer, were both under contract with Mercury Records. In May, Lowe recorded his own composition in Mercury's Chicago studio. Later the same month, standing approximately where Lowe stood, Draper covered the song, backed by David Carroll's orchestra. Lowe's rendition didn't sell; Draper's quickly sold a million copies. (Lowe and Draper were both born in 1923, a few months apart, in small Missouri towns only a couple hundred miles apart. But there's nothing that says they knew each other, other than both recording for Mercury.)[2] Lowe, who was 93 when he died in 2015, went on to a long career as a popular New York disc jockey, never having another hit recording as either a performer or a songwriter.[3]

I asked Michael Feinstein about one-hit songwriters. "There are tons of them," he said, and then he rattled off just a few from memory.[4]

I asked Peter Mintun, the New York pianist who once worked at the Fairmont Hotel, where Tony Bennett sang "I Left My Heart in San Francisco" for the first time in 1961, the same question as Feinstein.

"I've never been asked that before," said Mintun, who then, like Feinstein, was able to cite several by rote.[5]

I have a couple of one-hit wonders of my own. But my memory was wrong about Lowe. I have always had a sentimental interest in "The Green Door," because I thought that the song was inspired by The Shack, a dimly lit beer joint with a green front door on the University of Missouri campus, where Lowe went to school. When I visited a good friend at the school back in the ice age, we lifted a few schooners at The Shack one night while trying to romance a couple of coeds from Tennessee (when we told them we had never heard of Tennessee Ernie Ford, as a joke, we lost all chance). Later, however, I have learned that the idea for "The Green Door" came from Davie's visit to a Dallas club where a password was required for entry. Davie, by the way, played the catchy rinky-tink piano to Lowe's singing on "The Green Door."[6]

So Lowe doesn't qualify as a one-hit songwriting wonder for "The Green Door," but "Gambler's Guitar" lands him on the list. Not knowing he was very ill, I called Lowe in 2016, and he politely declined an interview. He sounded like a very nice man. It might have been just as well—I would have embarrassed myself, being so wrong about "The Green Door."

In 1965, a young English rocker, Ian Whitcomb, and the group Bluesville made the British charts with "You Turn Me On," a song Whitcomb wrote. That was the last hit he had. He moved to the U.S., started playing the ukulele and appearing at traditional jazz festivals—he got as far away from rock as a musician could get.[7] In the early 1990s, somebody connected with the ill-received movie *Encino Man* contacted Whitcomb to ask for permission to use "You Turn Me On" on the sound track.

"We can pay $25,000," they said, "but would it be all right if we changed a word or two?"

"For twenty-five grand, do anything you want," Whitcomb said. "Hell, there are only about ten words in the whole thing, anyway."[8]

"You Turn Me On," sung by Crystal Waters, couldn't save *Encino Man*. The critics called the film "formulaic" and said it "produced scant laughs." But how bad could it have been? A few years later, *Encino Woman*, a TV sequel, was made (scanter laughs, maybe a few chuckles).[9]

Alicia Bridges' only hit—singing or writing—was "I Love the Night Life," an infectious song with a disco beat, which was released in 1978. Bridges wrote it with her partner, Susan Hutcheson.[10] It's a song with a lot of lives—it was included in at least two 1990s movies, *Adventures of Priscilla Queen of the Desert* and *The Last Days of Disco*.[11] Bridges, who was the lyricist, and Hutcheson didn't visit the hit parade again, and their personal relationship ended around 2006.[12] In the 1990s, Bridges worked as a DJ at The Otherside Lounge in Atlanta, a club for lesbians which closed after it was bombed in 1997.[13]

One of the first one-hit wonders cited by Michael Feinstein was Einar Swan, who wrote "When Your Lover Has Gone," an immortal torch song, in 1931.[14] Except for true musicologists like Feinstein and Max Morath, even some of the most trenchant students of musical arcana have ever heard of Swan, who was 37 when he died in 1940. Swan, without exaggeration, was a child prodigy. He was playing the violin—a violin his father made for him—at four. By the time he was a teenager, he was playing piano, clarinet, flute, saxophone and drums for the high school band. He was composing for the violin at the age of eleven, and his work was good enough to be copyrighted.

The family, which came from Finland, had the surname of Joutsen, but Swan's father, who took on the first name of John, also changed the family name, using the Finnish meaning of the word *joutsen*. The second oldest of nine children, Einar William Swan, was born in 1903 in Fitchburg, Massachusetts. His father, who had emigrated to the U.S. in 1899, when he was 22, studied music, taught music, wrote music and directed orchestras. One of his children died at birth, but of the other eight, seven became musicians. When the family formed its own orchestra, Einar Swan played the cornet.

As Swan got older, he grew away from the classical music his father embraced, and started developing jazz inclinations. The son and the father argued philosophically about this change, and when Einar fell in love with a Jewish girl and changed his middle name to Aaron, the gap between them widened. When Swan married and converted to Judaism, his father wanted nothing to do with him.

"Jazz," Swan said when he was in his mid-twenties, "is the coming and perfectly legitimate development of modern music.... Jazz is now firmly established, the music of the future, and already has become classic in a certain way, the only difference being that it is more alive than the older type of music."

Many musicians—Red Nichols, Tommy and Jimmy Dorsey, Benny Goodman, Jack Teagarden—started out with the Sam Lanin orchestra in New York City, and Swan followed in this tradition when he was 21. He did some of the arranging as well as playing alto saxophone and the other reeds. Then Vincent Lopez, whose band was established on records, on the radio and toured, hired Swan. The violinist for Lopez was a 25-year-old Xavier Cugat. During a two-month trip to England with the Lopez organization in 1925, Swan was offered a permanent job conducting the house orchestra at the famed Savoy Hotel. But he returned to the U.S., where his wife soon delivered the first of his two children.

Back home, Swan turned down an offer to play with Paul Whiteman, the kingpin of U.S. orchestras at the time, and then Swan quit playing altogether to concentrate on composing and arranging. He said the earnings potential was much greater for arrangers, and who could argue with him? He was paid $400 for one of his early arrangements, and later received a $1500 bonus for the chart he wrote for an orchestral version of "Stormy Weather."

Songwriting was not Swan's bag. Some of his efforts included "White Ghost Shivers," "What Good Is Scheming," "Swan's Serenade" and "Closet Strut," all ignored. But then in 1930 he wrote "When Your Lover Has Gone." Warner Bros. put it in the 1931 James Cagney-Joan Blondell film, *Blonde Crazy*, and Gene Austin, the popular crooner, recorded it. *Blonde Crazy* was not a musical, but Warners in that era liked to use low background music throughout a movie, even when the dialogue was heavy. Moviegoers probably couldn't help walking out of *Blonde Crazy* without humming Swan's haunting melody. An unbilled tenor sang the song through the opening credits; an orchestra played it during a nightclub scene; it was background music as Cagney's character proposed to Blondell; and there were a few more refrains right at the end. As for Gene Austin, he was already a star, thanks in part to "My Blue Heaven," which would be the all-time seller until Bing Crosby's "White Christmas" came along. Austin's "When Your Lover Has Gone" shot to No. 10 on the charts. There were seven more recordings of the song in 1931 alone, including those of Louis Armstrong and his orchestra, and another single by Ethel Waters. When Frank Sinatra recorded "When Your Lover Has Gone" in 1945, five years after Swan's death, he gave the royalties to the composer's widow, Ann Kaufman Swan, who outlived him by more than fifty years.

Swan's doctor told him in 1935 that he had a serious high blood pressure problem. It was a family trait, and Swan did nothing. Five years later, while vacationing in Greenwood Lake, New York, Swan died of a cerebral hemorrhage. In 2002, Swan's name came up and Max Morath, the legendary stride pianist, said: "Who knows what he might have done?"[15]

Like Swan, George Bassman was classically trained, as a pianist, but he took up popular music, to his father's chagrin. At nineteen, Bassman, with lyricist Ned Washington, wrote his only hit song, "I'm Getting Sentimental Over You," and that launched a career that spanned the entertainment spectrum—scoring and arranging music for the movies, both musicals (*The Wizard of Oz, Cabin in the Sky*) and dramas (*The Postman Always Rings Twice*); television (*Omnibus, Caesar and Cleopatra, The Martha Raye Show*) when the Communist witch hunts drove him from Hollywood ("I tried to study the Marxist pamphlets," he testified, "but I couldn't make heads nor tails of them.")[16]; and the Broadway stage (*Guys and Dolls*) before he had a chaotic return to films.[17] Sydney Pollack, just starting out as a director, rejected Bassman's contribution, and Bassman and Sam Peckinpah had a loud shout-out. Mark Hellinger accused Bassman of copying Aaron Copland's work. Finally, Warren Beatty, doing *Bonnie and Clyde*, told Gassman his score wasn't good enough. Through it all, however, by the time of his death, he only had that lone blockbuster of a song, which he wrote in 1933. His songs, like "The Bicycle Song" and "I Didn't Have the Heart To Tell You," went by the wayside.[18] When Bassman died in 1997, at 83, divorced from his third wife, away from his four children and hooked on drugs, newspapers ignored his death. His family paid for a 42-word obituary in the *New York Times*. The only credit of his that they listed was "I'm Getting Sentimental Over You."[19]

The song became Tommy Dorsey's theme, after a studio blowup that was the *coup de grace* in the simmering feud with his brother Jimmy. They were still combining their musical talents in those days, and after the band had played Bassman's song, which was tailor-made for Tommy's patient trombone, Jimmy said:

"Hey, Mac [Tommy's nickname]. Isn't that a little fast?"

Tommy picked up the music off the stand, stormed out of the studio and assembled his own band.[20]

Not much later, on the night Tommy's orchestra had played the song as its theme on his radio show, he was sitting with his vocalist Edythe Wright at the Onyx Club, a hangout for musicians on 52nd Street in New York. Jimmy walked in, feeling no pain from a night on the town. He had launched his own band as well. The brothers were still speaking, but just barely.

"Did you hear the show?" Tommy asked, as Jimmy stood at his table.

"Yeah," Jimmy said.

"What did you think of the theme song?"

"The tempo was off."

Tommy caressed a sugar bowl that was on the table.

Perhaps anticipating the worst, Jimmy went to the bar to have another drink. When the Dorseys reunited years later, "I'm Getting Sentimental Over You" remained the band's theme song. There's no record of Jimmy Dorsey ever mentioning the pace of the piece again.[21]

In 1957, a couple of high school musicians rented a cracker-box recording studio at the corner of Seventh Avenue and 48th Street in Manhattan for $25. Sid Prosen, who had been collecting royalties for four years for "Till I Waltz Again with You," a composition of his that shot to the top of the charts after Teresa Brewer recorded it, was listening to the demo that Paul Simon and Art Garfunkel did. Prosen got together with the young singers' parents and signed their sons to a contract. The deal was 2 percent for Simon and Garfunkel and 98 percent for Prosen. The first song the two boys sang for Prosen's fledgling Big Records was "Hey, Schoolgirl." The names on the 45 recording were Tom & Jerry, artists, and

Tom Graph and Jerry Landis, songwriters. Garfunkel chose his last name because he was a mathematics scholar enamored with graphs; Simon had a former girlfriend named Sue Landis. Their singing names came from the cat and the mouse in the popular movie cartoons of the day.[22]

To his double-sworded credit, Prosen knew what it took to get a pop song off the ground. In an era rife with payola, he paid Alan Freed, the disc jockey, $200 a week to play "Hey, Schoolgirl" on the radio as often as he could.[23] He wrangled an appearance for "Tom & Jerry" on Dick Clark's new program, *American Bandstand*. Simon and Garfunkel went down to Philadelphia where they shared a show with Jerry Lee Lewis. Clark paid them $176 apiece, with the stipulation that they sign over the checks to him later. Their song quickly sold 100,000 copies. The singers' share was $2000 apiece. They continued recording for Big Records, but couldn't lasso another hit.[24] Without Garfunkel, Simon signed a contract with Prosen to record an album of songs. "We can't use Jerry Landis if you're solo," Prosen said to Simon. "You'll be True Taylor." True Taylor's album fell flat. A resentful Garfunkel didn't speak to Simon for five years, and on into the 1980s, after they had reunited, become icons and then split up again, Garfunkel couldn't forget. "For Christ sakes," Simon once said, "he brought it up after it was 25 years in the past. He said I betrayed him. For Christ sake, I was 15 years old."[25]

Prosen's Big Records went out of business. In the 1960s, Sid Prosen tried to release recordings of the now-successful Simon and Garfunkel, but they weren't having any, and took Prosen to court. Prosen's argument was that when they were teenagers, Simon and Garfunkel signed away lifetime rights to their material. That might have been true, but what they signed was lifetime rights to anything by Tom & Jerry; there was no mention of Simon and Garfunkel. This was an important legal distinction, and Prosen was foiled by his own cleverness.[26] He wrote other songs, stuff like "That Old River Line" and "The Rockin' Lady (from New Orleans)," but nothing caught on. While Teresa Brewer went on to more success, and Simon and Garfunkel rode off into the sunset, Prosen went broke and wound up driving a taxi.[27]

Doris Tauber once worked as a secretary in Irving Berlin's office. There's no greater testimony to osmosis than "Them There Eyes," a song written by Tauber and Maceo Pinkard. William G. Tracy is credited with the lyrics. Thelma Todd, working in a music store, sang the song in a Hal Roach film quickie in 1931, and Bing Crosby and the Rhythm Boys, as well as Duke Ellington's orchestra, recorded it the same year. Over time, some heavy hitters like Anita O'Day, Ella Fitzgerald, Sarah Vaughan, Peggy Lee and Carmen McRae have sung the song, but no one has really been able to take it away from Billie Holiday, who sang it in 1939. Tauber later teamed up with Johnny Mercer to write "Drinking Again," which wasn't bad. It caught the attention of Frank Sinatra, Dinah Washington and Bette Midler, but it wasn't a hit. Doris Tauber lived to be ninety, remembered in song for "Them Their Eyes" but nothing else.

In 1947, the song Anita Leonard Nye co-wrote, "A Sunday Kind of Love," was recorded by Claude Thornhill's orchestra and it became a breakthrough hit for the band's singer, Fran Warren. Also in 1947, Anita Leonard married the deadpan comic, Louie Nye. Their marriage lasted until 2005, when a 92-year-old Nye died, and the song may go on forever. In 1947 alone, Frankie Laine, Jo Stafford and Ella Fitzgerald all recorded "A Sunday Kind of Love." It was a truly collaborative effort, besides Anita Nye, sharing the credits for both words and music were Louie Prima, Stanley Rhodes and Babarba Belle, who was Fran Warren's manager.[28] At least 48 more recordings have been done of the song since its debut. When the Thornhill version hit the charts, the bandleader gave Warren a $5000 bonus. She left the band in 1948, began recording by herself and went on to a long career that included Broadway and films.[29] Anita Nye wrote several scores for ballets and tried writing some other numbers, such as "The Bee Song" and "William Didn't Tell," but "A Sunday Kind of Love" was her only pop hit.

In 1952, George Shearing, the London-born pianist, was ensconced at Birdland. The Birdland was only three years old but already considered one of Manhattan's most exclusive jazz clubs. Birdland was about to launch a regular radio program that would showcase many of the club's musical talents and needed a theme song. Morris Levy, owner of the club, commissioned someone to write the theme, but Shearing didn't think much of it.

"Why don't I try doing one?" Shearing said.

"I bet you want to do this because you have your own publishing company," Levy replied.

"That's not it. I just want to write something that I would feel comfortable playing."

Levy and Shearing worked out a deal: Birdland would own the publishing rights, and Shearing would own the composer's rights.

Shearing finished a draft, but didn't like his work. Then, after setting aside the composition for a couple of days, he had his eureka moment while he and his wife Trixie were just starting dinner one night at their home in Old Tappan, New Jersey. Shearing, the youngest of nine children and sightless since birth, jumped up, went to his piano and wrote "Lullaby of Birdland" in ten minutes. George David Weiss later added the words, and the song has resonated ever since.[30] It has been recorded almost 150 times.[31] Shearing never tired of playing it. "It's paid the rent," he said.[32] He recorded it as an instrumental as well as with Nancy Wilson and Mel Torme.[33] In 1962, Bill Haley and his Comets gave it a "Lullaby of Birdland Twist."[34]

Shearing, who died in 2011 when he was 91, tried many times to duplicate his one hit. "I must have written about three-hundred songs," he said. "Most people have never heard of two-hundred ninety-five of them."[35]

Appendix III

The Richest Songs of All Time

Del Mar Race Track, near San Diego, has always been a good place to happen across the show-business names of yesteryear. Jimmy Durante's widow used to stay at the hotel across the street. Outside another neighboring hotel one day sat Don Ameche, waiting for a cab. A visit to the Turf Club might find Tim Conway sitting at a table, looking funny without saying a word. One day I shook Tim's hand and mentioned my name in case he had forgotten. He had once emceed a horseshoe-pitching contest that I had a hand in.

"Bill Christine, Tim."

"You better be," he deadpanned. With Conway, there's no wiggle room for a comeback.

Bob Crosby liked to hobnob in the Del Mar press box. They had free ice cream up there and visitors really didn't have to talk to the turf writers unless they wanted to. Crosby told me the story one day about how he didn't get paid by either his brother Bing or Bob Hope for the non-speaking cameo he did with an elephant gun in *Road to Bali*. (Punch line, Bing Crosby to Hope: "I promised my brother Bob a shot in one of my pictures.")

One day in the crowd, there was Frankie Carle, the pianist and bandleader, trying to pick a winner.

After introducing myself to Carle, I said two words: "Sunrise Serenade." Carle smiled broadly. He wrote the song, with Jack Lawrence, in 1939, gave everybody else a chance to record it, then did it himself in 1946, and it shot to No. 1 on the charts. Glenn Miller's orchestra recorded it one year: "Sunrise Serenade" on the A-side and "Moonlight Serenade" (which became his theme) on the B-side.[1]

"That song is my annuity," Carle said at Del Mar. "My mailbox money."

Several years after Tony Bennett sang "I Left My Heart in San Francisco," George Cory said that he and his songwriting partner, Douglass Cross, had pulled in five million dollars apiece in residuals.[2] This was at a time when dozens of artists were recording the song, as though the proceeds from Bennett's recording alone weren't enough for a sinecure. While it is safe to say that the Cory/Cross song is well beyond the eight-figure mark in total royalties, it is still an also-ran on the overall musical moolah scoreboard. In 2012, the BBC did a TV documentary about the richest songs of all time.[3] While their research is murky, the exercise was a lot like what one guy said to another guy at the end of the bar: "I might not be right, but I'm close."

Here's the BBC's list:

1. "Happy Birthday to You," Mildred Hill and Patty Hill (1893). Estimated earnings: $50 million.[4] Mildred Hill was a teacher at a kindergarten in Louisville and her older sister Patty was principal. In 1893, they wrote a short song called "Good Morning to You." By the 1920s, after Mildred Hill had died, the song, with the same basic melody, had morphed into "Happy Birthday to You." After it became more popular in the 1930s, and was used in two major Broadway shows, *The Band Wagon* and *As Thousands Cheer*, Jessica Hill, sister of the songwriters, went to court and won a copyright for their work.[5] In 2015, when a documentary filmmaker objected to paying $1,500 for the rights, a judge, questioning whether the Hill sisters had written the song, declared the copyright null and void.[6] It was said that the song had been bringing in two million dollars a year for the Warner Music Group, which since 1988 had been sharing the royalties with a family foundation and a relative or two. The heavy betting is that "Happy Birthday" has not seen its last day before a judge. The song had been scheduled to become public domain in 2030.

2. "White Christmas," Irving Berlin (1940). $36 million.[7] Bing Crosby sang the song in the 1942 film *Holiday Inn* and it won the Oscar for the year's best song. It's interesting that Berlin, Mel Torme, and Bob Wells, who were all Jewish, have Christmas songs on the list. Berlin said that Christmas was as much an American holiday as a Catholic holy day, and he felt that as a patriot he was simply celebrating the day. The first three years "White Christmas" was out, it sold three million copies of sheet music and fourteen million records, most of them by Crosby, who came back to sing the song again in the movie *White Christmas*.[8]

3. "You've Lost That Lovin' Feelin'," Barry Mann, Cynthia Weil and Phil Spector (1964). $32 million.[9] After Phil Spector, the *wunderkind*, discov-

ered the Righteous Brothers at a concert in San Francisco, he asked Cynthia Weil and Barry Mann, the husband-wife team, to write a song for them. Before the record was released, Spector, in Los Angeles, played it over the phone for Mann in New York. To Mann, the melody sounded three ticks faster and a tone and a half higher than what he had written. "Phil," Mann said, "you've got it on the wrong speed." Spector said that that was the record and that was the way they were releasing it. The version Mann heard was not only faster, but longer. It was three minutes and 45 seconds, a long song for radio play. Spector put the time as 3:05 on the label, and got away with it.[10] Through 1999, the song had been played on the radio eight million times. (Spector went to prison, for what could be life, following the shooting death of an actress at his California mansion in 2003.)[11]

4. "Yesterday," John Lennon and Paul McCartney (1965). $30 million.[12] One night in a restaurant, a strolling violinist came by John Lennon's table. He began playing "Yesterday." There's no record of Lennon asking him to stop, nor has it been noted that Lennon tipped him, either. Lennon's name is on the song, but he had nothing to do with it; McCartney and Lennon, at the beginning of their careers as Beatles, agreed to put both names on their compositions, no matter how little one of them might have contributed. Asked to talk about "Yesterday" in 1980, Lennon said: "If you read the song, it doesn't say anything. You don't know what happened." Twenty years after Lennon was killed, McCartney asked his widow, Yoko Ono, if Lennon/McCartney on the credit line could be changed to McCartney/Lennon. Fat chance.[13]

5. "Unchained Melody," Alex North and Hy Zaret (1955). $27.5 million.[14] One newspaper said that Todd Duncan, a Broadway actor and operatic baritone, gave the "strongest performance" in the 1955 prison film *Unchained*.[15] He was also the best singer. In a bit that took just a little more than a minute, Duncan, to a guitar background, sang "Unchained Melody" to a group of inmates.[16] The song was released the same year, and at one time versions by Al Hibbler, Roy Hamilton and the Les Baxter orchestra were all in the top ten on the charts. The song has been covered by almost seven hundred musicians, including a top-drawer rendition by the Righteous Brothers in 1965.[17] The song got another boost in 1990 when it was used on the soundtrack for *Ghost*, a film that won Whoppi Goldberg an Oscar. In *Unchained*, Dexter Gordon appeared briefly, but George Auld played the saxophone for him.[18] That's like sending in Ty Cobb to bat for Babe Ruth.

6. "Stand by Me," Ben E. King, Jerry Leiber and Mike Stoller (1961). $27

million.[19] Ben E. King was a singer and songwriter for The Coasters when he wrote an early version of "Stand by Me." Shortly before he left The Coasters, King said, the group said it wasn't interested in the song. Then King began working with Jerry Leiber and Mike Stoller. Stoller said that the final composition was 50 percent King, whose recording turned into a hit. More than a quarter century later, King's singing of the song was used toward the end of the soundtrack for *Stand by Me*, Rob Reiner's 1986 film.[20] The movie was based on a Stephen King story called "The Body," but Paramount Pictures didn't like that. Reiner suggested that they use the same title as the King song. No one had any better ideas. "That's the least objectionable option," said Raynold Gideon, a co-writer on the picture.[21]

7. "Santa Claus Is Coming to Town," Haven Gillespie and Fred J. Coots (1934). $25 million.[22] In 1934, Eddie Cantor was going to do a remote radio show from the Macy's Thanksgiving Day parade. He needed a new Christmas song, and went to the publisher Leo Feist, who went to a friend, Haven Gillespie, who was a reporter for the *New York Times*. Gillespie had the recent death of his brother on his mind, but still wrote most of the words in fifteen minutes on a train. The veteran Broadway composer J. Fred Coots ran with the lyrics and finished the music in 24 hours. Cantor, who owned his own record company, was so certain of the result that he had records pressed even before the Macy's broadcast. But Gillespie cringed whenever he heard his song, because it still reminded him of his late brother.[23]

8. "Every Breath You Take," Sting (1983). $20.5 million. This is the only song written after 1965 that's on the list. At its peak, this song was bringing in more than $700,000 a year for Sting. Puff Daddy won a Grammy for his cover of the song in 1997, but had failed to get permission and forfeited his publishing royalties. "It was the major ripoff of all-time," said Andy Summers, whose guitar riff on the original song formed the core of Puff Daddy's cover. Sting was listed as the only composer, so Summers got nothing.[24]

9. "Oh, Pretty Woman," Roy Orbison and Bill Dees (1964). $19.75 million.[25] In 1964, Roy Orbison and the lyricist Bill Dees were at Orbison's home, trying to come up with another hit. Orbison's wife Claudette came into the room and said she was going shopping. Orbison asked if she needed money, and before she could answer, Dees blurted: "Pretty woman, she never needs any money." Before Claudette got back, they had written the song. A week later, they recorded it. The song was an instant hit,[26] and then, two years after Orbison died in 1988, the hit Richard Gere-Julia Roberts film *Pretty Woman* came out. The original title for the film was

3,000 (the amount of money Roberts' hooker character charged for an overnight), but it was changed after the producers obtained the rights to the Orbison song.[27]

10. "The Christmas Song," Mel Torme' and Bob Wells (1944). $19 million.[28] Mel Torme was twenty when, on a hot July day in Los Angeles, he went to the home of the lyricist Bob Wells to work on some songs. On the piano stand, Wells had left the first four lines of something that had popped into his head, including the immortal "Chestnuts roasting on an open fire...." Torme' liked what he saw, sat down at the piano and in 45 minutes they had finished. When Nat "King" Cole recorded it, he sang, "When reindeers really know how to fly...," incorrectly pluralizing reindeer. The record was released without anyone catching the error, but eventually someone did. When told, Cole was mortified, but he recorded the song over and over, and never made the same mistake. The so-called "reindeers" version is a collectors' item.[29]

Chapter Notes

Chapter 1

1. Ron Strowbridge, interview with author, August 19, 2016.
2. "'I Left My Heart' Composer Is Dead," *San Francisco Examiner*, April 12, 1978.
3. Rick Booth, telephone interview with author, September 10, 2016.
4. "Last Will and Testament of George Cory," Superior Court of the State of California, March 15, 1978.
5. Ron Strowbridge.
6. Lloyd Crenna, interview with author, August 19, 2016.
7. "Last Will."
8. Lloyd Crenna.
9. David Talbot, *Season of the Witch* (New York: Simon & Schuster, 2012), 14–15, 200–01.
10. Lloyd Crenna.
11. "Remember the Compton's Cafeteria Riot," thetender.us, accessed December 30, 2016.
12. Robert Lindsey, "Dan White, Killer of San Francisco Mayor, a Suicide," *New York Times*, October 22, 1985.
13. Ron Strowbridge.
14. Lloyd Crenna.
15. Rick Booth.
16. Marian Halley, "Mary Ellen Pleasant," sfcityguides.org, accessed December 30, 2016.
17. Tom Wolfe, telephone interview with author, September 21, 2016.
18. Aaron Dykes, "Bohemian Grove Roster Sent Along to Infowars," jonesreport.com, June 22, 2007.
19. Ron Strowbridge.
20. "Last Will."
21. "Percodan Overview," percodanabusehelp.com, accessed December 30, 2016.
22. "'I Left My Heart' Composer."
23. Ron Strowbridge, telephone interview with author, August 22, 2016.
24. "'I Left My Heart' Composer."
25. George Cleveland Cory, Coroner's Register, City and County of San Francisco, May 20, 1978.
26. Ron Strowbridge.
27. Richard Carpeneti, interview with author, August 23, 2016.
28. "George Cleveland Cory."
29. Lloyd Crenna.
30. Ron Strowbridge.
31. Jesse Stanton, telephone interview with author, September 18, 2016.
32. "George Cleveland Cory."
33. "'I Left My Heart' Composer."
34. "George Cleveland Cory."
35. Jesse Stanton.
36. "George Cleveland Cory."
37. Carl Apone, "Bennett Brings His Heart Here," *Pittsburgh Press*, June 8, 1978.
38. Tony Bennett, telephone interview with author, June 15, 2016.
39. Rick Booth.
40. Tony Bennett.
41. *Estate of George Cory and Cory Traver, et al., v. Walter K. Hinton, et al.*, Superior Court of California in and for the City and County of San Francisco, August 4, 1981.
42. Richard Carpeneti.
43. Lance Williams and Patrick Hoge, "Love and Money/Mayor's Fund-Raiser Got Millions," *San Francisco Chronicle*, July 13, 2003.
44. Richard Carpeneti.
45. "George Cleveland Cory."
46. Carolyn Carpenti, email to author, January 6, 2017.
47. Richard Carpenti.
48. "Declaration of Final Discharge and Order for Final Discharge," Estate of George Cory, Superior Court of the State of California in and for the City and County of San Francisco, June 28, 1988.
49. Richard Carpeneti.

50. "I Left My Heart in San Francisco Lyrics," metrolyrics.com, accessed December 30, 2016.
51. Ron Strowbridge.

Chapter 2

1. 1940 U.S. Federal Census, accessed December 28, 2016.
2. "'I Left My Heart' Composer Is Dead," *San Francisco Examiner*, April 12, 1978.
3. Ron Strowbridge, interview with author, August 18, 2016.
4. Daniela "Lela" Schwarz, telephone interview with author, January 5, 2017.
5. "Last Will and Testament of George Cory," Superior Court of the State of California, City and County of San Francisco, April 17, 1978.
6. Daniela "Lela" Schwarz.
7. U.S. Social Security Death Index, 1935–2014, accessed December 28, 2016.
8. Daniela "Lela" Schwarz.
9. 1930 U.S. Federal Census, accessed December 28, 2016.
10. Barbara Fluhrer Bauer, "Legendary Baritone Walter Hinton Passes," *The Post*, September 21–27, 2005.
11. Barbara Fluhrer Bauer, email to author, June 29, 2016.
12. "Estate of George Cory," Superior Court of the State of California, City and County of San Francisco, May 7, 1978.
13. Daniela "Lela" Schwarz, telephone interview with author, August 19, 2015.
14. William Rozel III, telephone interview with author, January 11, 2017.
15. Rick Booth, telephone interview with author, July 12, 2016.
16. "Claramae Turner, 92, Great American Contralto, Dead," operanews.com, May 31, 2013.
17. William Grimes, "Tessie O'Shea, Music-Hall Star and Tony Winner, Dies at 82," *New York Times*, April 22, 1995.
18. Ralph Sharon, interview with Les Tomkins, 1988–89.
19. Jerry Buckner Ford, *River of No Return: Tennessee Ernie Ford and the Woman He Loved* (Nashville: Cumberland House, 2008), 141.
20. Bill Christine, "Where the Heart Is: The Story Behind San Francisco's Official Ballad," *SF Weekly*, July 28–August 3, 2016.
21. Rev. Dorsey Blake, telephone interview with author, January 30, 2017.
22. Ron Strowbridge.
23. 1930 U.S. Federal Census, accessed January 1, 2017.
24. "This Day in 1914," Museum of Durham History, accessed January 1, 2017.
25. U.S. Social Security Death Index, 1935–2014, accessed January 1, 2017.
26. "Merola Alumni," merola.org, accessed January 14, 2017.
27. "Show Boat West Coast Tour (1960)," ovrtur.com, accessed January 2, 2017.
28. *The Visitation*, archive.sfopera.com, accessed January 2, 2017.
29. Leontyne Price, interview with Bruce Doffie, February 17, 1982.
30. "In Celebration of the Life of Walter K. Hinton," Western Addition Senior Center, September 20, 2005.
31. William Rozell III.
32. "Legendary Baritone."
33. Steve Rubenstein, "Dazzling Fireworks at Candlestick," *San Francisco Chronicle*, July 5, 1976.
34. "Last Will and Testament."
35. "Grant Deed, 833 Fillmore Street, San Francisco, California," Contra Costa, May 26, 1982.
36. Will White, interview with author, August 22, 2016.
37. "Last Will and Testament."
38. Shashi Dalal, email to author, February 2, 2017.
39. Onlinesearches.com, accessed January 3, 2017.
40. Psr.edu.com, accessed January 3, 2017.
41. Daniela "Lela" Schwarz, telephone interview with author, December 29, 2016.
42. "The Rosicrucian Teaching," rosicrucian.com, accessed January 3, 2017.
43. Will White.
44. Daniela "Lela" Schwarz.
45. David Talbot, *Season of the Witch* (New York: Simon & Schuster, 2012) 275–76, 290–92, 304–05.
46. Daniela "Lela" Schwarz.
47. *Osterberg v. Hinton*, Superior Court of California, San Francisco, November 30, 2004.
48. Daniela "Lela" Schwarz.
49. "In Celebration."
50. Daniela "Lela" Schwarz.
51. Ed Scott, telephone interview with author, June 8, 2016.
52. Jack Olsen, "Gone with the Gypsies," *Vanity Fair*, May, 1998.
53. Harvey Nehgila, "Foxglove Case Ends

with a Plea Bargain," *San Francisco Chronicle*, February 23, 2000.
54. Talbot, *Season of the Witch*, 345–46, 387–88.
55. Jack Olsen, *Hastened to the Grave: The Gypsy Murder Investigation* (New York: St. Martin's Press, 1998), 32–33.
56. Ibid., 20–26.
57. William Rozell III.
58. Benjamin Kaplan, telephone interview with author, January 11, 2017.
59. Fay Faron, email to author, January 11, 2017.
60. *Beesley v. Tene*, Superior Court of California, County of San Francisco, August 21, 1997.
61. Fay Faron.
62. Zillow.com, accessed January 13, 2017.
63. Daniela "Lela" Schwarz, emails to author, January 11, 2017.
64. Conservatorship of Walter K. Hinton, Superior Court of California, County of San Francisco, accessed January 8, 2017.
65. Arthur Park, telephone interview with author, January 11, 2017.
66. Debra Dolch, voice telephone message to author, January 9, 2017.
67. Lloyd Thomas, telephone interview with author, January 17, 2017.
68. Daniela "Lela" Schwarz.
69. Arthur Park.
70. Conservatorship of Walter K. Hinton.
71. Arthur Park.
72. Conservatorship of Walter K. Hinton.
73. Will White.
74. Arthur Park.
75. Daniela "Lela" Schwarz.
76. "In Celebration."
77. Daniela "Lela" Schwarz.

Chapter 3

1. Joe L. Martin, *The Journey of "Old Fremont": A Revolutionary War Rifle* (Bloomington: iUniverse, 2013), 66
2. "San Francisco Gold Rush Chronology 1846–49," sfmuseum.org, accessed February 13, 2017.
3. Martin, *The Journey*, 60, 66–67, 70–73, 75, 78.
4. Douglass Cross, "Elizabeth Cross of Pioneer Family Passes Away Here on Saturday," *Lake County Record-Bee*, October 19, 1967.
5. "Services Held Wednesday for Harry Cross," *Lake County Record-Bee*, August 6, 1949.

6. Martin, *The Journey*, 112.
7. Lewis Francis Byington, *History of San Francisco, Vol. 2* (Chicago: S.J. Clarke, 1931), 387–89.
8. "Elizabeth Cross."
9. Martin, *The Journey*, 108.
10. Elizabeth Hammack Cross, *Again to Earth* (New York: Exposition Press, 1956), front, back flaps.
11. Martin, *The Journey*, 111.
12. "Elizabeth Cross."
13. "Services Held."
14. Cross, *Again to Earth*, 220–23.
15. "Elizabeth Cross."
16. Cross, *Again to Earth*, 282–83.
17. Ibid., 280–81.
18. Elizabeth Hammack Cross, personal notes, May 4, 1967.
19. Letter from Elizabeth Hammack Cross, July 3, 1959, to California Historical Society, collection of Melinda Moranda and Ellen Humble.

Chapter 4

1. Ron Strowbridge, interview with author, August 19, 2016.
2. Rick Booth, telephone interview with author, July 12, 2016.
3. Ron Strowbridge.
4. "Elizabeth Cross of Pioneer Family Passes Away Here on Saturday," *Lake County Record-Bee*, October 19, 1967.
5. Ron Strowbridge.
6. "Eric Clapton—Cow Palace 1974," collectorsmusicreviews.com, accessed December 26, 2016.
7. David Evanier, *All the Things You Are: The Life of Tony Bennett* (Hoboken: John Wiley & Sons, 2011), 189.
8. Leonard Maltin, *Leonard Maltin's 2015 Movie Guide* (New York: Penguin, 2014), 284.
9. "Howard Graham Crawford, Jr.," *Lake County Record-Bee*, February 24, 2011.
10. *Crawford v. State Bar*, San Francisco No. 20290, In Banc, September 20, 1960.
11. Ron Strowbridge.
12. "Father Robert Wright: The Reverend in Rhythm," vinylamongotherthings.com, November 9, 2013.
13. "Pancho the Parrot—Johnny Carson Show," YouTube, September 16, 1981.
14. Ron Strowbridge.
15. Will of Douglass Cross, Lake County Superior Court, Case No. 6017, January 27, 1975.

16. "Sherley Mae Cross," 1940 U.S. Federal Census, search.ancestry.com, accessed December 22, 2016
17. Ron Strowbridge.
18. Will of Douglass Cross.
19. Ron Strowbridge.
20. "Henry Douglass Cross," County of Sonoma, Santa Rosa, California, Certificate of Death, January 9, 1975.
21. Ron Strowbridge.
22. "Henry Douglass Cross."
23. "Songwriter Cross Dies," *San Francisco Chronicle*, January 9, 1975.
24. "Where the Heart Is."
25. Ron Strowbridge.
26. "Where the Heart Is."
27. Peter Mintun, telephone conversation with author, April 5, 2016.
28. Ron Strowbridge.
29. Elizabeth Hammack Cross, *Again to Earth* (New York: Exposition Press, 1956), 1.

Chapter 5

1. Ron Strowbridge, telephone interview with author, July 20, 2016.
2. Usmilitariaforum.com, November 21, 2006.
3. "Ernest Bloch, 78, Composer, Is Dead," *New York Times*, July 16, 1959.
4. "Douglass Cross, Lyricist of 'I Left My Heart...,'" *San Francisco Examiner*, January 8, 1975.
5. Sfopera.com, accessed October 12, 2016.
6. Tim O'Rourke, "Chronicle Covers: It's True, San Francisco Opera's Founder Died Onstage," *San Francisco Chronicle*, August 31, 2016.
7. Ancestry.com, accessed October 13, 2016.
8. "'I Left My Heart' Composer Is Dead," *San Francisco Examiner*, April 12, 1978.
9. Ron Strowbridge.
10. Douglass Cross, "Elizabeth Cross of Pioneer Family Passes Away Here on Saturday," *Lake County Record-Bee*, October 19, 1967.
11. Woody LaBounty, email, January 4, 2017.
12. Internet Broadway Database, accessed October 8, 2016.
13. Songlyrics.com, accessed October 5, 2016.
14. John Bush, "Mabel Mercer," allmusic.com, September 14, 2006.
15. Billie Holiday and William Duffy, *Lady Sings the Blues 50th-Anniversary Edition* (New York: Random House, 2006), 136, 139–40.
16. "Douglass Cross, Lyricist of 'I Left My Heart...'"
17. Holiday and Duffy, *Lady Sings the Blues*, 136.
18. Leonard Maltin, *Leonard Maltin's Classic Movie Guide 2nd Edition* (New York: Penguin, 2010), 465.
19. John Szwed, *Billie Holiday: The Musician and the Myth* (New York: Penguin, 2015), 90–91.
20. Ninasimone.com, accessed September 14, 2016.
21. Songlyrics.com, accessed October 5, 2016.
22. Szwed, *Billie Holiday*, 182.
23. Thomas Conrad, "Kurt Rosenwinkel: Deep Song," Jazztimes.com, May 2005.
24. Carl Apone, "Bennett Brings His Heart Here," *Pittsburgh Press*, June 8, 1978.
25. Maltin, *Leonard Maltin's Classic Movie Guide 2nd Edition*, 465.
26. Szwed, *Billie Holiday*, 90–91.
27. Ninasimone.com, accessed September 14, 2016.
28. Szwed, *Billie Holiday*, 182.
29. Thomas Conrad, "Kurt Rosenwinkel: Deep Song," Jazztimes.com, May 2005.
30. Carl Apone, "Bennett Brings His Heart Here," *Pittsburgh Press*, June 8, 1978.
31. "Maggie Teyte Comes Back," musictime.com, July 23, 1945.
32. "Georgio Tozzi," allmusic.com, accessed September 16, 2016.
33. "Tozzi Sings George Cory Songs," YouTube, accessed May 29, 2016.
34. Anthony Tommasini, "Eileen Farrell, Soprano with a Populist Bent," *New York Times*, March 25, 2002.
35. "Douglass Cross, Lyricist of 'I Left My Heart...'"
36. Bernard Holland, "Gian Carlo Menotti, Opera Composer, Dies at 95," *New York Times*, February 2, 2007.
37. William Ruhlmann, "Tommy Dorsey," allmusic.com, accessed September 18, 2016.
38. Peter Levinson, *Tommy Dorsey, Livin' in a Great Big Way: A Biography* (Cambridge, MA: Da Capo Press, 2006), 171–72.
39. "Tommy Dorsey."
40. Jane Gross, "Note of Compromise Struck on Coast in Dispute Over City's Official Song," *New York Times*, May 19, 1984.
41. Rick Booth, telephone interview with author, April 22, 2016.
42. Peter Mintun, telephone interview with author, April 24, 2016.

43. Dick Bright, telephone interview with author, May 1, 2016.
44. Rick Booth.
45. Associated Press, "Jury Finds Robin Thicke, Pharrell Ripped Off Marvin Gaye Song in 'Blurred Lines,'" March 11, 2015.
46. "Zeppelin Happy 'Stairway' Riff Debate Settled," *Torrance* [CA] *Daily Breeze*, June 24, 2016.
47. "Gian Carlo Menotti."
48. Peter Dobrin, "Curtis Institute and the Case of Nina Simone," *Philadelphia Inquirer*, August 17, 2015.
49. Catalog of Copyright Entries, Third Series, Vol. 2, Part 5a, No. 1, Published Music, January–June 1948, Copyright Office, Library of Congress, Washington, D.C., 53.
50. "What She Said," Nathan Heller, *The New Yorker*, October 24, 2011.
51. Cynthia Haven, "The Bay Area's 'Activists' Shook Up Poetry in the 50s," sfgate.com, September 4, 2005.
52. "'I Left My Heart' Composer Is Dead."
53. Internet Broadway Database, accessed January 3, 2016.
54. "Spotlight on 'The Counsel,'" operasb.com, September 17, 2006.
55. "Claramae Turner, 92, Great American Contralto, Has Died," operanews.com, May 31, 2013.
56. Chris Smith and Brett Wilkison, "Claramae Turner," *Santa Rosa Press Democrat*, May 31, 2013.
57. "Claramae Turner: Tribute to a San Francisco Treasure," YouTube, accessed September 25, 2016.
58. Laurence Bergreen, *As Thousands Cheer: The Life of Irving Berlin* (New York: Viking, 1990), 155, 156, 160, 368–70.
59. Tim Panaccio, "Flyers at 50: The Story Behind the Tradition of Kate Smith's 'Gold Bless America,'" csnphilly.com, accessed January 3, 2017.
60. "The Golden Gate District of the Boy Scouts of America Serves the Communities of San Francisco and the Northern Half of Daly City," sfbac.org, accessed October 14, 2016.
61. Ron Strowbridge.
62. Martin, *The Journal of 'Old Fremont.'*
63. "Douglass Cross."

Chapter 6

1. Bill Christine, "Where the Heart Is." *SF Weekly*, July 28–August 3, 2016.
2. "I Left My Heart in San Francisco," secondhandsongs.com, accessed December 16, 2016.
3. "British-Born Jazz Prodigy Victor Feldman Dies," *Los Angeles Times*, May 14, 1987.
4. Victor Feldman, interview with Les Tompkins, 1987.
5. Evanier, *All the Things You Are*, 135.
6. Ted Gioia and William Claxton, *West Coast Jazz: Modern Jazz in California 1945–60* (Berkeley: University of California Press, 1998), 128, 172, 197–98, 200.
7. Steven Cerra, "Victor Feldman: A Career Overview," jazzprofiles.blogspot.com, accessed December 16, 2016.
8. "Victor Feldman," 45cat.com, accessed December 16, 2016.
9. "Victor Feldman," discogs.com, accessed December 16, 2016.
10. "Victor Feldman Discography," jazzdisco.org, accessed December 16, 2016.
11. "The Sixties…," ninoandapril.com, December 13, 2016.
12. "I Left My Heart in San Francisco, Victor Feldman Quartet," YouTube, accessed December 16, 2016.
13. Steven Cerra.
14. Nino Tempo, telephone interview with author, December 15, 2016.
15. 45cat.com, accessed December 16, 2016.
16. James Kaplan, *Sinatra: The Chairman* (New York: Doubleday, 2015), 478.
17. "Roberta Sherwood, 86, Singer at Top Clubs in 50's and 60's," *New York Times*, July 9, 1999.
18. Antolin Garcia Carbonell, "She Was the Most Famous Miami Entertainer You Never Heard Of," *Biscayne Times*, July, 2010.
19. "Robera Sherwood," 45cat.com, accessed December 14, 2016.
20. "Robera Sherwood," YouTube, accessed December 12, 2016.
21. Andrea Higbie, "Curse of the Oscar," *New York Times*, March 27, 1995.
22. "George Chakiris," secondhandsongs.com, accessed December 14, 2016.
23. "Claramae Turner," operanews.com, May 31, 2013.
24. "Silvertone Record Club," discogs.com, accessed December 16, 2016.
25. "Where the Heart Is."
26. Diller and Buskin, *Like a Lampshade in a Whorehouse*.
27. Stanley Turkel, "Washington Square Hotel," hotelinteractive.com, January 13, 2010.

28. Diller and Buskin, *Like a Lampshade in a Whorehouse*.
29. "Tessie O'Shea, Music-Hall Star and Tony Winner, Dies at 82," William Grimes, *New York Times*, April 22, 1995.
30. "Stodgy Brains, Fat Figures Go Together," *Daytona Beach Morning Journal*, May 9, 1952.
31. "Tessie O'Shea."
32. "Where the Heart Is."
33. Ford, *River of No Return*, 140–41.
34. "Where the Heart Is."
35. Ford, *River of No Return*, 141.
36. Ford, *River of No Return*, 140–41.
37. "The Incedible Talking Machine," *Time*, June 23, 2010.
38. "Songs That Elvis Turned Down or Became Hits for Others," elvis-collections.com, accessed December 15, 2016.
39. Maltin, *Leonard Maltin's 2015 Movie Guide*, 925.
40. "Rejected Movie Songs," yahoo.com, accessed December 15, 2016.
41. Barry Singer, "How Singers Fall in Love with Songs," *New York Times*, February 17, 2002.
42. James Gavin, *Is That All There Is? The Strange Life of Peggy Lee* (New York: Atria Books, 2014), 280–81.
43. "How Singers Fall in Love with Songs."
44. "Fats Waller," 45cat.com, accessed December 16, 2016.

Chapter 7

1. Al Schackman, telephone interview with author, November 29, 2016.
2. "Douglass Cross, Lyricist of 'I Left My Heart…,'" *San Francisco Examiner*, January 8, 1975.
3. Ron Strowbridge, telephone interview with author, November 27, 2016.
4. Gary Kramer, *Let's Misbehave*, liner notes, Prestige Records, 1962.
5. Al Schackman.
6. Ninasimone.com, accessed December 11, 2016.
7. "'He Was Too Good to Me,' Nina Simone," gaslightrecords.com, accessed December 11, 2016.
8. Al Schackman, telephone interview with author, December 9, 2016.
9. "Sally Rand Papers," chsmedia.org, 2008.
10. "Sally Rand Wins Case," *New York Times*, April 1, 1947.
11. Charles G. Bennett, "Cabaret-Card Use Ended by Council," *New York Times*, September 13, 1967.
12. "Prestige Records Discography: 1961," jazzdisco.org, accessed December 9, 2016.
13. Billy Dee Williams, telephone interview with author, December 9, 2016.
14. John S. Wilson, "When a Cellar Was the Place to Be," *New York Times*, September 22, 1991.
15. Billy Dee Williams.
16. Don Schlitten, *Let's Misbehave*, liner notes, Cherry Red Records, 2014.
17. "'Let's Misbehave,' Billy Dee Williams," cherryred.co.uk, accessed December 11, 2016.
18. Gary Groth, "The Jules Feiffer Interview," tcj.com, February 10, 2011.
19. Al Schackman, December 9, 2016.
20. "I Left My Heart in San Francisco," secondhandsongs.com, accessed December 12, 2016.
21. Al Schackman, email to author, December 9, 2016.
22. Ford, *River of No Return*, 141.
23. Douglass Cross, "Elizabeth Cross of Pioneer Family Passes Away Here on Saturday," *Lake County Record-Bee*, October 19, 1967.
24. Ron Strowbridge.
25. "Elizabeth Cross."
26. Elizabeth Hammack Cross, *Again to Earth* (New York: Exposition Press, 1956), 12, 414, 424.
27. Ron Strowbridge.
28. Evanier, *All the Things You Are*, 136–37.
29. "Great Moments at Carnegie Hall," carnegiehall.org, November 22, 2016.
30. Gary Marmorstein, *The Label: The Story of Columbia Records* (New York: Thunder's Mouth Press, 2007), 376.
31. John Marchese, "Pop Music: When He Covers, Slackers Listen," *New York Times*, May 1, 1994.
32. Ron Strowbridge.
33. Talbot, *Season of the Witch*, 234.
34. Lloyd Crenna, interview with author, August 18, 2016.
35. Talbot, *Season of the Witch*, 233–34.
36. Tony Bravo, "Armistead Maupin on Saying Goodbye to San Francisco and 'Tales of the City,'" kqed.org, January 29, 2014.
37. Ron Strowbridge, interview with author, August 18, 2016.
38. "Elizabeth Cross."

Chapter 8

1. Evanier, *All the Things You Are*, 84.
2. Tony Bennett with Will Friedwald, *The Good Life* (London: Simon & Schuster, 1998), 161.
3. Evanier, *All the Things You Are*, 67–68.
4. Ben Yagoda, *The B Side: The Death of Tin Pan Alley and the Rebirth of the Great American Song* (New York: Riverhead Books, 2015), 25.
5. Bennett with Friedwald, *The Good Life*, 102.
6. Yagoda, *The B Side*, 25.
7. Bennett with Friedwald, *The Good Life*, 148–49.
8. Ralph Sharon interview with Les Tomkins, 1988–89.
9. "Ted Heath, Bandleader, Dies," *New York Times*, November 20, 1969.
10. Les Tomkins.
11. Bennett with Friedwald, *The Good Life*, 148.
12. Les Tomkins.
13. Ancestry.com, accessed October 14, 2016.
14. Bennett with Friedwald, *The Good Life*, 147.
15. Les Tomkins.
16. Tony Bennett, telephone interview with author, July 12, 2016.
17. Matt Schudel, "Ralph Sharon, Longtime Accompanist to Singer Tony Bennett, Dies at 91," *Washington Post*, April 5, 2015.
18. Les Tomkins.
19. Bennett with Friedwald, *The Good Life*, 118.
20. "Me and My Shadow: A Life in Chicago," francesarcher.com, August 11, 2011.
21. Bennett with Friedwald, *The Good Life*, 118.
22. Youtube.com, accessed October 4, 2016.
23. Bennett with Friedwald, *The Good Life*, 118.
24. Ben Stewart, "Chess Records: A Brief History," plosin.com, 1998.
25. Bennett with Friedwald, *The Good Life*, 118–19.
26. "Chess Records: A Brief History."
27. Celebritynetworths.org, accessed October 16, 2016.
28. Youtube.com, accessed October 4, 2016.
29. Matt Miller, "Ralph Sharon, Tony Bennett's Longtime Pianist, Dies in Boulder at 91," *Denver Post*, April 5, 2015.
30. Bennett with Friedwald, *The Good Life*, 147.
31. "From the Vaults: Ralph Sharon," bopinbob.blogspot.com, accessed October 15, 2016.
32. Bennett with Friedwald, *The Good Life*, 84.
33. Charlotte Albert, "Ralph Sharon, Jazz Pianist Who Accompanied Tony Bennett, Dies at 91," world24monitor.com, April, 2015.
34. Les Tomkins.
35. Evanier, *All the Things You Are*, 114–15.
36. Ibid., 113.
37. Ibid., 115.
38. Les Tomkins.
39. "Tony Bennett: A Quality That Lets You In," jazzprofiles.com, April 20, 2012.
40. James Kaplan, *Sinatra: The Chairman* (New York: Doubleday, 2015), 478.
41. Evanier, *All the Things You Are*, 86–87.
42. Bennett with Friedwald, *The Good Life*, 161.
43. Evanier, *All the Things You Are*, 121.
44. Yagoda, *The B Side*, 204–05.
45. Les Tomkins.
46. Kaplan, *Sinatra*, 593.
47. Bennett with Friedwald, *The Good Life*, 93.
48. Erik Nelson, "*The Oscar*—Greatest Terrible Movie of All Time," salon.com, March 5, 2010.
49. Evanier, *All the Things You Are*, 6, 242–43.
50. Ancestry.com, accessed October 5, 2016.
51. Nancy Fischer, "Round 'n' Round, Star-Studded History of Melody Fair," *Buffalo News*, February 21, 2015.
52. "Ralph Sharon, Tony Bennett's Longtime Pianist, Dies in Boulder at 91."
53. Evanier, *All the Things You Are*, 250–51.
54. Tony Bennett with Scott Simon, *Just Getting Started* (New York: HarperCollins, 2016), 242.
55. "Ralph Sharon, Longtime Accompanist to Singer Tony Bennett, Dies at 91."
56. Elaine Woo, "Ralph Sharon Dies at 91; Pianist Brought Tony Bennett His Signature Song," *Los Angeles Times*, April 11, 2015.
57. Bennett with Simon, *Just Getting Started*, 242

Chapter 9

1. Yagoda, *The B Side*, 149–50.
2. Bennett with Friedwald, *The Good Life*, 269.

3. Maltin, *Leonard Maltin's Classic Movie Guide 2nd Edition*, 332.
4. The Interactive Tony Bennett Discography, accessed October 22, 2016.
5. Marmorstein, *The Label*, 187.
6. Bennett with Friedwald, *The Good Life*, 265.
7. Evanier, *All the Things You Are*, 129.
8. Ibid., 129–31.
9. Yagoda, *The B Side*, 204, 206.
10. Evanier, *All the Things You Are*, 131–33.
11. Marmorstein, *The Label*, 251.
12. Robert Shelton, "Bob Dylan: A Distinctive Folk-Song Stylist," *New York Times*, September 29, 1961.
13. Joseph Berger, "Dylan and New York Share a Complex, Fertile Romance," *New York Times*, October 15, 2016.
14. Evanier, *All the Things You Are*, 99.
15. Yagoda, *The B Side*, 210.
16. Evanier, *All the Things You Are*, 135.
17. Michael Hodge, Encyclopediaofarkansas.net, February 14, 2014.
18. Wallace Turner, "Hot Springs: Gamblers' Haven," *New York Times*, March 3, 1964.
19. "Gangland Connection," marydonovan.com, accessed October 23, 2016.
20. "Hot Springs: The Valley of The Vapors," buysellfind.com, accessed October 23, 2016.
21. Jim Jerome, "A Place Called Home," *People*, January 11, 1993.
22. David Maraniss, "The Place Where Clinton's Coming From," *Washington Post*, September 30, 1992.
23. *London Gazette*, April 2, 1946.
24. Ralph Sharon interview with Les Tomkins, 1988–89.
25. Rex Nelson, "Along Park Avenue," rexnelsonsouthernfried.com, July 21, 2014.
26. "Elaine Massacre," Encyclopedia of History and Culture, encyclopediaofarkansas.net, accessed October 28, 2016.
27. Carlotta Walls, "The Little Rock Nine," timeline.com, accessed October 28, 2016.
28. Robert H. Boyle, "The Hottest Spring in Hot Springs," *Sports Illustrated*, March 19, 1962.
29. Evanier, *All the Things You Are*, 90–91.
30. Ibid., 143–44.
31. Bennett with Friedwald, *The Good Life*, 164.
32. "A Place Called Home."
33. "The Hottest Spring in Hot Springs."
34. Tom Young, telephone interview with author, October 29, 2016.
35. Richard Craigo, telephone interview with author, May 15, 2016.
36. Rex Nelson, telephone interview with author, October 31, 2016.
37. Tom Young.
38. Evanier, *All the Things You Are*, 183–84.
39. "The Hottest Spring in Hot Springs."
40. "I Left My Heart in San Francisco," General Music Publishing Company, Inc., 1954.
41. Ralph Sharon.
42. Bennett with Friedwald, *The Good Life*, 164.

Chapter 10

1. "Douglass Cross, Lyricist of 'I Left My Heart…'" *San Francisco Examiner*, January 8, 1975.
2. Ron Strowbridge, interview with author, August 19, 2016.
3. Bennett with Friedwald, *The Good Life*, 164.
4. "Hotel," Imdb.com, accessed November 5, 2016.
5. Ken Belker, "The Fairmont Celebrates 100," sfcityguides.org, accessed November 6, 2016.
6. "Gypsy," Imdb.com, accessed November 6, 2016.
7. Jim Burroway, "Today in History, 1961," boxturtlebulletin.com, August 14, 2016.
8. Gary Kamiya, "1961 Police Raid Pivotal for Gay Rights in San Francisco," sfgate.com, June 21, 2013.
9. "1961," timeline.com, accessed November 6, 2016.
10. Ivan Paul, "Around Town," *San Francisco Examiner*, December 30, 1961
11. Bennett with Friedwald, *The Good Life*, 265–66.
12. "1961."
13. Bennett with Friedwald, *The Good Life*, 29, 33.
14. Stephen Schwartz, "Obituary—Ernest (Ernie) Heckscher," sfgate.com, April 20, 1996.
15. *Billboard*, October 27, 1958.
16. Tony Bennett, telephone interview with author, May 18, 2016.
17. Bruce Bellingham, "Venetian Room at the Fairmont Is Revitalized, Opens with a Touch of Triumph," northsidesf.com, October 10, 2010.
18. Jon Akselsen, telephone interview with author, April 26, 2016.
19. Lois Rosano, telephone interview with author, April 1, 2016.

20. Chad Jones, "The Venetian Room and the Way We Were," theaterdogs.net, October 18, 2010.
21. Evanier, *All the Things You Are*, 136.
22. Bennett with Friedwald, *The Good Life*, 168.
23. Evanier, *All the Things You Are*, 136.
24. Lynn Ludlow, "Columnists," tardytimes.com, September 2008.
25. Herb Caen, "Herb Caen," *San Francisco Chronicle*, September 4, 1967.
26. "Around Town."
27. Tony Bennett.
28. Christine, "Where the Heart Is."

Chapter 11

1. Evanier, *All the Things You Are*, 68.
2. Marmorstein, *The Label*, 187.
3. Bennett with Friedwald, *The Good Life*, 265.
4. Matt Schudel, "Mitch Miller, Record Executive and 'Sing Along' Host, Dies at 99," *Washington Post*, August 3, 2010.
5. Clive Davis with Anthony De Curtis, *The Soundtrack of My Life* (New York: Simon & Schuster, 2012), 49.
6. Richard Severo, "Mitch Miller, Maestro of the Singalong," *New York Times*, August 2, 2010.
7. Yagoda, *The B Side*, 143.
8. David Simons, *Studio Stories* (San Francisco: Backbeat Books, 2004), 38–39.
9. Yagoda, *The B Side*, 143–44.
10. Maltin, *Leonard Maltin's Classic Movie Guide 2nd Edition*, 739.
11. Yagoda, *The B Side*, 147.
12. Bennett with Friedwald, *The Good Life*, 123.
13. Marmorstein, *The Label*, 194.
14. Yagoda, *The B Side*, 141.
15. Simons, *Studio Stories*, 33.
16. Yagoda, *The B Side*, 140.
17. Evanier, *All the Things You Are*, 85.
18. Bennett with Friedwald, *The Good Life*, 123–24.
19. Marmorstein, *The Label*, 208.
20. *Ibid.*, 258.
21. Wolfgang Saxon, "Frank DeVol, 88, a Composer for Movies and TV Sitcoms, Dies," *New York Times*, October 30, 1999.
22. Marmorstein, *The Label*, 428, 430.
23. Bennett with Friedwald, *The Good Life*, 277.
24. Evanier, *All the Things*, 85.
25. Maltin, *Leonard Maltin's Classic Movie Guide 2nd Edition*, 739.
26. Yagoda, *The B Side*, 147.
27. Bennett with Friedwald, *The Good Life*, 123.
28. Marmorstein, *The Label*, 194.
29. Yagoda, *The B Side*, 141.
30. Simons, *Studio Stories*, 33.
31. Yagoda, *The B Side*, 140.
32. Evanier, *All the Things You Are*, 85.
33. Marmorstein, *The Label*, 196.
34. Simons, *Studio Stories*, 37.
35. Bennett with Friedwald, *The Good Life*, 164.
36. Dan Daley, "Classic Tracks: Tony Bennett's 'I Left My Heart in San Francisco,'" mixonine.com.
37. Tony Bennett, telephone interview with author, May 18, 2016.
38. "Classic Tracks."
39. Christine, "Where the Heart Is."
40. "Top 10 'B-side' Hits," classicpopicons.com, April 15, 2010.
41. Gene Stevens, interview with author, October 25, 2008.
42. "Session Note: The Splish Splash Session," bobbydarin.net, accessed November 15, 2016.
43. Gene Stevens.
44. "Session Note."
45. "Where the Heart Is."
46. Terry Teachout, "The Three Lives of Tony Bennett," commentarymag.com, October 1, 2011.
47. Tony Bennett with Scott Simon, *Just Getting Started* (New York: HarperCollins, 2016), vii–ix, 39, 52–54.

Chapter 12

1. "Wells Twombly, Prize-Winning Sports Columnist," *New York Times*, May 31, 1977.
2. Author's recollection.
3. "Songwriter Cross Dies," *San Francisco Chronicle*, January 9, 1975.
4. "Timeline 1974," Times of History, timelines.ws, accessed October 17, 2016.
5. Talbot, *Season of the Witch*, 193.
6. Will White, interview with author, San Francisco, August 23, 2016.
7. Talbot, *Season of the Witch*, 169.
8. Steven Short, "San Francisco's Two Official Songs or, the Day Tony Bennett Hid in His Hotel," kalw.com, February 14, 2012.
9. Gladys Hansen, "San Francisco's Official Songs," The Virtual Museum of the City

of San Francisco, sfmuseum.org, accessed June 5, 2016. 10. "Bob Grimes," Imdb.com mini-biography, accessed July 13, 2016. 11. Edwin Baron Turk, *Hollywood Diva: A Biography of Jeanette MacDonald* (Berkeley: University of California Press, 1998), 185–86. 12. *Judy at Carnegie Hall: Fortieth Anniversary Edition*, liner notes, February 27, 2001. 13. "Cinema. The New Films," *Time*, July 6, 1936. 14. "Woody Van Dyke," pinterest.com, accessed July 13, 2016. 15. Sean Martin, "*San Francisco*, Starring Jeanette MacDonald, to Be Featured at Castro Theatre's 90th Anniversary," *Huffington Post*, August 3, 2012. 16. Merla Zellerbach, "Do We Need a New Song?" *San Francisco Chronicle*, March 25, 1974. 17. Peter Mintun, email to author, June 20, 2016. 18. Bob Grimes, letter to Peter Mintun, March 26, 1977. 19. Certificate of Death, Sonoma County, Santa Rosa, California, June 24, 1975. 20. George Cory, letter to Bob Grimes, February 11, 1975. 21. Coroner's Register, Record of Death, City and County of San Francisco, May 10, 1978. 22. Warren Hinckle, "Big Night for Song Historian As City Hall Looks for a Tune," *San Francisco Chronicle*, May 3, 1984. 23. "San Francisco Needs Updated Song," *Sumter* [South Carolina] *Daily Item*, April 14, 1984. 24. "San Francisco City Officials Want To Drop Bennett Hit, Sing New Song," *Bangor* [Maine] *Daily News*, April 25, 1984. 25. Max DeNike, "Revisiting 'Dump Dianne,'" *SF Weekly*, July 28–August 3, 2016. 26. Peter Mintun, telephone interview with author, April 28, 2016. 27. Jane Gross, "Note of Compromise Struck on Coast in Dispute Over City's Official Song," *New York Times*, May 18, 1984. 28. Susan Cheever, *Note Found in a Bottle* (New York: Simon & Schuster, 1999), 117. 29. "San Francisco to Sing Its Heart Out for Tony Bennett," lanow.com, February 13, 2012. 30. Steve Turner, "I Left My Heart in San Francisco: Touring the Vibrant City That Inspired a Song," *London Daily Mail*, January 4, 2010. 31. KPIX Eyewitness News, San Francisco, interview, October 6, 1969. 32. Gerald Nachman, "Hometown Tourist," *Nob Hill Gazette*, June 8, 2010. 33. Peter Mintun. 34. "Scott McKenzie Dies at 73; His 'San Francisco' Caught Flower-Power Wave," *Los Angeles Times*, August 21, 2012.

Chapter 13

1. Joe Nocera, "Top of the Heap in the Bronx," *New York Times*, December 12, 2015. 2. "Theme from 'New York New York,'" steynonline.com, November 27, 2015. 3. Nocera, "Top of the Heap." 4. "Theme from 'New York New York.'" 5. Evanier, *All the Things You Are*, 254. 6. James Kaplan, *Sinatra: The Chairman* (New York: Doubleday, 2015), 863. 7. "Top of the Heap." 8. "The Last Train to Clarksville," songfacts.com, accessed December 8, 2016. 9. Steve Ember, "Vermont Is Small in Size, Big in Beauty," learningenglish.vop.com, April 14, 2014. 10. Jesse McKinley, "Fred Ebb, 76, Lyricist Behind 'Cabaret' and Other Hits, Dies," *New York Times*, September 13, 2004. 11. Valerie Scher, "There Is No Shortage of Tunes About San Diego or Nearby Spots, But They All Fall Short of Memorable," *San Diego Union-Tribune*, August 13, 2007. 12. Willis Conover, *Billboard*, November 30, 1968. 13. "Billy Sunday Quotes," goodreads.com, accessed December 8, 2016. 14. "Hit Songs' Author Suicide by Hanging," *New York Times*, January 15, 1942. 15. "Do You Know the Way to San Jose," songfacts.com, accessed December 8, 2016. 16. Serene Dominic, *Burt Bacharach, Song by Song* (New York: Schirmer Trade Books, 2003), 115. 17. "Kansas City," songfacts.com, accessed December 8, 2016. 18. Andy Greene, "Songwriter Jerry Leiber Dies at 78," *Rolling Stone*, August 22, 2011. 19. James Kaplan, "The King of Ring-A-Ding-Ding," *Vanity Fair*, February 14, 2015. 20. "My Kind of Town (Chicago Is)," songfacts.com, accessed December 8, 2016. 21. "Ding Dong Days History," dumasar.com, accessed December 8, 2016. 22. "I'm a Ding Dong Daddy from Dumas," songfacts.com, accessed December 8, 2016.

23. "Ding Dong Days History."
24. "I'm a Ding Dong Daddy from Dumas."
25. Ricky Riccardi, "85 Years of 'Ding Dong Daddy (from Dumas),'" dippermouth.blog.spot.com, July 21, 2015.
26. "'I'm a Ding Dong Daddy From Dumas' Lyrics and Chords," classic-country-songs-lyrics.com, accessed December 8, 2016.
27. Sandy Spirtas, telephone interview with author, November 20, 2016.
28. Maltin, *Leonard Maltin's 2015 Movie Guide*, 914.
29. Maltin, *Leonard Maltin's Classic Movie Guide 2nd Edition*, 465.
30. "Eddie DeLange Songs," eddiedelange.com, accessed December 8, 2016.
31. Eric Scott Strother, "The Development of Duke Ellington's Compositional Style: A Comparative Analysis of Three Selected Works," University of Kentucky, 2001.
32. "Duke Ellington," redhotjazz.com, accessed December 8, 2016.
33. Allen Morrison, "Behind the Song: 'Wichita Lineman,'" americansongwriter.com, January 9, 2012.
34. "Wichita Lineman," songfacts.com, accessed December 9, 2016.
35. Maltin, *Leonard Maltin's Classic Movie Guide 2nd Edition*, 570.
36. "Allentown," songfacts.com, accessed December 9, 2016.
37. Maltin, *Leonard Maltin's 2015 Movie Guide*, 452.
38. Ralph Blumenthal, "Bob Merrill, Composer and Lyricist, Dies," *New York Times*, February 17, 1998.
39. "Knight: 'I Wish't I Was in Peoria Should Get a New Recording,'" peorian.com, March 25, 2013.
40. Stephen Holden, "Jerome (Doc) Pomus, 65, Lyricist for Some of Rock's Greatest Hits," *New York Times*, March 15, 1991.
41. Maltin, *Leonard Maltin's 2015 Movie Guide*, 1517.
42. Ross Farrow, "Residents Proud to Be Stuck in Lodi," *Lodi News-Sentinel*, August 12, 2004.
43. "Streets of Laredo," balladsofamerica.com, 2012.
44. Bill Friskics-Warren, "Merle Haggard, Country Music's Outlaw Hero, Dies at 79," *New York Times*, April 6, 2016.
45. "Tony Bennett With Dean Martin, 1965," YouTube, accessed December 27, 2016.
46. "Tony Bennett With Andy Williams, 1965," YouTube, accessed December 27, 2016.

Chapter 14

1. Laurence Bergreen, *As Thousands Cheer: The Life of Irving Berlin* (New York: Viking, 1990), 370.
2. Yagoda, *The B Side*, 146.
3. "Nice One, Tessie," discogs.com, accessed January 24, 2017.
4. Ford, *River of No Return*, 141; Kaplan, *Sinatra*, 478.
5. Evanier, *All the Things You Are*, 136.
6. Kelly-Ann Franklin, "Norwich Native, Grammy-Winning Musician, Lived Generously and Humbly, Friends Say," *The Bulletin*, April 6, 2011.
7. "I Left My Heart in San Francisco," secondhandsongs.com, accessed January 24, 2017.
8. Bill Crandall, "Surf Legend Jan Berry Dies," *Rolling Stone*, January 29, 2004.
9. Kaplan, *Sinatra*, 478.
10. Nancy Sinatra, "Frank Remembered," sinatrafamily.com, August 7, 2001.
11. "Obituaries—Dorothy Squires Dies at 83," bbc.com, April 1, 1998.
12. Will Friedwald, *A Biographical Guide to the Great Jazz and Pop Singers* (New York: Pantheon Books, 2010), 15.
13. "This Time by Basie!" 45cat.com, accessed January 24, 2017.
14. David Denby, "Naughty Nibbles," *New York*, October 11, 1982.
15. "Yes, Georgio," rogerebert.com, September 24, 1982.
16. Friedwald, *A Biographical Guide*, 378.
17. "Chet Baker Discography," jazzdisco.org, accessed January 24, 2017.
18. Jon Pareles, "Chet Baker, Trumpeter, Dies," *New York Times*, May 14, 1988.
19. Scott Yanow, "Sarah Vaughan—Sassy Swings Again," ltunes.apple.com, accessed January 24, 2017.
20. "Rosemary Clooney: Demi-Centennial," jazzdisco.org, accessed January 24, 2017.
21. Deborah Wilker, "Clooney Gives Peek at Soul in TV Special," *Fort Lauderdale Sun-Sentinel*, November 9, 1995.
22. Friedwald, *A Biographical Guide*, 269–96.
23. John Lewis, "Bobby Womack Obituary," *The Guardian*, June 28, 2014, and David Edwards, "Bobby Womack (1944–2014)," *Rolling Stone*, June 28, 2014.
24. Jason Newman, "Soul Legend Bobby Womack Dead at 70," *Rolling Stone*, June 27, 2014.

25. "Bobby Womack: My Prescription," discogs.com, accessed January 24, 2017.
26. "Dean Martin: I Left My Heart in San Francisco," YouTube, accessed January 24, 2017.
27. Beth Berlo, "Jerry Lewis Talks About His Career and Friendship With Dean Martin," butoday.com, November 1, 2005.
28. *Live and Swingin': The Original Rat Pack Collection*, Bear Family Records, 2003.
29. "Bobby Darin," ntl.matrix.com, accessed January 24, 2017.
30. "Bobby Darin," discogs.com, accessed January 24, 2017.
31. Friedwald, *A Biographical Guide*, 135, 137.
32. William Grimes, "Buddy Greco, Singer Who Had That Swing, Dies at 90," *New York Times*, January 13, 2017.
33. "Last But Not Least: Marilyn Monroe's Last Photo," lomography.com, August 25, 2011.
34. Friedwald, *A Biographical Guide*, 199.
35. Brenda Lee, with Robert Koermann and Julie Clay, *Little Miss Dynamite: The Life and Times of Brenda Lee* (New York: Hyperion Books, 2002), 66, 151, 215.
36. Jeremy Fish, "I Left My Heart in San Francisco," stereofat.blogspot.com, April 17, 2010.
37. Lee, Koermann, Clay, *Little Miss Dynamite*, 144, 175, 188, 193, 206, 228, 230.
38. Davy Rothbart, "Q & A: Mayer Hawthorne," grantland.com, December 13, 2011.
39. "Mayer Hawthorne Video," YouTube, April 5, 2010.
40. Johnnymathis.com, accessed January 24, 2017.
41. Johnnymathis.com, accessed January 25, 2017.
42. "Johnny Mathis," discogs.com, accessed January 24, 2017.
43. Jim Bawden, "She Juggled Two Careers in Films and on Records," thecolumnists.com, June 1972.
44. Friedwald, *A Biographical Guide*, 141.
45. "Sammy Davis, Jr.," discogs.com, accessed January 24, 2017.
46. Lindsay Planer, "Sammy Davis, Jr. Sings the Big Ones for Young Lovers," allmusic.com, accessed January 24, 2017.
47. "Sammy Davis, Jr. Sings the Big Ones for Young Lovers," discogs.com, accessed January 26, 2017.
48. Associated Press, "Dinah Washington, Blues Singer, Is Found Dead," *New York Times*, December 15, 1963.
49. "Dinah '63," discogs.com, accessed January 24, 2017.
50. Nadine Necohodas, *Queen: The Life and Music of Dinah Washington* (New York: Random House, 2004), 434.
51. Brett Smiley, "The 13 Scariest NFL Players of All Times," foxsports.com, October 31, 2016.
52. "Dinah Washington."
53. Necohodas, *Queen*, 434.
54. "Dinah Washington: Dinah '63," allmusic.com, accessed January 24, 2017.

Chapter 15

1. Dick Golden, telephone interview with author, August 26, 2016.
2. Richard Carpeneti, interview with author, Olympic Club, San Francisco, August 22, 2016.
3. Dick Golden.
4. Mark Olsen, "Deep Questions for Jerry Lewis," *Los Angeles Times*, September 8, 2016.
5. Kathryn Vercillo, "Lombard Crooked Street—San Francisco," sftodo.com, accessed October 21, 2016.
6. Gerald Harris, "Kaepernick's Political Football," *New York Times*, September 1, 2016.
7. Jay Barmann, "Legendary Trans Performer Vicki Marlane Gets Tenderloin Block Named After Her," sfist.com.
8. Jane Gross, "Note of Compromise Struck on Coast in Dispute Over City's Official Song," *New York Times*, May 18, 1984.
9. Sam Whiting, "Tony Bennett Sculpture Going Up in Heart of San Francisco," *San Francisco Chronicle*, August 14, 2016.
10. Tony Bennett, telephone interview with author, June 15, 2016.
11. Leah Garchik, "San Francisco Shines Its Golden Sun on Tony Bennett," *San Francisco Chronicle*, August 23, 2016.
12. "Songwriter Cross Dies," *San Francisco Chronicle*, January 9, 1975; "'I Left My Heart' Composer Is Dead," *San Francisco Examiner*, April 12, 1978.
13. Jeff Lunden, "The Composer Who Tested Fighter Planes and Partied With Sinatra," nprmusic.org, January 26, 2013.
14. Paul Willistein, "Sinatra Is Still the Sinatra of the 1980s," *Allentown [Pennsylvania] Morning Call*, May 10, 1986.
15. "Tony Bennett Sculpture Going Up in the Heart of San Francisco."

16. Johnny Miller, "Wayback Machine," *San Francisco Chronicle*, August 21–27, 2016.
17. Oscar.go.com, accessed August 30, 2016.
18. Dick Golden.
19. Bennett with Friedwald, *The Good Life*, 109.
20. Evanier, *All the Things You Are*, 229.
21. Marian Halley, "Don't Call Her Mammy," newfillmore.com, September 2, 2016.
22. "Pancho the Parrot," YouTube, accessed December 21, 2016.
23. Richard Carpeneti.
24. Sheldon M. Siegel, *Judgment Day* (San Francisco: MacAdams Cage, 2008), 1–2, 5.
25. Quentin Kopp, telephone interview with author, August 30, 2016.
26. Noah Griffin, telephone interview with author, August 29, 2016.
27. Richard Carpeneti.
28. Quentin Kopp.
29. William Grimes, "Warren Hinckle, 77, Ramparts Editor Who Embraced Gonzo Journalism, Dies," *New York Times*, August 25, 2016.
30. Gil Jacobs, *Harold Jones: The Singer's Drummer* (Bloomington,: AuthorHouse, 2013), ix.
31. Noah Griffin.
32. Bennett with Friedwald, *The Good Life*, 22.
33. Noah Griffin.
34. Dick Golden.
35. Rick Booth.
36. "*Vertigo*—Scottie's House," citysleuth@reelsf.com, April 26, 2011.
37. Rick Booth.
38. John Marchese, "'I Just Love What I'm Doing,'" *New York Times*, December 18, 2016.

Appendix II

Other One-Hit Wonders

1. Daniel E. Slotnik, "Jim Lowe, 93, Singer and Radio Disc Jockey," *New York Times*, December 15, 2016.
2. Michael Ruppli and Ed Novitsky, *The Mercury Labels 1945–56* (Westport, CT: Greenwood Press, 1993), 383.
3. "Jim Lowe."
4. Michael Feinstein, email to author, July 13, 2016.
5. Peter Mintun, email to author, July 13, 2016.
6. Michael Jack Kirby, "Jim Lowe," waybackattack.com, accessed January 30, 2017.
7. "Ian Whitcomb," picklehead.com, accessed January 30, 2017.
8. Ian Whitcomb, conversation with author, January 20, 2006.
9. Maltin, *Leonard Maltin's 2015 Movie Guide*, 415–16.
10. "Alicia Bridges," aaronshore@hotmail.com, January 30, 2017.
11. Maltin, *Leonard Maltin's 2015 Movie Guide*, 11, 790.
12. "Special Interviews with Horse and Alicia Bridges," J.D. Doyle, queermusicheritage.com, 2008.
13. Jon Michaelson, "The Otherside Lounge Bombing, Atlanta," manasticfiction.com, October 10, 2013.
14. Michael Feinstein.
15. Sven Bjerstedt, "Who Was Einar Swan? A Study in Jazz Age Fame and Oblivion," essay, January 2007.
16. "House Probers Continue Their Check on Reds," *Wilmington News*, January 29, 1952.
17. Charles Goldman, "George Bassman: Rhapsody in Black," *Film Score Monthly*, July 2007.
18. "George Bassman Biography," Imdb.com, July 30, 2016.
19. "Deaths: Bassman, George," *New York Times*, July 1, 1997.
20. "Tommy Dorsey," jazzstandards.com, accessed February 4, 2017
21. Levinson, *Tommy Dorsey*, 74
22. "George Bassman."
23. Caroline Howe, "Paul Simon the Music Thief?" *London Daily Mail*, October 9, 2016.
24. Tony Schwartz, "Paul Simon Interview," *Playboy*, February, 1984.
25. Jordan Runtaugh, "Paul Simon's Early Years," *Rolling Stone*, October 12, 2016.
26. "Paul Simon Interview."
27. "Tom & Jerry Released in Japan as Simon and Garfunkel," wordpress.com, February 13, 2012.
28. Dick Jacobs and Harriet Jacobs, *Who Wrote That Song?* (Cincinnati: Writer's Digest Books, 1994), 239.
29. Linda Dahl, *Stormy Weather: The Music and Lives of a Century of Jazzwomen* (New York: Pantheon, 1984), 299.
30. "A Sunday Kind of Love," secondhandsongs.com, accessed February 5, 2017.
31. Peter Keepnews, "Fran Warren, Singer in Big-Band Era, Dies at 87," *New York Times*, March 21, 2013.

32. George Shearing and Alyn Shipton, *Lullaby of Birdland: The Autobiography of George Shearing* (New York: Continuum, 2004), 137–38.
33. "Lullaby of Birdland," secondhandsongs.com, accessed February 5, 2017.
34. Shearing and Shipton, *Lullaby*, 138.
35. Peter Keepnews, "George Shearing, 'Lullaby of Birdland' Jazz Virtuoso, Dies at 91," *New York Times*, February 14, 2001.

Appendix III

The Richest Songs of All Time

1. William H. Honan, "Frankie Carle, Band Leader Who Wrote 'Sunrise Serenade,'" *New York Times*, March 10, 2001.
2. Rick Booth, telephone interview with author, October 1, 2016.
3. "The Richest Songs in the World," BBC Four, December, 2012.
4. Brian Warner, "The 10 Richest Songs of All Time," celebritynetworth.com, March 12, 2014.
5. Alice Vincent, "Happy Birthday Song and Its Strange Past," *The Telegraph*, February 19, 2016.
6. Joe Mullin, "Federal Judge: Copyright Invalid," arstechnicia.com, September 22, 2015.
7. "The 10 Richest Songs."
8. Laurence Bergreen, *As Thousands Cheer: The Life of Irving Berlin* (New York: Viking, 1990), 414.
9. "The 10 Richest Songs."
10. Yagoda, *The B Side*, 149–50.
11. Alan Duke, "Phil Spector Gets 19 Years to Life for Murder of Actress," cnn.com, May 29, 2009.
12. "The 10 Richest Songs."
13. J.T., "Fifty Years of 'Yesterday,'" *The Economist*, September 11, 2015.
14. "The 10 Richest Songs."
15. H.T.T., "Screen: Prison Film; 'Unchained' Presented at Victoria Theatre," *New York Times*, January 28, 1955.
16. Murray Burbidge, "The Origin and History of Unchained Melody," YouTube, October 12, 2012.
17. "The 10 Richest Songs."
18. Maltin, *Leonard Maltin's Classic Movie Guide 2nd Edition*, 711.
19. "The 10 Richest Songs."
20. Jerry Leiber, Mike Stoller, with David Ritz, *Hound Dog: The Jerry Leiber and Mike Stoller Autobiography* (New York: Simon & Schuster, 2010), 174.
21. Roger Cormier, "Nostalgic Facts About 'Stand By Me,'" mentalfloss.com, accessed February 11, 2017.
22. "The 10 Richest Songs."
23. Ace Collins, *Stories Behind the Hits of Christmas* (Grand Rapids: Zondervan, 2003), Chapter 4.
24. "10 Richest Songs."
25. *Ibid.*
26. "(Oh) Pretty Woman, by Roy Orbison," songfacts.com, accessed February 11, 2017.
27. Kate Erbland, "The True Story of *Pretty Woman's* Original Dark Ending," *Vanity Fair*, March, 2015.
28. "The 10 Richest Songs."
29. Bill DeMain, "The Christmas Song," performingsongwriter.com, December, 2000.

Bibliography

Http://allmusic.com.
Http://ancestry.com.
Apone, Carl. "Bennett Brings His Heart Here." *Pittsburgh Press*, June 8, 1978.
Http://arstechnicia.com.
Associated Press. "Jury Finds Robin Thicke, Pharrell Ripped Off Marvin Gaye Song in 'Blurred Lines.'" March 11, 2015.
Http://balladsofamerica.com.
Http://bbc.com.
Http://bbcfour.com.
Bear Family Records. *Live and Swingin': The Original Rat Pack Collection*. 2003.
Bennett, Charles G. "Cabaret-Card Use Ended by Council." *New York Times*, September 13, 1967.
Bennett, Tony, and Will Friedwald. *The Good Life*. London: Simon & Schuster, 1998.
Bennett, Tony, and Scott Simon. *Just Getting Started*. New York: HarperCollins, 2016.
Berger, Joseph. "Dylan and New York Share a Complex, Fertile, Romance." *New York Times*, October 15, 2016.
Bergreen, Laurence. *As Thousands Cheer: The Life of Irving Berlin*. New York: Viking, 1990.
Billboard, October 27, 1958.
Blumenthal, Ralph. "Bob Merrill, Composer and Lyricist, Dies." *New York Times*, February 17, 1998.
Http://bobbydarin.net.
Http://bopinbob.blogspot.com.
Http://boxturtlebulletin.com.
Boyle, Robert H. "The Hottest Spring in Hot Springs." *Sports Illustrated*, March 19, 1962.
Bravo, Tony. "Armistead Maupin on Saying Goodbye to San Francisco and 'Tales of the City.'" Kqed.org, January 29, 2014.
"British-Born Jazz Prodigy Victor Feldman Dies." *Los Angeles Times*, May 14, 1987.
Http://buysellfind.com.

Byington, Lewis Francis. *History of San Francisco, Vol. 2*. Chicago: S.J. Clarke, 1931.
Caen, Herb, "Herb Caen." *San Francisco Chronicle*, September 4, 1967.
Carbonell, Antolin Garcia. "She Was the Most Famous Miami Entertainer You Never Heard Of." *Biscayne Times*, July, 2010.
Http://carnegiehall.org.
Cheever, Susan. *Notes Found in a Bottle*. New York: Simon & Schuster, 1999.
Http://cherryred.co.uk.
Christine, Bill. "Where the Heart Is: The Story Behind San Francisco's Official Ballad." *SF Weekly*, July 28–August 3, 2016.
Http://chsmedia.org.
"Cinema. The New Films." *Time*, July 6, 1936.
Citysleuth@reelsf.com.
Http://classic-country-songs-lyrics.com.
Http://classicpopicons.com.
Http://cnn.com.
Http://collectorsmusicreviews.com.
Collins, Ace. *Stories Behind the Hits of Christmas*. Grand Rapids: Zondervan, 2003.
Cory, George, Coroner's Register, City and County of San Francisco, May 20, 1978.
Cory, George, Last Will and Testament, Superior Court of the State of California, March 15, 1978.
Crandall, Bill. "Surf Legend Jan Berry Dies." *Rolling Stone*, January 29, 2004.
Crawford v. State Bar, San Francisco No. 20290, September 20, 1960.
Cross, Douglass, Certificate of Death, County of Sonoma, January 7, 1975.
Cross, Douglass, Last Will and Testament, Lake County Superior Court, January 27, 1975.
Cross, Elizabeth Hammack. *Again to Earth*. New York: Exposition Press, 1956; letter, July 3, 1959, to California Historical Society, collection of Melinda Moranda and Ellen, Humble; personal notes, May 4, 1967.

Dahl, Linda. *Stormy Weather: The Music and Lives of a Century of Jazzwomen*. New York: Pantheon, 1984.

Davis, Clive, and Anthony De Curtis. *The Soundtrack of My Life*. New York: Simon & Schuster, 2012.

"Deaths: Bassman, George." *New York Times*, July 1, 1997.

DeNike, Max. "Revisiting 'Dump Dianne.'" *SF Weekly*, July 28-August 3, 2016.

Diller, Phyllis, and Richard Buskin. *Like a Lampshade in a Whorehouse*. New York: Penguin, 2006.

"Dinah Washington, Blues Singer, Is Found Dead." *New York Times*, December 15, 1963.

Http://dippermouth.blog.spot.com.

Http://discogs.com.

Dobrin, Peter. "Curtis Institute and the Case of Nina Simone." *Philadelphia Inquirer*, August 17, 2015.

Dominic, Serene. *Burt Bacharach, Song by Song*. New York: Schirmer Trade Books, 2003.

"Douglass Cross, Lyricist of 'I Left My Heart...'" *San Francisco Examiner*, January 8, 1975.

Http://dumasar.com.

Http://eddiedelange.com.

"Elizabeth Cross of Pioneer Family Passes Away Here on Saturday." *Lake County Record-Bee*, October 19, 1967.

Http://elvis-collections.com.

Http://encyclopediaofarkansas.net.

Erbland, Kate. "The True Story of *Pretty Woman*'s Original Dark Ending." *Vanity Fair*, March 2015.

"Ernest Bloch, 78, Composer, Is Dead." *New York Times*, July 16, 1949.

Evanier, David. *All the Things You Are: The Life of Tony Bennett*. Hoboken: John Wiley & Sons, 2011.

Farrow, Ross. "Residents for Proud To Be Stuck in Lodi." *Lodi News-Sentinel*, August 12, 2004.

Fischer, Nancy. "Round 'n' Round, Star-Studded History of Melody Fair." *Buffalo News*, February 21, 2015.

Ford, Jerry Buckner. *River of No Return: Tennessee Ernie Ford and the Woman He Loved*. Nashville: Cumberland House, 2008.

Http://45cat.com.

Http://foxsports.com.

Http://francesarcher.com.

Franklin, Kelly-Ann. "Norwich Native, Grammy-Winning Musician, Lived Generously and Humbly, Friends Say." *The Bulletin*, April 6, 2011.

Friedwald, Will. *A Biographical Guide to the Great Jazz and Pop Singers*. New York: Pantheon Books, 2010.

Friskics-Warren, Bill. "Merle Haggard, Country Music's Outlaw Hero, Dies at 79." *New York Times*, April 6, 2016.

Garchik, Leah. "San Francisco Shines Its Golden Sun on Tony Bennett." *San Francisco Chronicle*, August 23, 2016.

Http://gaslightrecords.com.

Gavin, James. *Is That All There Is? The Strange Life of Peggy Lee*. New York: Atria Books, 2014.

General Music Publishing Co., Inc., "I Left My Heart in San Francisco," 1954.

Gioia, Ted, and William Claxton. *West Coast Jazz: Modern Jazz in California 1945-60*. Berkeley: University of California Press, 1998.

Goldman, Charles. "George Bassman: Rhapsody in Black." *Film Score Monthly*, July 2007.

Http://goodreads.com.

Http://grantland.com.

Greene, Andy. "Songwriter Jerry Leiber Dies at 78." *Rolling Stone*, August 22, 2011.

Grimes, William. "Tessie O'Shea, Music-Hall Star and Tony Winner, Dies at 82." *New York Times*, April 22, 1995.

Gross, Jane. "Note of Compromise Struck on Coast in Dispute Over City's Official Song." *New York Times*, May 19, 1984.

Groth, Gary. "The Jules Feiffer Interview," tcj.com, February 10, 2011.

Harris, Gerald. "Kaepernick's Political Football." *New York Times*, September 1, 2016.

Haven, Cynthia. "The Bay Area's 'Activists' Shook Up Poetry in the 50s." Sfgate.com, September 4, 2005.

Heller, Nathan. "What She Said." *The New Yorker*, October 24, 2011.

H.H.T. "Screen: Prison Film; 'Unchained' Presented at Victoria Theatre." *New York Times*, January 28, 1955.

Higbie, Andrea. "Curse of the Oscar." *New York Times*, March 27, 1995.

Hinckle, Warren. "Big Night for Song Historian as City Hall Looks for a Tune." *San Francisco Chronicle*, May 3, 1984.

"Hit Songs' Author Suicide by Hanging." *New York Times*, January 15, 1942.

Holden, Stephen. "Jerome (Doc) Pomus, 65, Lyricist for Some of Rock's Greatest Hits." *New York Times*, March 15, 1991.

Holiday, Billie, and William Duffy. *Lady Sings the Blues 50th Anniversary Edition*. New York: Random House, 2006.

Bibliography

Holland, Bernard. "Gian Carlo Menotti, Opera Composer, Dies at 95." *New York Times*, February 2, 2007.

Honan, William H. "Frankie Carle, Band Leader Who Wrote 'Sunrise Serenade.'" *New Times*, March 10, 2001.

"House Probers Continue Their Check on Reds." *Wilmington News*, January 29, 1952.

"Howard Graham Crawford, Jr." *Lake County Record-Bee*, February 24, 2011.

Howe, Caroline. "Paul Simon the Music Thief?" *London Daily Mail*, October 9, 2016.

"'I Left My Heart' Composer Is Dead." *San Francisco Examiner*, April 12, 1978.

Http://ibdb.com.

Http://imdb.com.

"The Incredible Talking Machine." *Time*, June 23, 2010.

The Interactive Tony Bennett Discography, discography.bloggingtonybennett.com.

Jacobs, Dick, and Harriet Jacobs. *Who Wrote That Song?* Cincinnati: Writer's Digest Books, 1994.

Jacobs, Gil. *Harold Jones: The Singer's Drummer*. Bloomington: AuthorHouse, 2013.

Http://jazzdisco.org.

Http://jazzprofiles.blogspot.com.

Http://jazzstandards.com.

Http://jazztimes.com.

Jerome, Jim. "A Place Called Home." *People*, January 11, 1993.

Http://johnnymathis.com.

Jones, Chad. "The Venetian Room and the Way We Were." Theaterdogs.net, October 18, 2010.

Http://jonesreport.com.

J.T. "Fifty Years of 'Yesterday.'" *The Economist*, September 11, 2015.

Judy at Carnegie Hall: Fortieth Anniversary Edition.

Kamiya, Gary. "1961 Police Raid Pivotal for Gay Rights in San Francisco." Sfgate.com, June 21, 2013.

Kaplan, James. "The King of Ring-A-Ding-Ding." *Vanity Fair*, February 14, 2015.

Kaplan, James. *Sinatra: The Chairman*. New York: Doubleday, 2015.

KPIX Eyewitness News, San Francisco, interview, October 6, 1969.

Kramer, Gary. *Let's Misbehave*. Liner notes, Prestige Records, 1962.

Http://lanow.com.

Http://learningenglish.com.

Lee, Brenda, with Robert Koermann and Julie Clay. *Little Miss Dynamite: The Life and Times of Brenda Lee*. New York: Hyperion Books, 2002.

Leiber, Jerry, and Mike Stoller with David Ritz. *Hound Dog: The Jerry Leiber and Mike Stoller Autobiography*. New York: Simon & Schuster, 2010.

Levinson, Peter. *Tommy Dorsey, Livin' in a Great Big Way*. Cambridge, MA: Da Capo Press, 2006.

The Library of Congress, Washington, D.C., Catalog of Copyright Entries.

Lindsey, Robert. "Dan White, Killer of San Francisco Mayor, a Suicide." *New York Times*, October 22, 1985.

Http://lomography.com.

London Gazette, April 2, 1946.

Http://manasticfiction.com.

Maltin, Leonard. *Leonard Maltin's Classic Movie Guide 2nd Edition*. New York: Penguin, 2010.

Maltin, Leonard. *Leonard Maltin's 2015 Movie Guide*. New York: Penguin, 2014.

Maraniss, David. "The Place Where Clinton's Coming From." *Washington Post*, September 30, 1992.

Marchese, John. "Pop Music: When He Covers, Stackers Listen." *New York Times*, May 1, 1994.

Marmorstein, Gary. *The Label: The Story of Columbia Records*. New York: Thunder's Mouth Press, 2007.

Martin, Joe L. *The Journal of 'Old Fremont,' a Revolutionary War Rifle*. Bloomington: iUniverse, 2013.

Martin, Sean. "*San Francisco*, Starring Jeanette MacDonald, To Be Featured at Castro Theatre's 90th Anniversary." *Huffington Post*, August 3, 2012.

Http://marydonovan.com.

Http://mentalfloss.com.

Http://merola.org.

Http://metrolyrics.com.

Miller, Johnny. "Wayback Machine." *San Francisco Chronicle*, August 21–27, 2016.

Miller, Matt. "Ralph Sharon, Tony Bennett's Longtime Pianist, Dies in Boulder at 91." *Denver Post*, April 5, 2015.

Http://mixonine.com.

Museum of Durham History. "This Day in 1914."

Http://musictime.com.

Nachman, Gerald. "Hometown Tourist." *Nob Hill Gazette*, June 8, 2010.

"Naughty Nibbles." *New York*, October 11, 1982.

Necohodas, Nadine. *Queen: The Life and Music of Dinah Washington*. New York: Random House, 2004.

Nehgila, Harvey. "Foxglove Case Ends With a Plea Bargain." *San Francisco Chronicle*, February 23, 2000.
Nelson, Erik. "*The Oscar*—Greatest Terrible Movie of All Time." Salon.com, March 5, 2010.
Nelson, Rex. "Along Park Avenue." Rexnelsonsouthernfried.com, July 21, 2014.
Http://newfillmore.com.
Newman, Jason. "Soul Legend Bobby Womack Dead at 70." *Rolling Stone*, June 27, 2014.
Http://ninasimone.com.
Http://ninoandapril.com.
Nocera, Joe. "Top of the Heap in the Bronx." *New York Times*, December 12, 2015.
Http://nprmusic.org.
Http://ntl.matrix.com.
Olsen, Jack. "Gone With the Gypsies." *Vanity Fair*, May 1998.
Olsen, Jack. *Hastened to the Grave: The Gypsy Murder Investigation*. New York: St. Martin Press, 1998.
Olsen, Mark. "Deep Questions for Jerry Lewis." *Los Angeles Times*, September 8, 2016.
Http://onlinesearches.com.
Http://operanews.com.
Http://operasb.com.
O'Rourke, Tim. "Chronicle Covers: It's True, San Francisco Opera's Founder Died Onstage." *San Francisco Chronicle*, August 31, 2016.
Http://oscar.co.com.
Http://ovrtur.com.
Tim Panaccio. "Flyers at 50: The Story Behind the Tradition of Kate Smith's 'God Bless America.'" Csnphilly.com, accessed January 3, 2017.
Paul, Ivan. "Around Town." *San Francisco Examiner*, December 30, 1961.
Http://peorian.com.
Pereles, Jon. "Chet Baker, Trumpeter, Dies." *New York Times*, May 14, 1988.
Http://performing songwriter.com.
Http://picklehead.com.
Http://pinterest.com.
Http://psr.edu.com.
Http://queermusicheritage.com.
Http://redhotjazz.com.
"Roberta Sherwood, 86, Singer at Top Clubs in 50's and 60's." *New York Times*, July 7, 1999.
Http://rogerebert.com.
Http://rosicrucian.com.
Rubenstein, Steve. "Dazzling Fireworks at Candlestick." *San Francisco Chronicle*, July 5, 1976.
Runtaugh, Jordan. "Paul Simon's Early Years." *Rolling Stone*, October 12, 2016.
Ruppli, Michael, and Ed Novitsky. *The Mercury Labels 1945–56*. Westport, CT: Greenwood Press, 1993.
"Sally Rand Wins Case." *New York Times*, April 1, 1947.
"San Francisco Needs Updated Song." *Sumter* [South Carolina] *Daily Item*, April 14, 1984.
Saxon, Wolfgang. "Frank DeVol, 88, a Composer for Movies and TV Sitcoms, Dead." *New York Times*, October 30, 1999.
Scher, Valerie. "There Is No Shortage of Tunes About San Diego or Nearby Spots, But They All Fall Short of Memorable." *San Diego Union-Tribune*, August 13, 2007.
Schlitten, Don. *Let's Misbehave*. Cherry Red Records, liner notes, 2014.
Schudel, Matt. "Ralph Sharon, Longtime Accompanist to Singer Tony Bennett, Dies at 91." *Washington Post*, April 15, 2015.
Schwartz, Stephen. "Obituary—Ernest (Ernie) Heckscher." Sfgate.com, April 20, 1996.
Schwartz, Tony. "Paul Simon Interview." *Playboy*, February, 1984.
"Scott McKenzie Dies at 73; His 'San Francisco' Caught Flower-Power Wave." *Los Angeles Times*, August 21, 2012.
Http://secondhandsongs.com.
"Services Held Wednesday for Harry Cross." *Lake County Record-Bee*, August 6, 1949.
Severo, Richard. "Mitch Miller, Maestro of the Singalong." *New York Times*, August 2, 2010.
Http://sfbac.org.
Http://sfist.com.
Http://sfmuseum.org
Http://sfopera.com.
Shearing, George, and Alyn Shipton. *Lullaby of Birdland: The Autobiography of George Shearing*. New York: Continuum, 2004.
Shelton, Robert. "Bob Dylan: A Distinctive Folk-Song Stylist." *New York Times*, September 29, 1961.
Short, Steven. "San Francisco's Two Official Songs or, the Day Tony Bennett Hid in His Hotel." Kalw.com, February 14, 2012.
Siegel, Sheldon M. *Judgment Day*. San Francisco: MacAdams Cage, 2008.
Simons, David. *Studio Stories*. San Francisco: Backbeat Books, 2004.
Sinatra, Nancy. "Frank Remembered," sinatrafamily.com, August 7, 2001.
Singer, Barry. "How Singers Fall in Love with Songs." *New York Times*, February 17, 2002.

Bibliography

Slotnik, Daniel E. "Jim Lowe, 93, Singer and Radio Disc Jockey." *New York Times*, December 15, 2016.
Smith, Chris, and Brett Wilkison. "Claramae Turner." *Santa Rosa Press Democrat*, May 31, 2013.
Http://songfacts.com.
Http://songlyrics.com.
"Songwriter Cross Dies." *San Francisco Chronicle*, January 9, 1975.
State of California, Grant Deed, 833 Fillmore Street, San Francisco, May 26, 1982.
Http://stereofat.blogspot.com.
Http://steynonline.com.
Strother, Eric Scott. "The Development of Duke Ellington's Compositional Style: A Comparative Analysis of Three Selected Works." University of Kentucky, 2001.
Superior Court of San Francisco. Declaration of Final Discharge and Order for Final Discharge, Estate of George Cory. June 28, 1988.
Szwed, John. *Billie Holiday: The Musician and the Myth*. New York: Penguin, 2015.
Talbot, David. *Season of the Witch*. New York: Simon & Schuster, 2012.
Http://tardytimes.com.
Teachout, Terry. "The Three Lives of Tony Bennett." Commentarymag.com, October 1, 2011.
"Ted Heath, Bandleader, Dies." *New York Times*, November 20, 1969.
Http://thecolumnists.com.
Http://thetender.us.
Http://timelines.ws.
Tomkins, Les. Interview, Victor Feldman. 1987.
Tomkins, Les. Interview, Ralph Sharon. 1988–89.
Tommasini, Anthony. "Eileen Farrell, Soprano With a Popular Bent." *New York Times*, March 25, 2002.
Turk, Edwin Baron. *Hollywood Diva: A Biography of Jeanette MacDonald*. Berkeley: University of California Press, 1998.
Turkel, Stanley. "Washington Square Hotel." Hotelinteractive.com. January 13, 2010.
Turner, Steve. "I Left My Heart in San Francisco: Touring the Vibrant City That Inspired a Song." *London Daily Mail*, January 4, 2010.
Turner, Wallace. "Hot Springs: Gamblers' Haven." *New York Times*, March 3, 1964.
U.S. Federal Census 1930.
U.S. Federal Census 1940.
U.S. Social Security Death Index.
U.S. Social Security Index.
Vincent, Alice. "Happy Birthday Song and Its Strange Past." *The Telegraph*, February 19, 2016.
Http://vinylamongotherthings.com.
Walls, Carlotta. "The Little Rock Nine." Timeline.com, accessed October 28, 2016.
Http://waybackattack.com.
"Wells Twombly, Prize-Winning Sports Columnist." *New York Times*, May 31, 1977.
Western Addition Senior Center. "In Celebration of the Life of Walter K. Hinton." September 20, 2005.
Whiting, Sam. "Tony Bennett Sculpture Going Up in Heart of San Francisco." *San Francisco Chronicle*, August 14, 2016.
Wilker, Deborah. "Clooney Gives Peek at Soul in TV Special." *Fort Lauderdale Sun-Sentinel*, November 9, 1995.
Williams, Lance, and Patrick Hoge. "Love and Money/Mayor's Fund-Raiser Got Millions." *San Francisco Chronicle*, July 13, 2003.
Willistein, Paul. "Sinatra Is Still the Sinatra of the 1980s." *Allentown [Pennsylvania] Morning Call*, May 10, 1986
Wilson, John S. "When a Cellar Was the Place to Be." *New York Times*, September 22, 1991.
Woo, Elaine. "Ralph Sharon Dies at 91; Pianist Brought Tony Bennett His Signature Song." *Los Angeles Times*, April 11, 2015
Http://wordpress.com.
Yagoda, Ben. *The B Side: The Death of Tin Pan Alley and the Rebirth of the Great American Song*. New York, Riverhead Books, 2015.
Http://yahoo.com.
Yanow, Scott. "Sarah Vaughan—Sassy Swings Again." Ltunes.apple.com, accessed January 24, 2017.
Http://youtube.com.
Zellerbach, Merla. "Do We Need a New Song?" *San Francisco Chronicle*, March 25, 1974.
"Zeppelin Happy 'Stairway' Riff Debate Settled." *Torrance [California] Daily Breeze*, June 24, 2016.
Http://zillow.com.

Index

Numbers in **_bold italics_** indicate pages with photographs

A-side 105, 108, 131, 167
Abbott, Shirley 84
Academy Award 55, 59
Adams, Lee 98, 104
Adams, Robert 46
Adderley, Nat "Cannonball" 53, 77
Adventures of Priscilla Queen of the Desert 160
Again to Earth 33, 42, 67
Aida 20
Aiken, Conrad Potter 46
Akselsen, Jon 94–95
Albritton, Dub 137
Alcatraz 9, 132
Alioto, Joseph 69–70, 95, 113, 118
All-American 98–104
"All the Way" 116, 141
Allen, Steve 55, 118
"Allentown" 124, 128
Ambassador Hotel 85
Ameche, Don 167
American Bandstand 42, 164
Ames Brothers 84
Anchor Steam beer 120
Ann Dee's 440 Club 138
Annie 64
Anthony, Garland 86
"April in Paris" 66
Arden, Eve 7
"Are You Lonesome Tonight?" 93
Argo Records 74
"Arkansas State Prison" 135
Arlen, Harold 37, 64
Arlington Hotel 84, 86, 87
Armenian Greek Orthodox Church 106
Armistice Day 50
Armstrong, Louis 45, 74, 127, 162
Army III Corps 43
"Artificial Flowers" 136
As Thousands Cheer 168
ASCAP 118
Astaire, Fred 138
AT&T Park 140
The Atmosphere 86
Auden, W.H. 44

Auld, George 169
"Aunt Jemima" 23, 27
Austin, Gene 145, 162
"Autumn in New York" 122
Avakian, George 60, 137

B-side 105, 108–109, 131, 167
Babcock, Chester Edward 142
"Baby, I Don't Cry Over You" 45
Bacharach, Burt 52, 60, 125
Baer, Larry 144
Baez, Joan 129
Bailey, Colon 54
Bailey, F. Lee 8
Bailey, Pearl 70
Baillet, Whitney 78
Baker, Chet 52, 134
"Bali Hai" 38
Ballad for Voices and Orchestra 61
Baltimore News-American 22
The Band Wagon 168
Barbary Coast, 116
Barber, Samuel 48
Bari, Joe 71; *see also* Bennett, Tony
Basie, Count 52, 76, 86, 96
Bassman, George 162–163
"Battle Hymn of the Republic" 118
Bauer, Barbara Fluhrer 18
Baxter, Phil 126
BBC 52, 168
"Be-Bop-A-Lula" 108
Beach Boys 132
Beale, Margaret **_23_**, 24, 27–28
Beat Generation 69
The Beat of My Heart 77
the Beatles 68, 138
Beatty, Warren 162
"Because of You" 145
Becket 48
"The Bee Song" 165
Beesley, Hope Victoria 26–27
Beesley v. Tene 27
Belafonte, Harry 94
Belle, Barbara 165
Belli, Melvin 7

193

Index

Bellingham, Bruce 94
The Belmonts 108
Benedetto, Anna 93–94, 111
Benedetto, Anthony Dominic, 70; *see also* Bennett, Tony
Benedetto, John 93, 106, 111.
Bennett, Patricia 88
Bennett, Tony 1–3, 5, 10, 13, 19, 37–38, 45–47, 49–50, 52, 54–55, 57, 59, 61, 65–66, 68, 71–90, 92–99, 103–109, **110**, 111, 114, 116, 118–121, 123, 125, 129, 131–138, 140–141, **143**, 144–148, **149**, 150–152; *see also* Bari, Joe; Benedetto, Anthony Dominic
Benny, Jack 127
Bentley 149
Berle, Milton 74
Berlin, Irving 50–51, 55, 131, 164, 168
Bernstein, Geri 83
Bernstein, Leonard 68
Bernstein, Sid 82–83
Berry, Chuck 75, 79
Berry, Jan 132
"The Best Is Yet To Come" 79, 93
Betford Corporation 57
"The Bicycle Song" 163
Biederbicke, Bix 82
Big Records 163–164
Bill Haley and the Comets 166
Billboard 59, 94, 103, 125, 136
"Bim Bam Baby" 72
Birdland 165
Black Hawk Indian War 31
Black Orchid Lounge 87
"Black Rock" 106
Blackburn, John 124
Blackstone Hotel 94
Blake, Dorsey 19, 21
Blakey, Art 77
the Blitz 73
Bloch, Ernest 43
Blonde Crazy 162
Blondell, Joan 162
Blue Angel 64
"Blue Velvet" 139
"Blues in the Night" 77
Bluesville 160
"Blurred Lines" 47
"Boat Song" 46
Bob Willis and the Texas Playboys 127
"The Body" 170
Bohemian Club 10
Bolger, Ray 98, 104
Bonnie and Clyde 162
Booth, Rick 10, 13, 47, 150
Bornstein, Saul 51
"Boulevard of Broken Dreams" 71, 82, 92, 99
Boulton, Derek 80
Boy Scout Handbook 51
Boy Scouts of America 33, 44, 51

Boyce, Tommy 124
Brazzi, Rosano 46
Brewer, Teresa 163–164
Brewis, Laurie 56
Brian's Song 64
Bridges, Alicia 160
Bright, Dick 47
Brill Building 5, 52
Broadway 44, 47–50, 55, 60 64–66, 80, 82, 92, 98–99, 122, 128, 136, 159, 162, 165, 168–170
Brooks, Mel 98, 105
Brooks, Pamela 119
Brown, James 92
Brown, Joe E. 20
Brown, Willie 14, 142
Brubeck, Dave 85, **105**
Brunswick Record Company 128
Bryan, John 97
Brynner, Yul 9–10
Buffett, Jimmy 127
Burke, Joe 46–47
Burnett, Carol 64
Burns, Roy Edward 128
Burton, John 122
Buttons, Red 55
"Bye Bye Birdie" 104
Byron, Lord 46

Cabaret 122
cabaret cards 62–63
Cabin in the Sky 162
Caen, Herb 10, 16, 22, 93, 97, 112
Caesar and Cleopatra 162
Cagney, James 162
Cahn, Sammy 55, 126
Calamari Club 148
California Street 21, 145, 156
"Call Me Irresponsible" 126
Callas, Maria 68
The Cameo 86
Camero, Candido 75
Camp Upton 50
Campbell, Glen 128
Candlestick Park 20, 144
Capitol Records 55, 99, 133, 136
Capone, Al 84, 86
Capote, Truman 44
"The Capricorn" 48
"Carey," George 55
Carle, Frankie 167
Carlin, George 62
The Carmel Strings 134
Carmichael, Hoagy 118
Carnegie Hall 68, 82–83, 86, 109, 116
Carney, Art 127
Carousel 48–49, 55
Carpenetti, Carolyn Mundt 14
Carpenetti, Richard 11, 13–16, 18, 24, 28, 148
Carroll, David 159

Index

Carson, Johnny 38, 109, 147
Caruso, Enrico 68
Cash, Johnny 129
Castro Theatre 116
Catholics 124, 168
CBS 102
CBS Symphony 99
Cernik, Al 100; *see also* Mitchell, Guy
Chakiris, George 54-55
The Champs 108
Channel, Bruce 108
Charlap, Bill 152
Charlie Byrd Trio 66, 133
Chavez, Cesar 113
Checker, Chubby 108
Cherry Red Records 65
Chess, Leonard 75
Chess, Philip 75
Chet Baker Suite 134
Chez Paree 74-75
Chiappa, Mary 109
"Chicago Cubbies" 126
"Chicago (That Toddlin' Town)" 125, 129
Chicago World's Fair 63
"Chim Chim Cher-ee" 126
Chinese-American International School 119
Christine, Bill 167
Christine, Laura 134
Christmas 139, 168, 170-171
"The Christmas Song" 170
Christopher, George 93
"Chugga Lugga Choo Choo" 53
Clapton, Eric 37
Clark, Dick 42, 164
Clearlake, California 9, 36, 57-58, 66-67, 69-70, 90
Cline, Patsy 136
Clinton, Billy Blythe 84-86
Clinton, Raymond 84-85
Clive, Fannie 19
Clooney, Rosemary 79-80, 83, 101-106
"Closet Strut" 161
The Coasters 170
Cohen, Andrew Mayer 137; *see also* Hawthorne, Mayer
Cohen, Maxwell 62
"Cold, Cold Heart" 54, 78, 104
Cole Porter Society 148
Coleman, Cy 79
Collins, Ted 50
Coltrane, John 63
Columbia Records 50, 54, 59, 71-72, 75, 78-80, 82-83, 93, 97-99, 101-104, 107, 127, 131, 137-138, 145
Columbia University 49
"Come Fly with Me" 129
"Come-on-a-My-House" 101
Como, Perry 83
Connor, Chris 73-74
Conover, Willis 125

The Conversation 37
Conway, Tim 167
Cook, Barbara 48
Cooke, Sam 135
Copland, Aaron 55, 162
Coppola, Francis Ford 37
Cory, Edward M. 40, 154
Cory, George: Army duty 43-44; ashes 2, 9, 119, 157; and Bohemian Club 10; Brooklyn Heights 2, 5, 28, 37, 44, 56, 65, 85, 88, 90, 131, 142; and Claramae Turner 49, 55-56, 134; and Cory Sound Co. 42; covers of song 133; cremation 16, 157; death 1, 2, 5, 11-14, 17, 40-41, 46, 62, 69, 118, 142, 146, 149; description of song **115**-116; in Douglass Cross' will 39-40, 153-155; drinking 36; ego 47; favorite drink 9-10; feud with Bob Grimes 117-18; and Frank Sinatra cover of song 55, 132-133; friends 47; in Japan **120**; and Lombard Street 151; and Marty Manning 105; and May Cross' art collection 41; medication 10, 12; melodies 94, 110; in New York 62; as organist 43; other songs 64; as pianist 37, 44, 46, 49, 56, 61; piano 28; as poet 48; possible plagiarism 18-19; possible suicide 1, 2, 12, 17, 118; in Poughkeepsie **132**; public performance 20; and Ralph Sharon 79, 85, 98; remembered 141; return to San Francisco 68-70, 93, 113; and San Francisco's official song **114-115**; as seen by Mae Cross 69; separation from Douglass Cross 8, 17, 36-37, 69; and sheet music 147; talent 41; and Tessie O'Shea 56; and title of song 52; under-appreciation 147-148; wealth 42, 168; will 2, 5-8, 11, 13-17, 20-21, 113, 155-158; working with Douglass Cross 45-46
Cory, George, Sr. 44
Cory, Gertrude 40, 44, 154
Cossato, Walden Robert 108; *see also* Darin, Bobby
the Cotton Club 84
Cow Palace 37
Coward, Noel 56
Crawford, Howard G. 37-38
Crawford, Phil 37-39, 42, 155
"Crazy Rhythm" 71
Creedence Clearwater Revival 128
Crenna, Lloyd 7, 8, 12, 69
Crenna, Richard 7
Crosby, Bing 72, 78, 80, 82, 162, 167-168; and the Rhythm Boys 164
Crosby, Bob 167
Cross, Douglass: ancestors 30; Army duty 43-44; birth 34, 51; and Brooklyn Heights 2, 5, 28, 37, 44, 56, 65, 85, 88, 90, 131; and Claramae Turner 49, 134; covers of song 133; cremation 16, 41; death 1, 2, 5, 16, 36, 41, 70, 90; description of song 121; drinking 36, 62, 69, 90; father 41; and Frank

Sinatra cover of song 55, 132–133; in Japan *120*; as lyricist 16, 45–46, 61, 66, 90, 94, 109–110; and Marty Manning 105; mother 32; opinion of San Francisco 113; other songs 64; piano 28; possible plagiarism 18–19; in Poughkeepsie *132*; and Ralph Sharon 79, 85, 98; relationship with nephew 11; remembered 141; return to San Francisco 68, 93; and San Francisco's official song *114–115*; separation from George Cory 8, 17, 36–37, 69; sheet music 147; as singer 43; and Tennessee Ernie Ford 57–59; and Tessie O'Shea 56; and title of song 52; under-appreciation of 147–148; wealth 168; will 2, 6, 36–41, 70, 90, 153–155
Cross, Elizabeth Mae Hammack 12, 16, 30, 32–34, 38–39, 41–42, 44, 51, 57–58, 66–67, 69–70, 90, 154
Cross, Harry 12, 16, 32–33, 37, 41, 44, 51, 67
Cugat, Xavier 161
Curtis Institute 48
Curtiss, Lou 125

Dagmar 72
Dailey, Dan 145
Dalal, Shashi 21
Damone, Vic 83
"Dardanella" 125
Darin, Bobby 108–109, 136; *see also* Cossato, Walden Robert
David, Hal 125
David Trimble Recordings 50
Davie, Bob 159–160
Davis, Miles 52–53, 63, 78, 106
Davis, Sammy, Jr. 74, 92, 135, 138
Day, Doris 79, 101, 133
"Days of Wine and Roses" 139
"Dear Heart" 59
Decca Records 45–46, 55, 136–137
"Deep Purple" 54, 139
"Deep Song" 46
Dees, Bill 169
De Lange, Eddie 127
Del Mar Race Track 167
The Den 62
De Niro, Robert 122
DeVol, Frank 103
Dietrich, Marlene 60, 92
Dietz, Howard 45
Diller, Phyllis 56, 64, 84
"Ding Dong Day" 126
Dion 108
Dixon, Mort 128
"Do You Know the Way to San Jose" 125
"Do You Know What It Means to Miss New Orleans" 127, 130
Dolch, Debra 27–28
Domino, Fats 127
"Don't Cry for Me, Argentina" 47
Dorsey, Jimmy 161, 163

Dorsey, Tommy 18, 46, 70, 161, 163
Down Beat 73
Draper, Rusty 159
"Dream On for Me, Little Solider Boy" 50
"Drinking Again" 165
"Drown in My Tears" 139
"The Drowned Wife" 48
Drummond, Bill 182
Duane Hotel 62
Dubin, Al 99
Duke University 19
Duncan, Isadora 141
Duncan, Tommy 127
Dunn, Ann 11
Durante, Jimmy 74, 167
Dylan, Bob 59, 83, 106; *see also* Zimmerman, Robert

"East St. Louis Toodle-oo" 127–128
Eastman School of Music 99
Eastwood, Clint 144
Ebb, Fred 122, 124
Eckstein, Billy 76, 86
Edison, Thomas 159
Edwards, Frances L. 40, 155
Eisenhower, Dwight 74
Elbert, H 13
Ellington, Duke 53, 127–128, 164
"Embraceable You" 134
Emmy Award 54, 150–151
Encino Man 160
Encino Woman 161
The End of the World 138
Entratter, Jack 101
Ermey, John 84
Ertola, John 15
Estes, Simon 20
Evanier, David 76
Evans, Bill 38, 76
Everly Brothers 59
"Every Breath You Take" 170
"Everybody's Talkin'" 59
"Everything's Up to Date in Kansas City" 130
Evita 47
Exiner, Billy 75, 77

Fair, James 91
Fairmont Hotel 6, 19, 45, 47, 50, 59, 66, 83, 88–89, 91–92, 95, 104, 131, 140, 148–150, 159; Fairmont Towers 92; Venetian Room *6*, 10, 19, 55, 90, 92–95, *96*, 97, 103, 114, 147
Falk, Peter 80
Fantasy Records 63
Faron, Fay 26–27
Farrell, Eileen 46
Fascinato, Jack 58–59
Faye, Mart 125
Feiffer, Jules 37, 65
Feinstein, Dianne 9, 118, 120–121, *143*, 144, 147

Index

Feinstein, Michael 121, 159–160
Feist, Leo 170
Feldman, Victor 53–54
Ferrante & Teicher 66
Ferrer, Jose 101
"Fever" 55
Fields, Dorothy 45
Fields, Gracie 118
52nd Street 45, 163
Figlio, Mike 107–108
Fisher, Eddie 133
Fisher, Fred 125
Fisherman's Wharf 3
Fogerty, John 128
"A Foggy Day in London Town" 129
"Fools Rush In" 139
Ford, Betty 57
Ford, Gerald 107–108
Ford, Jeffrey Buckner 57
Ford, Phil 74
Ford, Tennessee Ernie 19, 41, 52, 57–59, 66, 131–132, 159–160
Forest Hills 82
48th Street 163
Fountain, Pete 127
"Four Songs in the Night" 46
Fourgeaud, Victor John 30
"Foxglove Deaths" 25
Foy, Eddie, Jr. 20
Frank Sinatra Orchestra 55
Freed, Alan 79, 164
French Foreign Legion 125
Friedwald, Will 133, 138
From Here to Eternity 91

Gable, Clark 115–116
Gallagher, Bill 82
"Gambler's Guitar" 159–160
Garchik, Leah 142
Gardner, Ava 101
Garfunkel, Art 163–164
Garland, Judy 68, 77, 109, 115–116
"Gary, Indiana" 128
Gastoni, Lina 7, 14, 156
Gavin, Steve 22
Gay Men's Chorus 119
Gaye, Marvin 47
Gaylord, Billy 9
Gene Compton Cafeteria 141
General Artists Corporation 82
George Cory Ensemble 63–65
George Washington Bridge 61
Gere, Richard 170
German Navy 125
Gershwin, George 68
Getz, Stan 63, 76
Ghost 169
Gibbs, Georgia 127; *see also* Lipschitz, Frieda
Giddens, Gary 68

Gideon, Raynold 170
Gilbert and Sullivan 44, 49
Gillespie, Dizzy 73, 78
Gillespie, Haven 170
Ginsberg, Allen 69
Girl Scouts of America 51
Gleason, Jackie 127
Glenn Miller Army Air Force Band 53
"God Bless America" 50, 51, 139
"God Bless the Child" 77
Goerner, Fred 116
Goldberg, Whoopi 169
Goldberg Variations 106
Golden Gate Bridge 9, 16, 25, 29
Golden Gate Heights 145
Golden Gate Park 56
"Good Morning to You" 168
Goodbye, Mr. Chips 76
Goodman, Benny 68, 127, 136, 161
Gordon, Dexter 169
Gordon, Max 64
Gould, Glenn 106
Goulet, Robert 80
Grace Cathedral 10, 144
Graceland 59
Grammy Awards 60, 80, 125, 139, 140, 170
Granat, Mynna 50–51
Grand Central Station 48
Grant, Rudy 63
The Grateful Dead 10, 37
Gray, Elizabeth 30–31, 33
Great American Songbook 121
Greco, Buddy 136
"The Green Door" 159–160
Grey, Joel 92
Griffin, Noah 119, 148–149
Grimes, Bob 115–118, 119, 121
Grossman, Felix 82
Guerin, Johnny 54
Guest, Edgar A. 29
Guys and Dolls 82, 162
Gypsy 92

Hacienda Convalescent Hospital 40
Haggard, Merle 129
Haley, Bill 108
Haley, Jack, Jr. 124
Hallinan, Terry "Kayo" 8
Hallinan, Vincent 7–8
Hamilton, Chico 77
Hammack, Benjamin Franklin 35
Hammack, Brice Martin 30–32
Hammack, Eleanor 31
Hammack, Elizabeth Gray 32, 35
Hammack, George Washington 30, 32, 35
Hammack, Helen Theis 32–33
Hammack, John 30
Hammack, Martin 30–32
Hammack, Minnie Jane 33
Hammack, Sara Eleanor 32

Index

Hammack, Valentine 32
Hansel and Gretel 23, 55
Hanson, Winifred 13
"Happiness Is a Thing Called Joe" 103
"Happy Birthday" 168
Harper's 48
Harris, Dane 84
Harris, Phil 127
Harrison, Wilbert 126
Hart, Bobby 124
Hartley Cemetery 41
Hartman, Johnny 74
Harvard 18, 94
Hastings College of Law Rugby Club 119
"Hava Nagila" 85
Hawn, Robert 134
Hefti, Neal 55
Hellinger, Mark 162
"Hello, Dolly!" 59
Hemingway, Ernest 56
Henderson, Florence 80
Herlie, Eileen 104
Herman, Pee Wee 137
Herman, Woody 45, 53
Hertelendy, Paul 20
"Hey! Baby!" 104
"Hey, Schoolgirl" 163–164
"High Hopes" 126
Hill, Jessica 168
Hill, Mildred 168
Hill, Patty 168
Hinckle, Warren 118–119, 121, 148
Hinton, Martha 19
Hinton, Walter 1–2, 6–8, 10–11, 13–14, 17–22, **23**, 24–29, 114, 148, 156
Hirt, Al 127
Hodges, Eddie 128
Holiday, Billie 13, 45–46, 60, 62, 74, 76, 127, 165
Holiday Inn 81, 168
Holly, Buddy 102, 137
Hollywood 66, 80, 82, 103, 162
The Honeymooners 127
Hoover, Herbert 10
Hope, Bob 71–72, 74, 167; *see also* Hope, Leslie Townes
Hope, Leslie Townes 72; *see also* Hope, Bob
Hopkins, Gerald Manley 41
Horan, Robert 48
Horne, Lena 92
Horowitz, Vladimir 68, 106
Hot Springs swimming pools 86
Hotel 91
Hotel Earle 56
Hotel Edison 129
"Hound Dog" 60, 126
The House I Lived In 86
"Houston" 129
"How Long Has This Been Going On" 75
"How High the Moon" 66

Howard, Ron 128
Howard Rumsey All-Stars 53
Huckleberry Hound 138
"The Hucklebuck" 72
Hudson, C.B. "Sonny" 7, 87–89
Hudson, Grace Carpenter 12, 41
Hudson, Will 127
Hughes, Barry 26–27
"Hung on You" 108
Huston, Walter 66
Hutcheson, Susan 160
Hyman, Dick 66

"I Can't Give You Anything But Love" 82, 99
"I Didn't Know What Time It Was" 103
"I Didn't Have the Heart to Tell You" 163
"I Guess the Lord Must Live in New York City" 59
"I Left My Heart in San Francisco" 1–3, 5, 9, 10, 14–21, 23, 26, 28, 32, 38, 45–47, 49, **50**, 52, 54, 56–59, 61–62, 65–68, 71, 78–79, 81–82, 85–86, 88–89, 93–97, 103, 106–109, 111, 114–119, 121, 123–125, 129–140, 145, 147, 148, 150, 159, 168.
"I Left My Nose in San Diego" 118
"I Love Paris" 129
"I Love the Night Life" 160
"I Wanna Be Around" 111
"I Wanna Be Loved" 99
"I Wish't I Was in Peoria" 128
"I'd Rather Be Blue" 125
"If I Were a Carpenter" 136
"I'll Look Around" 45
"I'll Take Manhattan" 129–130
"I'm a Ding Dong Daddy from Dumas" 126, 130
"I'm Coming, Virginia" 82
"I'm Getting Sentimental Over You" 162–163
"I'm Walking Behind You" 133
"In the Middle of an Island" 72
Ind, Peter 63
Infinity Records 53
Internal Revenue Service 80, 139
"Is That All There Is?" 60, 126
"It's Springtime in the Rockies" 38

Jacoby, Herb 64
"Jailhouse Rock" 60, 128
Jamal, Ahmad 75
The Jazz Singer 82
Jerome, Henry 132
Joel, Billy 123, 128
The Joker Is Wild 125
Jolson, Al 82, 125
Jones, Harold **149**
Jones, Jack 90, 94
Jones, Jim 22, 113
Jones, Quincy 133

Index

Jones, Shirley 49
Jones Street 146
Joutsen, Einar 161 *see also* Swan, Einar
Joyce, James 150
Judaism 161
"Judy Don't Be Moody" 109
"June Is Bustin' Out All Over" 49
Jurmann, Walter 115, 128
Jurmann, Yvonne 119
"Just in Time" 93, 98, 133
"Just One of Those Things" 77
Juster, Norton 65

Kael, Pauline 48
Kahn, Gus 115, 117, 128
Kander, John 122
"Kangaroo Hop" 53
"Kansas City" 126, 130, 139
Kaper, Benjamin 10
Kaper, Bronislaw 115, 128
Kaplan, James 78–79, 123
Kapralik, Dave 103
Keel, Howard 48
Kelley, Virginia Clinton 87
Kennedy, John F. 86
Kennedy, Willie 119, 121
Kern, Jerome 45
KGO Radio 119
KGO-TV 57
The King and I 9
Kissinger, Henry 10
"Kitchen Police" 50
KMPX Radio 117
Knickerbocker Holiday 66
Kopp, Quentin 119, 121, 148–149
Krouse, Morton 45
Krupa, Gene 63

Lady Gaga 150
Lady Sings the Blues 64
Laennec's cirrhosis 40
Laico, Frank 104, 106–107
Laine, Frankie 79, 84, 127, 165
Lake County, California 8, 16, 32, 34, 37, 41, 67, 153, 154
Lake County Superior Court 153
Lakeport, California 32, 153, 155
Lamb, Palmer 144
Lane, Dick "Night Train" 139
Lanin, Sam 161
Lansbury, Angela 64
Larkin Street 57, 150
The Last Days of Disco 160
"The Last Train to Clarksville" 124
Latin Casino 133
Lawrence, Jack 167
"Lay Lady Lay" 59
Lazar, Michael J. 63
Lazarus, Jim 113–114
Led Zeppelin 47

Lee, Brenda 52
Lee, Edwin M. 11
Lee, Julie 136
Lee, Peggy 9, 60, 79, 90, 164
Lee, Ruta 20
Leiber, Jerry 60, 126, 169–170
Leigh, Carolyn 79
Lennon, John 169
Lenya, Lotte 66
Leslie, Edgar 46–47
"Let Me Go, Devil" 105–106
"Let Me Go, Lover" 105
"Let's Face the Music and Dance" 77
"Let's Misbehave" 64, 65
Levy, Morris 165
Lewis, Jerry 11, 135, 140
Lewis, Jerry Lee 164
Lewis, Joe E. 125
Lewis, Ramsey 75
Liberace 52, 80, 84
Liberty Records 138
Lieberson, Goddard 99, 102–103
Liebling, A.J. 52
"Life's a Holiday" 64
The Lighthouse 53
Lipschitz, Frieda 127 *see also* Gibbs, Georgia
Loakes, Jim 57–59
"Lodi" 128
Loesser, Frank 64
Lombard Street 9, 36, 47, 150–151
London, Jack 134
London, Julie 138
"The Look of Love" 55
Lopez, Vincent 161
The Lord's Prayer 29
Los Angeles Airport 135
Loudon, Dorothy 64
"Love Me or Leave Me" 75
Lowe, Jim 159–160
Luciano, Lucky 84
"Lullaby of Birdland" 165
"Lullaby of Broadway" 77, 133
LuPone, Patti 60
Lyceum Theatre 64

MacDonald, Jeanette 46, 101, 114–117, 119, 121, 129–130, 138, 148
Mack, Allan 75
MacRae, Gordon 49
Macy's Thanksgiving Parade 151, 170
Madame Butterfly 43
Madden, Owney "the Killer" 84–85
Madison Avenue 150
Mafia 73
Maguire Sisters 84
Mailbox Money 167
Mailer, Norman 44
"Make Someone Happy" 139
"Mama Will Bark" 72

The Mamas & the Papas *121*
The Man Who Had All the Luck 44
Mancini, Henry 53
"Mandy" 50
Mann, Barry 168–169
Mann, Herbie 77
Mann, Shelly 53
Mardi Gras 24
"Maria" 55
Mark Hopkins Hotel 91–92, 94
Marlane, Vicki 141
The Martha Raye Show 162
Martin, Dean 79, 129, 135
Mary Poppins 126
Mathis, Clem 137
Mathis, Johnny 137–138
Matthews, Chris 10
Maupin, Armistead 70
May, Elaine 64
Mays, Willie 145
Mazander, Earl 87
McCartney, Paul 169
McKee, Ken 11
McKenzie, Scott 121
McRae, Carmen 73–74
The Medium 48, 49, 55
"Meet Me in St. Louis" 127
Melody Maker 137
Melson, Joe 59
Menotti, Giancarlo 46, 48
Mercer, Johnny 37, 64, 111
Mercer, Mabel 45
Mercury Records 72, 134, 159
Mercy Hospital 122
Merman, Ethel 92
Merola, Gaetano 43
Merola Opera Program 20
Merrill, Bob 128
Metro-Goldwyn-Mayer 114–117, 127
"Michelle" 138
Midnight Cowboy 59
The Mikado 55
Miley, James "Bubber" 128
Milk, Harvey 8, 25
Miller, Arthur 37, 44
Miller, Glenn 167
Miller, Mitch 54, 71–72, 76, 78–79, 83, 97–104, **105**, 106–108, 111, 131–132, 138
Mills, Irving 127
Mills, Kerry 127
Minnelli, Liza 122–124
Minnelli, Vincent 127
Mintun, Peter 47, 159
"Miss Me But Let Me Go" 29
Miss Piggy 151
Mitchell, Guy 100, 128; *see also* Cernik, Al
Mitchell, Joni 53
Mitchell, Karen 15
Mitchum, Robert 138
Monk, Thelonius 63

The Monkees 124
Monroe, Marilyn 44
Monroe, Vaughn 127
Moody, James 75
"Moon River" 53, 55
"Moonglow" 127
"Moonlight in Vermont" 66, 124, 134
"Moonlight Serenade" 167
Moore, Marvin 159
Morath, Max 160, 162
Morgan, Julia 91, 95
Morgenthaler, Mr. and Mrs. Paul 7, 13–14, 156
Moscone, George 8, 20, 25, 95, 145
Mulligan, Gerry 53
Muscarella, Ray 73, 99
"Music I Heard with You" 46
The Music Man 127, 130
"My Blue Heaven" 137, 145, 162
My Favorite Things 59
"My Favorite Things" 66
"My Funny Valentine" 103, 134
"My Heart Cries for You" 101
"My Kind of Town (Chicago Is)" 126, 142
"My Way" 78, 123

"Nabob of Nob Hill" 94, 151
Nachman, Gerald 121
National Guard 86
NBC 102
Neil, Fred 59
Neilson, Shirley May (Mae) Cross 37, 39, 90, 153–154
Nelson, Ricky 127
Nesbit, Evelyn 91
New Year's Day 136
New Year's Eve (1961) 93
New York City Council 63
New York City Opera 55
New York Giants 145
New York magazine 20
New York Metropolitan Opera 20, 46, 48–49
New York New York 122
"New York, New York" 122–124
New York Philharmonic 61
New York Times 83, 163, 170
New York Yankees 124
The New Yorker 48, 56
"Nice 'n' Easy" 133
Nichols, Mike 64
Nichols, Red 161
Nilsson, Harry 59
Noises Off 64
Nola Rehearsal Studio 73
Noone, Linda 80
North, Alex 169
Nye, Anita Leonard 165
Nye, Louie 165

Oakland Park 84, 87–88
Oakland Tribune 20
O'Day, Anita 164
Oedipus Rex 55
Office of War Information 44
"Oh, Pretty Woman" 170
"Okee from Muskogee" 129
"Ol' Man River" 75
Olivier, Laurence 48
Omnibus 162
"On Treasure Island" 18, 46–47
"Once Upon a Time" 55, 68, 98, 104–105, 108
"The Only Pal I Ever Had Came From Frisco Town" 119
"Only the Lonely (Know the Way I Feel)" 59
Ono, Yoko 169
Onyx Club 163
Oppenheim, Mathilde 7, 158
Orbison, Claudette 170
Orbison, Roy 59, 170–171
Ory, Kid 45
The Oscar 80
Oscars 122, 125–126, 144, 168
O'Shea, Tessie 19, 52, 56, **57**, 97, 131
the Osmonds 127
Osterberg, Craig 24–25
The Otherside Lounge 160
Our Miss Brooks 7

Pac Bell 26
Pacific Bandstand 42
Pacific Gas & Electric Co. 32
Pacific Ocean 53
Pacific School of Religion 21
Page, Patti 84
Palm Springs Airport 126
Palmer, Arnold 144
"Pancho the Parrot" 38
Paramount Pictures 170
Park, Arthur 27–28
Park Avenue 60, 83
Parker, Charlie 62, 73
Patrick & Co. Office Supplies 117
Paul, Ivan 97
Pavarotti, Luciano 133
payola 164
Peckinpah, Sam 162
"Peg o' My Heart" 125
"Pennies from Heaven" 133
Peoples Temple 22, 113
Pepper, Art 53
Percodan 11, 12
Perfectly Frank 81
"The Phantom" 75
The Phantom Tollbooth 65
Phillips, John 121
Piaf, Edith 92
Picasso, Pablo 111
Pillow Talk 103

Pinkard, Maceo 164
Pitney, Gene 125
plagiarism 18, 19, 47
Playboy Club 65, 68
Pleasant, Mary Ellen 10, 146
Pleasant Street **6**, 8–13, 36, 146
Plowright, Joan 64
Polk, James 30
Pollack, Sydney 162
Polo Grounds 145
Pomo Indians 12
Pomus, Doc 128
Porgy and Bess 20
Porter, Charles 88
Porter, Cole 37, 64
Post Street 10, 137
The Postman Always Rings Twice 162
Potter, Harry 137
Powers, Marie 48–49, 61
Presidio 37, 43, 62
Presley, Elvis 59–60, 79, 93, 102, 128, 138
Prestige Records 63
Pretty Woman 170
Price, Leotyne 20, 68
Prima, Louie 90, 165
Prince 10
Prins Hendrik Hotel 134
prohibition 62, 74, 84
Prosen, Sid 163–164
Pryce, Jonathan 112
Prysock, Arthur 133
Psychic Horizons 23
Puff Daddy 170
Pulitzer Prize 46, 65
"Put on a Happy Face" 98

Quaker Oats 23
Queen Mary 63
"Quierme Mucho" 47
Quigley family 34
Quinn, Anthony 48

Radio City Music Hall 122
Rae, Penny 53
"Rags to Riches" 93, 139
"Raindrops Keep Fallin' on My Head" 125
Ralph Sharon Quintet 75
Ralph Sharon Sextet 53
Ramsey Properties 24
Rand, Sally 63, 70
Ranier, Tom **149**
Rat Dog Dick Detective Agency 26
Rat Pack 136
RCA Victor 133
"Red Roses for a Blue Lady" 59
Redwood Valley 22
Reggie Cravens Quartet 87–88
Reid, Billy 133
Reiner, Rob 170
Reprise Records 54, 55, 123, 138

Republican National Convention 74
Resquiescat 48
the Rhineland 43
Rhodes, Stanley 165
Ricketts, Lois M. 40
Riddle, Nelson 55
Riggio, Nick 123
Righteous Brothers 108, 168
The Ring A Dings 53
RKO vaudeville circuit 94
Roach, Hal 164
Road to Bali 167
Robbins, Marty 129
Roberts, Julia 170–171
Robeson, Paul 68
Robin and the 7 Hoods 126
Robinson, Ted 17, 21, 24–25, 28
"Rock Around the Clock" 108
Rockefeller, Winthrop 88
"The Rockin' Lady (from New Orleans)" 164
Rodgers, Richard 119
Rodgers and Hammerstein 49
Rollins, Jack 150
Rollins, Sonny 63
Rooney, Mickey 84
Rosano, Lois 95
Rose, Billy 121
Rosemary Clooney: Demi-Centennial 134
Rosenwinkel, Kurt 46
Rosicrucian Order 22
Roulette Records 139
Round Table Restaurant 86
"The Roving Kind" 101
Royal Society Jazz Orchestra 119
Rozell, William, III 26
Ruth, Brett 169
Ryan, Joan Perry 50

Sachs, Manie 102
Sahl, Mort 64
St. Julien Hotel 81
St. Louis Beer 127
St. Louis World's Fair 127
St. Luke's Hospital Nursing School 33
Sammy Davis Jr. Sings the Big Ones for Young Lovers 138
Samson and Delilah 55
San Francisco 5, 30, 32–33, 36–37, 44, 155; Bay 9, 119, 151; Board of Supervisors 8, 113, 119; Castro district 69; Chinatown 3, 51; City Hall 120; coroner 1, 11–12, 17; decline 21, 113; discovery of gold 30, 43, 119; earthquake 33, 90, 94, 116–117, 119; Fillmore district 3, 7, 17, 21–25, 28 Fisherman's Wharf 3; and gays 8–9, 69, 141, 147–148; growth 30; as muse 5; Nob Hill 3, 5, **6**, 36, 115, 140; North Beach 149; Olympic Club 15; Opera Company 20, 49; police 2, 11–13, 25, 69; Russian Hill 3, 9, 14; Stern Grove 43, 56; Sunset district 26; Superior Court 14, 26, 148; Symphony 8; Union Square 3
"San Francisco" 46–47, 114, 116–117, 119, 121, 128, 130, 147–148
San Francisco 114–115, 128
"San Francisco (Be Sure to Wear a Flower in Your Hair)" 121
San Francisco Boys and Girls Chorus 144
San Francisco Chronicle 20, 22, 41, 70, 93, 116, 118, 141, 145, 148, 151
San Francisco Examiner 12, 97, 112
San Francisco Giants 140
San Francisco Jazz Combo 144
Sands Hotel 101, 135
"Santa Claus Is Coming to Town" 151, 170
Santa Fe Trail 31, 51
Sargent, Gary **149**
Sargent, Greg 20
Sargent, John Singer 111
Savoy Hotel 161
Schackman, Al 61, 65–66
Schizophrenia 21
Schlitten, John 64–65
Schmidt, Doug 25
Schwalb, Harry Abraham 85
Schwartz, Arthur 45
Schwartz, Jonathan 123
Schwarz, Daniela "Lela" 17–18, 21, **23**, 25, 27, 29
Scorsese, Martin 122
Sears 56
Separate Tables 144
"September Song" 66
Seventh Avenue 163
The Shack 159
Shacklett, Ronnie 137
The Shadow of Your Smile 138
Shakespeare, William 71
Shapiro, Bella 85
Sharon, Joyce 80
Sharon, Ralph 1–2, 53, 13, 19, 37, 44, 53, 57, 70, 72–81, 83, 85, 86, **87**, 88–89, 93–95, 98, 104, 111, 131, 138, 142
Shaw, Arnold 83
Shaw, Artie 63
Shearing, George 53, 73, 77, 165–166
Shearing, Trixie 165
Shelley, John 95
Shelley, Percy Bysshe 46
Sherman House 9
Sherwood, Roberta 54–55, 90
Shirly, Jimmy 45
Short, Bobby 90, 147
Show Boat 29
"The Show Must Go On" 139
Shultz, Charlotte 142, **143**, 144
Shultz, George 142, 144
Shuman, Mort 128
"Sidewalks of New York" 122

Siegel, Stephen 148
Silk Stockings 82
The Silver Lining: The Songs of Jerome Kern 150
Silvertone Record Club 56
Simon, Paul 163–164
Simone, Nina 45, 48
Sinatra, Frank 37, 54, 63, 72, 74, 78–80, 86, 99, 102, 122–126, 132–133, 135–136, 138, 141, 165
Sinatra, Nancy 133
Sinclair, Lou 42
Sing Sing 84
"Sing You Sinners" 93, 99
"Sixteen Tons" 132
Skelton, Red 92
Smith, George 91
Smith, Greer 28
Smith, Kate 50–51, 131
Smith, Keely 90
Smothers Brothers 128
"Snacky Poo" 53
Society for Individual Rights 142
Socolow, Frank 63
Soft and Gentle 136
"Some Enchanted Evening" 20
Sony/ATV Music Publishing 28
South Michigan Avenue 74–75
South Pacific 46
Southern Christian Leadership Council 86
Specht, Minnie Jane 32
Spector, Phil 168–169
"Splish Splash" 108–109
Spoleto Festival 69
Squires, Dorothy 133
Stafford, Jo 165
"Stairway to Heaven" 47
"Stand by Me" 12, 169–170
Stand by Me 170
Stanford University 94
Stanton, Jesse 12–13
"Stardust" 66
State Street (Brooklyn Heights) 65
State Street (Chicago) 125
Statue of Liberty 66
Steely Dan 53
Steiner, Mary Tene 25
Step Brothers 74
Sterling, Andrew 127
Stevens, April 54
Stevens, Gene 108–109
Stewart, James 151
Stockholm Syndrome 8
Stoller, Jerry 60, 126, 169–170
"Stormy Weather" 161
"Strangers in Paradise" 98
"Strangers in the Night" 78
"Street of Dreams" 103
"Streets of Laredo" 128
"String of Pearls" 127

Strouse, Charles 98, 104
Strowbridge, Ron 2, 11–12, 19, 36, 39–42, 61, 68, 70, 90, 154
Stumpe, Lou 42
Styron, William 121
Sullivan, Ed 49, 55
Summers, Andy 170
Sunday, Billy 125
"A Sunday Kind of Love" 165
"Sunrise Serenade" 167
Superior Court of California 155
Swahili 118
Swan, Ann Kaufman 162
Swan, Einar 160–162; *see also* Joutsen, Einar
"Swan's Serenade" 162
Swig, Benjamin 91–92, 94–95
Symbionese Liberation Army 7, 112–113

"Take the 'A' Train" 128
Talbot, David 113
"Tales of the City" 70
"A Taste of Honey" 53, 55, 64
A Taste of Honey 64
Tatum, Art 73
Tauber, Doris 164–165
Tay-Bush 92–93
Taylor Street 10, 141, 146
"Teach Me Tonight" 75
Teachout, Terry 109
Teagarden, Jack 161
Tempo, Nino 5
Tenderloin 3, 8, 29, 118, 141
Tenderloin 136
Tene, Danny 25–27
"Tequila" 108
Teyte, Maggie 46
"That Old River Line" 164
Thatcher, Margaret 144
Thaw, Harry 91
"Them There Eyes" 164
"There's a Pawnshop on a Corner in Pittsburgh, Pennsylvania" 128
Thicke, Robin 47
Third Baptist Church 23
"Thirteen Women (and Only One Man in Town)" 108
"This Could Be the Start of Something Big" 133
This Time by Basie!: Hits of the 50s and 60s 133
Thom McAn Shoes 103
Thomas, Dylan 56
Thomas, Lloyd 28
Thompson, Kay **96**
Thornhill, Claude 73, 165
"Till I Waltz Again with You" 163
Time 122, 142
Tin Pan Alley 37, 70
Todd, Thelma 164
Tom & Jerry 163–164

Index

Tonight Show 109
Tony Award 92
Tony's Greatest Hits 75
Tony Sings for Two 103–104
"Toot, Toot Tootsie (Goodbye)" 82
Torme, Mel 92, 94, 166, 168, 171
Tormey, Paul 147
Torrence, Dean 132
Toscanini, Arturo 55
Tozzi, Georgio 46
Tracy, Spencer 115
Tracy, William G. 164
"Train to Nowhere" 108
Traver, Cory 13
Traver, David 13
Traver, Warren 13
Trebek, Alex 1
"Tried and Convicted" 135
Trilogy: Past, Present, Future 123
Troup, Bobby 138
Truman, Harry 92
Tucker, Bobby 76
Tucker, Sophie 52, 74
Turk Street 141
Turner, Claramae 19, **49, 50**, 52, 55, 97, 131, **132**, 134
Turner, Steve 121
Twelfth Street and Vine 126
"Twenty-Four Hours From Tulsa" 125
2:38 a.m. 75
Twombly, Wells 112–113

Uggams, Leslie 60, 103
Unchained 169
"Unchained Melody" 108, 169
Union Square 113
Union Stockyards 126
United Nations 92
U.S. Army 32, 62, 147
U.S. Congress 30
U.S. Justice Department 84
U.S. Navy 125
University of Alabama 21
University of California–Berkeley 43, 48, 57
University of Michigan 44
University of Oklahoma 33
University of Oregon 94
University of Texas 33

Van Dyke, W.S. 115
Van Gelder, Rudy 61
Vanguard 64–65
Van Heusen, Jimmy 37, 55, 126, 142
The Vapors 83–84, 86, 87
Vaughan, Sarah 38, 134, 164
Velda Rose Motel 86, 89
Vertigo 151
Verve Records 46
Victor Feldman: A Taste of Honey and a Taste of Bossa Nova 53

Victor Feldman Quartet 53–54
Vietnam 124–125, 128
Villa Venice 135
Village Gate 62, 133
Village Voice 65
Vimmerstedt, Sadie 111
Vincent, Gene 108
The Visitation 20
"Viva Las Vegas" 128
voodoo 22

Wade, Agnes 7, 20–21, 158
Wade, Ernest V. 7, 20–21, 158
Waldorf Astoria Hotel
Walker, Vaughn 10
Wallace, Henry 7
Wallace, Jerry 64
Wallander, Arthur W. 63
Waller, Fats 60, 73
War Memorial Opera House 20, 43
War of 1812 31
War of the Worlds 99
"Warm Tonight" 64
Warner Bros. 162
Warner Music Group 168
Warren, Fran 165
Warren, Harry 99
Warwick, Dionne 125
Washington, Dinah 139, 165
Washington, Ned 162
Waters, Crystal 160
Waters, Ethel 92, 162
Waverly Lounge 56
"Way Down Yonder in New Orleans" 129–130
Wayne, Chuck 73
Webb, Jack 138
Webb, Jimmy 128
Weil, Cynthia 168–169
Weill, Kurt 66
Weinstock, Bob 63–64
Weir, Frank 73
Weisman, Ben 105
Weiss, George David 166
Welles, Orson 99
Wells, Bob 168, 171
"We're on Our Way to France" 50
West, Mae 63
West End 53
West Side Story 55, 106
Western Addison Senior Center 21, 29
Wexler, Jerry 101
"What a Difference a Day Makes" 139
"What Good Is Scheming" 162
"When I Come Home" 52
"When I Return to San Francisco" 52, 110
"When Your Lover Has Gone" 160, 162
Whitcomb, Ian 160
White, Dan 8, 25–26, 95
White, Robert 38

White, Stanford 91
White, Will 21, 28
"White Christmas" 168
White Christmas 168
"White Ghost Shivers" 162
White House 74, 86
White Panther Party 120
Whiteman, Paul 82, 161
Whiting, Sam 141
Whitlock, Bob 54
Whitman, Edwin 95
Whitman, Walt 44
"Wichita Lineman" 128
Wilde, Oscar 48
Wilder, Alec 78
"William Didn't Tell" 165
Williams, Andy 79, 129–130
Williams, Hank 78, 104
Williams, Pharrell 47
Williams, Roger 53, 66
Williams, Tennessee 24
Willie Mays Plaza 141
Willistein, Paul 142
Willson, Meredith 128
Wilson, Earl 55
Wilson, Jackie 137
Wilson, Julie 20
Wilson, Nancy 80, 166
Wilson, Pete 10
Winchell, Walter 55
Winding, Kai 77
"Witchcraft" 55, 79
"Without a Song" 133
The Wizard of Oz 137, 162

WNEW Radio 123
Wolfe, Bruce 141, 144
Wolfe, Thomas 44
Wolfe, Tom 10
Womack, Bobby 135
"Woman Love" 108
Wood, Marshall **149**
Woods, Harry 128
World War I 50
World War II 33, 43, 62, 73, 82, 112, 125
Wright, Edythe 46, 163

The Yale Review 48
Yes, Georgio 133
"Yesterday" 138, 169
Yip! Yip! Yaphank 50
"You Always Hurt the One You Love" 55
"You Turn Me On" 160
You'll Never Walk Alone" 49, 55
"Your Feet's Too Big" 60
Your Hit Parade 127
"You're Not the Only Oyster in the Stew" 60
"Yours" 47
"You've Lost That Lovin' Feelin'" 168

Zaret, Henry 169
Zebra murders 113
Zellerbach, Merla 116–117
Zimmerman, Robert 83; *see also* Dylan, Bob
Zito, Torrie 80
Zodiac killer 113
Zorro, Johnny 53